You are More than you t...

The return to your authentic Self

Andrew Jenkins

You are more than you think
The return to your authentic self © Andrew Jenkins
ISBN 978-1-909116-07-8

www.pdx-consulting.com
www.youaremorethanyouthink.co.uk

Published in 2014 by SRA Books

The right of Andrew Jenkins to be identified as the author
of this work has been asserted by him in accordance with the
Copyright, Designs and Patents Act 1988.

A CIP record of this book is available from the British Library.

Printed in the UK by TJ International, Padstow

- Contents -

Dedications and acknowledgements

I dedicate this book to my fabulous wife Sarah, and my three beautiful children, Katie, Hannah and Charlotte. These wonderful girls have made me, inspired me and delighted me. Through them I have found love and a love for life. Thank you.

Thank you, too, to Sarah Williams, and to all of you who helped me to have the confidence to put pen to paper and to write this book, you know who you are. I couldn't have done this without your support.

Thank you to the superb teaching of Roger Terry, an expert in helping people to help themselves get the most from their lives and reach their full potential. You helped me to find myself and woke me up out of my rigid thinking.

This book is also especially dedicated to those people contending with all sorts of learning issues, from when you are young and at school, to anyone who is struggling further along the journey of life, unsure of their bearings – I salute you. Keep going, never give up and always pursue life vigorously. I hope that this book offers you a ray of hope to illuminate your true path and to change yourself for the better. We can all make these kinds of changes inside us. No one needs to be stuck. So to all those determined and dedicated souls who wish to make change happen, and find authenticity, God bless you.

Some readers' views

"A one stop shop for personal development. If you want to have more, become more and live a more authentic and fulfilling life, this is the book for you." Bev James, CEO of The Coaching Academy, Best Selling Author of *Do it! or Ditch it.*

"A passionate, insightful and practical guide to how to think and act differently in our ongoing 'present point of power' - and so change ourselves and our lives for the better." Emmy Yeadon - Transformational Leadership and Team Coach

"For those who feel they are stuck with what life hands out – I strongly encourage you to read this book and take action!" Merete Langler - Business Development Coach

"A fascinating insight into how the mind works... accessible to anyone who wants to understand how what's going on in their head is shaping their life." Nikki Wild, Executive and Business Strategy Coach, Wild Empowerment Ltd

"Using the techniques and advice within this book you will not only unlock your potential and achieve your ambitions but become a better, more respected person for it." Paul Bates MBA, CMgr. Production Manager at Siemens

"I have never spent so much time pondering over words inside a book as this one. I love the way my mind would just take me off to dig deep in how what I was learning showed up in me. FAB!" Lisa Baker

"Andrew guides the reader to develop deeper understanding of themselves, the person they are now and how that relates to their authentic self - and provides guidance on how to use intentions to reconnect with that authenticity to live a more fulfilling life." Emma Brassington - Business Development Manager, University of York

"I particularly liked the inclusion of Andrew's own naturalistic artwork and diagrams which personalise the whole reading experience. A fascinating journey about aligning our life's purpose with our true selves." Jason Fletcher, MindWorks Therapy Training

"Throughout the chapters, Andrew offers his own views and makes good use of practical examples to illustrate a wide range of methods and tools, some rooted in convention and others that will undoubtedly challenge some received wisdom." Martin Care - Bid Director at Bombardier Transport

- Introduction -

One day in the heavenly realms, God summoned together the entire angelic host for an important decision to be made about humankind. There was a subdued silence amongst the host, as God announced: 'Humankind is becoming very clever and advancing rather more quickly than expected.' The entire angelic host responded with resounding agreement. God continued: 'So we have a problem and we need to agree a solution to it today. How do we go about hiding the keys to the Kingdom of God, until humankind is suitably ready to deserve the right to find them?'

For a while there was great consternation in the heavenly realm as the angels wrestled with God's dilemma.

Then one very bright angel announced a solution: 'The solution is to hide the keys to the Kingdom of God at the very top of the highest mountain. Surely humankind will *never* find them there?' There was a loud assent, like the sound of the roaring sea in a storm, as the angelic host agreed and applauded in great celebration that a solution had been found.

God, too, nodded in agreement for a moment. But then he furrowed His great brow, and said: 'This is a great idea, but I am afraid that humankind's cleverness will soon mean that they will climb the highest peaks to explore the roof of the world.' He added: 'Surely in so doing, they would therefore discover the keys to the Kingdom of God.'

God beseeched the entire angelic host to resolve their tricky predicament.

Again there was subdued silence amongst the host, as they muttered their agreement that the proffered solution would not work after all. Vexed, they bowed their heads in deep thought for an age, an aeon and then another age.

After a great silence, another bright angel announced a different solution: 'The solution is to hide the keys to the Kingdom of God at the very bottom of the deepest ocean. Surely humankind will *never* find them there?' There was a mighty, loud sound like the rumble of thunder and the howling of the wind as the angelic host agreed and applauded in great celebration that this time the solution had indeed been found.

God, too, nodded in agreement for a moment. But then he again furrowed His great brow, and said: 'This is a great idea, but I am afraid that humankind's cleverness will soon mean that they explore the ocean floor to the depths of the deepest oceans of the world.' He said: 'Surely in so doing, they would therefore discover the keys to the Kingdom of God.'

God once more beseeched the entire angelic host to resolve their tricky predicament.

The angelic host muttered their agreement that this solution would not work either, and then lapsed into a subdued silence.

Perplexed and frustrated, they bowed their heads in deep thought.

Suddenly the silence was broken by God Almighty and All That Is as He raised his gleaming sceptre in great joy. His great height towered over the host as they lifted their heads in joyous response to God as He proclaimed the great solution to humankind's cleverness: 'Great joy to the world and to the host of the heavenly realm, I have discovered a solution.'

He proclaimed: 'We will put the keys to the Kingdom of God in each man, woman and child on the planet, and they will *never* find them there!'

This book's purpose is to be a guide for you and a sort of practical do-it-yourself manual that is easy to learn from and follow. In it I describe a journey that contrasts two realities you can create for yourself. One reality defaults to the conditioning of the acquired self and the other is built from the uniqueness of your authentic self.

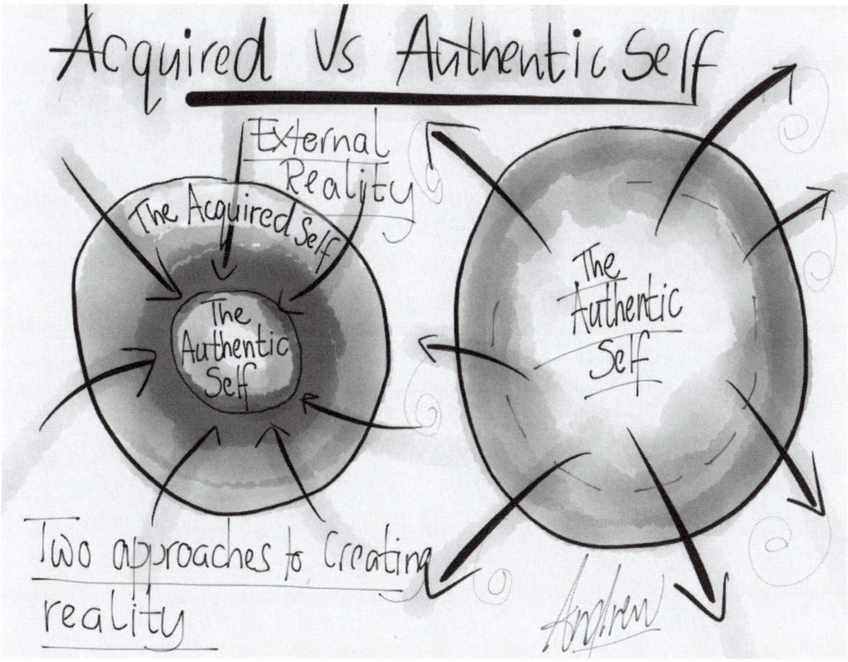

Figure 1: Acquired versus authentic self

My intention is to give you a heading and a bearing, to allow you to set a course that will direct you and take you on your own personal journey of self-discovery. Along the way my hope for you is that you will find the keys to your own kingdom – keys that unlock the doors to your own potential and uniqueness and your own true authentic self.

Along the way you will encounter all sorts of obstacles, pitfalls and traps. What you will, however, come to recognise is that these are merely your own inner demons, and your self-limiting projections; these are the negative forces and default reactions that you have acquired along the pathways of your life so far. They become forms of conditioning. I use a concept called your acquired self to collectively describe this conditioning and succumbing to negative forces and limitations. And they are your own personal dragons that need to be slain by you. To do this you have to find the resources within yourself that give you the know-how, tools and techniques and the courage to overcome yourself and get out of your own way. In this way you can fight against your own conditioning and deserve the right to access your authentic self. So this book is intended to guide you along your way. Once you start along this intention, then step by step, you begin to return to your true authentic self. These are the keys to your kingdom.

Every day in every way you get better and better.

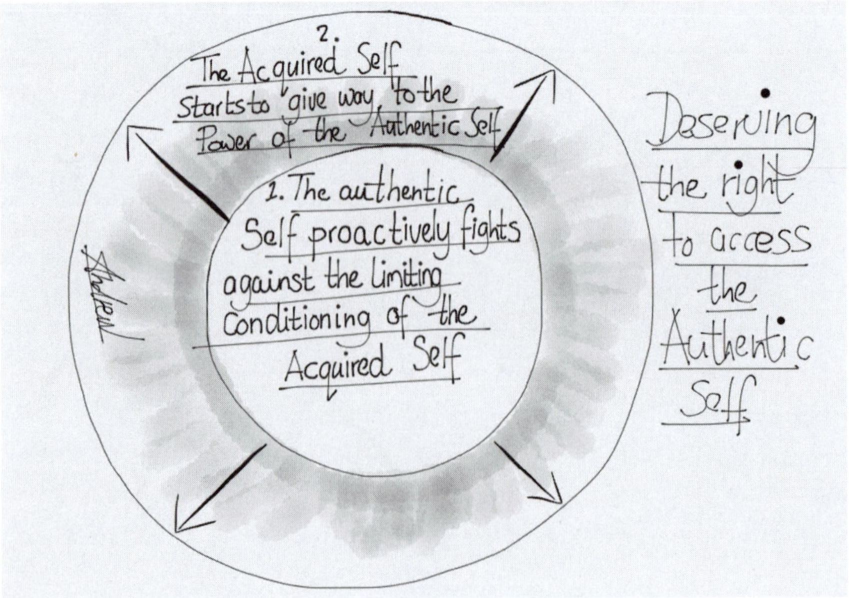

Figure 2: Deserving the right to access your authentic self

Changing your mind

If I said to you, 'We make our reality', I have a feeling the answer might come back, fairly forcefully, 'Oh, yeah? And what about if I stub my toe on a rock, is that something I've made?' And, of course, a reply like that would be entirely reasonable – your toe, and the rock, have an irresistible physical presence, particularly when one is brought painfully into contact with the other. But is the physical world the only world we know? And, indeed, how do we know it?

Before you throw your hands in the air, chuck this book across the room and take yourself for a long walk, let me reassure you: this is, above all, a really practical book, providing you with a logical process to follow, a series of insights, principles, exercises and tools that will help you understand change, get rid of the negative forces in your life that are holding you back, and allow you to rediscover and return to the true you – your original authentic self.

The amazing thing about the way the world works on a physical, scientifically documented level, is that we really can, quite literally, change our minds and, by changing our minds, we can change our lives as well.

This book is the fruit of careful observation and long practical experience. I have spent many years working with people, executives, managers and leaders in all sorts of walks of life and organisations across the world, helping them to develop and change. As my experience and expertise has grown, I have noticed certain consistent truths. What has become apparent, time and again, is that, deep down, we all want to shine, be happy and be the best we can be in life – but that far too many people find themselves trapped in dead, default and conditioned ways of being that limit them and stop them achieving this desire. I believe that millions of people feel trapped in this way, and that, deep down, what they are truly seeking is to rediscover and return to an authenticity that they know is there. It's inside or outside there somewhere, but always seems just out of reach. Somehow, along their way through life, they feel as if they have lost the connection to who they really are and who they were really meant to be.

Through my work with others, helping them to make this reconnection, I have gradually developed and honed a set of principles and created my own unique process that, when followed and adopted, powerfully enable people to return to their true authentic selves. This book provides you with those principles and that process.

What this book is not:

This book is not about magic, or 'out-there' concepts or simple quick fixes, nor is it about ways of overcoming deep trauma, stress or any type of severe psychological condition or disturbance – if this is what you are seeking, then this is not your book; there are other books and authors that can better help you instead.

Who this book is for...

If you are seeking an understanding of yourself and why you regularly find yourself getting in your own way, and want to find out how you can change this, then this book is for you.

If you are looking to understand how to overcome your limiting beliefs and the negative forces of conditioning, then again this book is for you.

This book is intended to help you to return you to your true authentic self by being inspired, following a process and going on a journey of personal discovery.

Importantly, though, this book is for all ordinary people everywhere and anywhere, just like me and you, who want the tools to help them to change, overcome their conditioning and return to who they are meant to be, and simply be the best they can be.

Look around you and what do you see?

Looking back on most of my adult life, I seem to have spent a great deal of my time noticing people and observing human behaviour around me. One of the things that struck me again and again is that, for many people, human existence is not all that it could be. I felt, and feel, there could be so much more. Many people, it seems, feel trapped and imprisoned in their lives, while at the same time doing everything they can to resist any kind of change. I get a profound sense of sadness and uneasiness, a feeling I find very hard to put into words when I look around at us as human beings. It really does seem as though we all have an almost overpowering tendency to restrict ourselves and to get in our own way, as it were.

I wondered if these were just my crazy thoughts at the time, the fruits of an overactive imagination, or a paranoid inclination towards some sort of plot or conspiracy (like in the film *The Matrix*). However, despite all this, I kept coming back to the central theme of human beings limiting themselves; that we all become, in some shape or form, conditioned to believe that this is simply just the way life is for each of us. I do wonder if others get similar fleeting thoughts, too, from time to time? In my work helping others I often have profound conversations that support this notion. So I do get the feeling that I'm not entirely alone in these thoughts. Perhaps you too may have pondered and reflected on thoughts such as these occasionally? And yet it is very easy to shake ourselves out of this state of mind, and say to ourselves, 'Come on, get real.'

However, having been through this journey, I do believe that there can be so much more to our lives, that we can, indeed, reach and achieve our deepest desires. That there is a profound sense that life must have a purpose to it, for each and every man, woman and child on this planet: that we are here for a reason. I do believe that life is a miracle, that our lives can be absolutely phenomenal and that somehow it is our life's journey to discover this for ourselves, and find our own meaning and purpose.

To get to this I also believe that we have to fight against ourselves first for a while, to believe we deserve the right to have this. I get the sense that we have to dare to reach out, and have the mindset and courage to become deliberate and purposeful and to want more to get the lives that we desire and deserve.

So that is really the intention of this book. My hope for you is that you will connect to its message and dare yourself to be inspired to get the most out of your own life, to lead your life deliberately and with determination and purpose, so that it takes you on a journey to fulfilment, wisdom and joy.

Over time I have become aware that so many people I have met, worked with, been friends with, had deep conversations with, as well as others I have simply just been acquainted with, bumped into, or simply rubbed shoulders with, seem to be journeying along pathways that often seem to lead to dissatisfaction, disappointment and sadness, living lives constrained by mediocrity of self or of others, burdened by coping strategies, lack of control, or over-control, unhelpful habits, unwarranted and uncontrollable emotions, and attitudes such as unworthiness, and generally leading profoundly unfulfilled lives. And yet at times each of us yearns deep down for something more, something different to happen to transform our lives.

As I've already mentioned, I fully acknowledge that this might just be a product of my own overactive imagination. However, over the years this belief in the unhappiness of some people I meet has developed into an increasingly acute awareness that as human beings we have to wake up and transform. Helping people do this has become the central purpose of my work.

To this end, I have spent many years working with, researching, learning, observing, trying out and testing various approaches to personal change that have been effective and successful for other people. Continually refining my approach and honing what works, I have augmented my method by using wisdom, principles and techniques from other sources too. For example, using philosophy and principles of faith from ancient scriptures have provided other useful points of view. Most importantly further insights have come from deeply researching into emerging understandings from within the neurological sciences. I have applied elements from all these sources, as well as supporting them with lessons learned and applied from my own journey towards transformation, and discovering what it means to strive to be enlightened, and to achieve a true sense of freedom.

From all these studies, I have over the years developed a unique expertise in developing and applying approaches that help people to make personal changes for themselves that simply work.

I am privileged to spend a significant part of my life helping others to become aware that they can change and transform themselves and lead lives for the better; to realise that they too can challenge their perceptions of the world (a construct they have actually created for themselves) and that they can do something different and consequently change their reality; to live a life that brings profound authenticity, enthusiasm, joy and contentment that enhance all aspects of their own personal success and achievement.

The question of the human condition

In my varied work as a development specialist, management change consultant, coach and mentor I have been privileged to meet, work and share experiences with many different people across the world. I work with and help many different organisations, often supporting managers, directors, executives and other individuals all doing things of importance and significance. They all seem to tell similar stories about themselves as individuals and as groups that correlate to my own observations.

For example…

So many people I meet seem to have found themselves trapped in self-created limiting strategies and habits around coping with life in general, gradually becoming aware that they are living restricted, increasingly joyless lives.

I began to see the underlying patterns to these types of conditioning, and I started to ask myself the following questions.

Why is it that…
so many of the potentially gifted and fantastic people I meet often can't seem to free themselves from their problems and fail to choose to take steps and make changes for the better in their lives?

Why is it that…
people appear to choose to be constrained by the very thing that they need to free themselves from and so remain controlled by it?

So why is it that…
so many of us seem to have the same sorts of unhelpful things keep happening to us, over and over, time and time again?

How come…
we keep having the same sorts of relationship issues?

Why is it that…
it seems there is an increase in background health issues, such as skin irritations, asthma and general allergic reactions?

How is it that…
people apparently buy the idea that they have no control of what 'seems to happen to them'?

Why is it that…
many people feel they need to micro-control events and everything that happens around them?

Why is it that…
so many people believe they have little or no ability to break out of the vicious circles of negative behaviour that affect their lives?

Why is that…
some people go about their lives in ways that actually create misery and discomfort?

How come…
issues of unhappiness, stress, anxiety, depression and mental illness seem to be increasing at an alarming rate?

And why do…
so many people seem to have lost hope in themselves and their dreams and passions?
so many people seem lethargic to life, half asleep, counting out time in their daily lives, being continually in some sort of comfortably numb, mindless stupor?
so many people not believe that they deserve the right to experience life as being magical and full of wonder, and instead don't care if they miss out or don't want to be part of the awesomeness of being alive and being able to free themselves?
others still refuse to lift themselves out of the ordinary, as they don't believe they are special and unique?

And why…
do many people feel racked by guilt in their lives over one thing or another?
do others feel a gnawing sense of insecurity about themselves and lack confidence?
for whatever reason do people deny themselves joy or don't allow themselves to receive praise from others in their lives?
do some people go to great lengths to avoid facing up to, or doing, something that has to be done and instead project before themselves a façade of denial?

What is it that drives some of us in negative ways…

to a constant and unnecessary need for pursuing perfection and feeling that it is wrong to ever make mistakes?

into feeling that whatever happens we must not show weakness, and that we must be strong at all times instead?

to over-strive to achieve, and push through to get what we want?

to become a people pleaser, believing that others are somehow always better than us, and that it is important to meet the needs and wants of others, that we are not important, that we don't count and don't matter?

The gods of the ages…

Throughout man's history, writers of ancient scriptures, wisdom and religious texts have referred to the predicaments above.

The wisdom and teachings from some of the ancient scriptures describe this predicament as 'man's fallen state' or the 'human condition'. Their messages are, at a high level, essentially intended to give hope to mankind: that all humans can be delivered, redeemed and liberated from this sort of conditioning. So, by abiding by certain principles, humankind can free itself, from itself, and reach beyond itself to higher ideals. To do this many ancient scriptures and religions point to reaching such higher ideals through worship and surrendering ourselves to a god, or gods: supernatural omnipresent beings, which are not of this world but are somehow on a higher plane, or order of reality than us physical beings. The ancient wisdom of the scriptures over the ages point us to gods, deities, angelic immortal beings, for example, that live on higher spiritual planes than us mortal humans and are somehow intimately involved with, influence and guide humankind. Many of the religions of the ages tell us that by deliberately submitting to God, human life, whether of the individual or of others (the community), will be fulfilled, worthwhile, will have purpose, be rich in experience and be connected to a greater sense of being, blessed and peaceful. That the generations to come will be blessed also, and so on through future ages.

And that life-long worship leads to a greater deserving in this life, which ultimately leads to a promise of a better life to come in eternity, in the afterlife, after the physical life is done.

The other underlying message of the ancient scriptures is that if we choose not to follow the ways of whatever god(s), and live life by our own rules and principles, this will lead to its own undesirable consequences: to smaller, less significant, lesser lives that have a propensity for misery, suffering of self and others around us. They tell the story that in the long run, such a life will lead to separation and disconnection, falling from favour and not being fulfilled. Ultimately some religions go further still and point to exclusion and damnation in an eternal afterlife of some sort.

I want you to know that my view is that any journey to self-fulfilment and freedom doesn't need any higher reason, purpose or mystical, spiritual calling.

I know that many people find fulfilment simply an end in itself, and that is absolutely fine and perfectly good enough. So in my opinion, it doesn't matter if you don't believe in any form of spirituality at all. To get to fulfilment and freedom, it isn't contingent on you having to believe in any religion, or system. I hope this brings you a sigh of relief.

Having got that important and significant point cleared up and out of the way we are then set free to discover what we can learn from the wisdom of formal spirituality and how those principles might be applicable, useful and beneficial to us along our journey. It seems that on many levels such stories can be easily dismissed by modern rationalism as being outdated and irrelevant. That such beliefs merely play to deep-rooted fears of not belonging, being separate from. That such held positions and creeds are not rational and instead are more about subjugation and methods of mass control etc. They play on your primary emotions, such as fear, separation, intolerance and guilt. Or if you don't believe or refuse to submit to the gods laid down by the culture and society of the day, then you don't belong, you have no right to live alongside everyone else that does and has. That you are a minority outcast and therefore need to be excluded. These viewpoints have been part of our history for thousands of years and can be still observed today, with many fundamentalists, sects and advocates of religions worldwide espousing similar views. So I completely understand why it is that, in our modern times, many people are moving away from such views as controls, and therefore desiring to free themselves from their grip. I feel that we need to move beyond getting trapped in such static and limited approaches, and evolve towards more resourceful views, which create more dynamic motivations, such as joy, happiness, enthusiasm and compassion. Such wisdom is also found in these same ancient scriptures and in the wisdom of the ages.

So my view is also to try to work with seeing such concepts from other perspectives. That our understanding of our place in the universe is not a fixed construct but rather that we are continuing to evolve our understanding of spirituality and existence, and further developing wisdom. That what was at one time considered irrefutable isn't necessarily fixed knowledge at all. That our understandings are forever changing and adapting as we advance through different ages and eras of humankind.

I would argue that as our understanding changes, our concepts of God and spirituality and what that means must also adapt and transform. That doesn't mean that we abandon what has gone before us, but rather that we build on it instead, and reach further into the deeper meanings of ancient writings and what message they have for humankind today. It is also fair to say that many traditionally held views and tightly adhered to opinions once held by many denominational faith groups are making headway to change and adapt to reflect the spirit, sentiment and wisdom of this age. As individuals, I believe there is an important need for us to do the same, and see things with different eyes. In that way we don't reject the benefits of what has gone before, but see it with fresh eyes and new understandings and we may interpret what was once understood to mean this or that in different ways that reflect humankind's advancements. Again, to do this we don't have to acquiesce to any religious thought or belief system: I am suggesting instead that we simply learn from their wisdom about applying timeless human principles that have worked through the ages.

All That Is…

So I feel that the concept of spirituality and connection to greater things beyond us is connected to the principles of human growth and as such is important to acknowledge. Perhaps spirituality in its broadest sense needs to be held in tension, acceptance and in wonder with an attitude of openness; not rejected or dismissed too readily but instead its possible impact and benefit to us as human beings considered. That in our everyday lives being lived out in this era, we might understand and interpret what was, against what is now, in new ways. And see things from the spirit of our times, rather than through the perceptions of bygone eras. So I make no apology for the fact that I am beginning to appreciate and support the idea that our own personal journeys are somehow inextricably interwoven with a connection to things greater than ourselves – and all their myriad meanings and interpretations.

Having said this I deliberately make no reference or leaning towards any particular faith, dogma, denomination or religion at all, as I believe that in this book it is important to remain free from and thereby not limited to any particular formal (or otherwise) belief system. I believe that if you combine all the key religious principles and take them to their highest level, you will find profound commonality, agreement and synergy. In this way one avoids getting caught up with the ways and means of their more traditional nuances of application.

Throughout this book I will be using the principle of mind, brain, body and, sometimes, spirit as a holistic concept to try to convey the process of personal change and its impact on us as individuals. In addition, I dare to hypothesise that consciousness itself is highly organised and goes far beyond our physical beings. That consciousness extends beyond us as individuals and is much, much bigger than we dare to dream, and is an eternal construct. That we are all somehow intimately connected to each other and everything around us, including things that are much bigger than we can currently comprehend. In the ancient scriptures and religions this is attributed to the concept and understanding contained in the word used for (the spirit of) God, as has been already outlined. However, to avoid prejudices and misunderstandings, or wrong perceptions, I have found it preferable to use an all encompassing 'universal' term, 'All That Is', instead. This term will be used to describe our connection to greater consciousness outside ourselves, the connectivity that we share with each other as well as with physical and mental reality.

My story

Looking back at my own life, I can remember the lessons I learned to overcome my own early experiences that created my own conditioning. Many of these were based around being different. These caused fitting in issues for me, which over the following years led to acute self-doubt in myself, my abilities and simply just getting on with others, all of which I desperately wanted. Especially to be accepted and liked.

From an early age, I acutely sensed that I was very different from the other children in my class at school. I was aware of thinking and acting differently from my classmates. I have always been a very sensitive person, and I found perceiving this very painful. My earliest experiences of school were of being labelled by my teachers as being dim, and a slow learner. I was told I was 'thick', 'stupid', 'dumb' and a 'no hoper'.

The reason for this, I found out later, was that I am dyslexic, particularly around sequencing of verbal information. I went through the school system during the 1960s and 70s. Dyslexia, however, was not at all understood or even acknowledged within the education system at the time. I have contended with this condition all my life, although my spelling, writing and maths did improve dramatically at around the age of 19. For most of my life I have been deeply ashamed and embarrassed about this condition. In fact in my early to mid-career I learned to hide it well. It just took lots of energy and psychic bandwidth to keep it in check and out of sight. Throughout this time, I devised a number of clever coping strategies to ensure that I was never exposed as being dyslexic. However, today I am actually very secure and okay to be who I am. I have learned to be proud to celebrate the huge advantages it has given me. I have learned, too, to simply laugh at myself if its downsides get in my way or become noticed. And so despite this, I have continued to strive towards achievement and being the very best I can be – with some considerable success.

Throughout my whole school life (all the way from infants' school to leaving at 17), dyslexia meant I found it almost impossible to learn by rote and by sequence. I still find this hard, even as an adult. Back then, I could not learn in the same way the other kids seemed to. I was also a very restless boy and could not settle. This meant that I couldn't concentrate on learning at school. Like many dyslexics, my writing was shockingly bad, as was my spelling. I could never remember my times tables, couldn't add up or take away – my maths was abysmal. Long division at school took me years to get even moderately okay with. Concepts like 'push' and 'pull', 'clockwise' and 'anticlockwise' were mysteries to me. As were phrases like 'my mother's brother' or my 'brother's mother'. I was left-handed and, at the time, pretty awkward too. I hated the structure of learning at school, and the way it kept building sequentially from one thing to another meant that I was constantly being left trailing behind in my class.

My adverse response to schooling sowed the seeds for shaping a number of limiting beliefs about myself and my abilities that conditioned much of my adult life (a common enough story for many dyslexic people). Limiting beliefs are perceptions that condition us to believe in and focus on our learned behavioural restrictions. Limiting beliefs then establish consistent behavioural responses and once developed become default responses that we automatically react to. My own limiting beliefs formed a powerful part of my own inner self-talk at the time, which in turn then conditioned me into believing that this was who I was. That there was no getting away from these inadequacies and deficiencies, even as I matured into adulthood. This is typical of how limiting beliefs inhibit us and our growth. More of this later.

Through these events in my early life I mistakenly believed that my identity was now indelibly, irreversibly and inexorably flawed for life – this is an example of what is meant by conditioning. The Christian religion calls this the human condition.

A poignant moment, I remember from senior school, was my parents being told at parents' evening that I would never, ever be capable of taking maths or English O levels. I remember my mother, in exasperation, telling me that I would become a *dustbin man*. I left school, as predicted, with virtually no (in the world's eyes anyway) useful qualifications. My self-confidence level was at ankle height.

An inner truth that whispers

Despite all the above, however, something that was always deeply buried in my psyche, even as a young boy, was another far more profound inner truth… It would quietly whisper and gently stroke me during times of soulful reflection. Whenever I took time to listen to my true inner self, it gave me the feeling that I am actually very bright, despite my school experiences informing me otherwise. I knew, even then, that all I needed to do was to simply trust and believe in it. My true inner self had an authenticity that seemed to whisper to me that it had always been part of me. Somehow, beyond all the evidence suggesting otherwise, I kind of felt its deep truth, but at the same time the evidence I'd accumulated through life's experiences meant I ignored and denied it. Occasionally though, I would get glimmers of its existence. For example, I have always been very creative, even as a young boy. I have a gift and a talent for art and was well practised. I have also always been very insightful and extremely intuitive. I would just know things would turn out in certain ways ahead of time. And, when things were right, they seemed to be very simple and easy to me.

However, it seemed the world around me was informing me otherwise. It seemed to me, at that time, that things had to be difficult, and complicated to be real. Furthermore, something I didn't believe, as it seemed hidden from my awareness at the time, was a natural ability to get on with other people. As it turned out, this ability along with all my above virtues would come into awareness and mature much later on in life. For now they appeared to me as glimmers of 'impossible possibilities'. During my schooling, these attributes of my character were not seen as being of any value or future worth.

Interestingly, we all have access to our true authentic selves. Our true inner selves have a fantastic natural ability to access unlimited wisdom from deep within our unconscious minds. This only gets expressed, though, when we are playing to our true strengths. It is our unconscious that has access to All That Is. Our true authentic selves attain this and know us completely, are able to gather and use our talents and gifts, as well as knowing us intimately. Most often it is merely a feeling that prompts us, or calls to us in gentle tones and quietly whispers at times in our lives.

To become aware of our true authentic selves we need to learn to tune into it. This is because it is more a 'feeling' than actual words. It is understood to be the more intuitive right side of our brains that make this unlimited resource available to us. Such revelations may only be passing glimmers and they may feel uncertain to us. In addition they are certainly easily ignored, inhibited, denied or rejected. This is because the more logical and factual left side of our brains often denies such feelings permission to enter into full consciousness. This is then justified by copious amounts of inner chatter that again forms part of our human conditioning.

Our inner true authentic self is always there and always tells the truth. The key is to access it more of the time. To do this successfully we need to make available more of our conscious bandwidth. However, any spare bandwidth is usually being consumed unnecessarily by the conditioning that forms part of our acquired selves. This therefore makes it harder to access such ultimate wisdom. As we will see later meditative interventions can provide a pathway that allows us to learn and gain access to this seemingly fragile phenomenon. The approaches in this book are all aspects of rebalancing our available psychic bandwidth to enable us to listen more to our true inner selves.

Sometimes you get a lucky break and someone who believes in you

In my youth, I had always assumed I would end up at art college doing a foundation degree somewhere – like my mum had before me. When I left school, with next to no decent qualifications, I decided that I wasn't good enough, or sufficiently talented, to make it as an artist. This was in spite of the fact that, at that time, it was all that I felt I was good at. In hindsight, turning my back on the art world turned out to be a good decision. Even though I am talented and creative, and to this day still use my artistic abilities, I prefer creating things by thinking and structuring things differently.

For whatever reason, at 17 years old I decided that engineering would be my starting point in life. My dad was an engineer, and an apprenticeship route appealed to me at the time. It seemed secure and a good grounding to start from. Despite my lack of prerequisite qualifications in the four main educational subjects, I embarked on this route. At that time it was possible to sit the IQ entrance tests for those like me who hadn't made the educational grade. However, because these were all based on sequenced learning, speed and other techniques I struggled with, I kept failing these too, time after time.

Out of the scores of rejection letters I received there was one that stood out. This one letter invited me to an interview for a company that worked with my dad at the time.

The person who interviewed me was called Mr Hinds. As soon as we shook hands he said that, although he knew my dad, I had actually failed the entrance test. He went on to explain that there must have been some sort of mix up and I shouldn't have received an interview letter at all because of the failed entrance test. But, since I had come all this way and I had actually got an interview letter, he would honour this and interview me anyway.

It turned out that this was my lucky break.

While academically I was considered wanting, conversationally was another matter entirely. As an only child, I had learned to be good at talking to adults. The more we talked the more Mr Hinds liked me. Eventually he looked at me seriously and said, 'You know what? I really like you, Andrew, because there is something about you. I believe you are going to make something of yourself in life. So I'm going to take a risk in offering you an apprenticeship.'

I was amazed. He then continued to say, 'As part of your apprenticeship you must attend day release at technical college. That means more academic work for you. I know you will find that hard. And it is a lot more demanding than school work. And here's where there is sting in this tale, Andrew. The deal is, because I am making a special case about you having no suitable qualifications, in addition to which you did not pass the entrance tests either, so, because of these two issues, you must prove to me that you are worthy of this chance I am giving you. So you must pass your first year exams with good grades. When you have these grades I want you to present them to me personally. Only then will I let you continue for the next three years of your apprenticeship. If you don't do this, you will be out of the apprenticeship scheme, and out of a job. Do you understand?'

Naturally I gladly agreed to our deal. What I found amazing about this conversation with Mr Hinds was that he actually believed in me. And this was the first time anyone had ever said anything like this to me. I had never had a conversation like this one ever before. And it made a profound impact on my life as a 17-year-old lad who, seemingly for the first time, had been given a lucky break.

A Mr Foster moment

It was 1979. I had had my lucky break. I found myself in the world of work, and I loved every moment of it. The company I worked for was booming and busy and that meant plenty of opportunities to learn. And I threw myself into it and immersed myself totally in the experience.

I loved working for a living, but technical college was another matter. It brought back for me all the bad associations of my school years – feeling dumb and stupid. This was exacerbated by the technical aspects: science and maths-based content. My feelings of inadequacy were rife. As a coping strategy I became the class clown and messed about a lot. While this made me a popular lad with my peers, the lecturers merely put up with me.

I clearly remember a profound and fundamental pivot point in my life at this time.

This was the encounter with Mr Foster. He was a senior maths and science lecturer and very strict and seemingly hot-tempered. I clearly remember his small stature, long white lab coat and chalky, chubby fingers. Blackboards were the teaching medium of the day. Personal computers were still a few years away from mainstream education. He had a no-messing nature and was very strict with us.

Unfortunately, my messing about and class-clown antics were not tolerated by him at all. One day it came to a head. I remember glibly announcing to Mr Foster that a group of us were going to leave his class early because we wanted to celebrate an 18th birthday and go drinking early that evening and later on go nightclubbing. This proved too much for Mr Foster to take and he blew up. Red-faced, he started by shouting at me. When I answered back, he grabbed me out of my chair and lifted me clean off my feet. I was six foot tall and he was considerably smaller, but his stocky frame made this feat seemingly easy. He dragged me kicking and screaming outside the classroom. In the corridor, he forced me up against the wall and began prodding me with his chubby, chalky index finger and berating me at the same time. He told me how I was throwing away my future by being stupid. He then changed pace, and said something that turned out to be a profound turning point moment for me, something that made all the difference to me, and deeply affected me. He paused, looked at me, and started underlining each of the next words by prodding me in the chest while slowly delivering each word at the same time prod by prod. He told me... that... I... could... go... to... university... if... only... I... concentrated... and focused! He also told me I was bright, and much cleverer than I believed. He told me that I needed to believe in myself and aim for better things. He suggested that I started to plan ahead a bit more and start to shape my life. Because if I did I could make something more of myself. I needed to break the model of class clown and classic underachiever and start doing something for myself and my future.

From that moment on everything changed

From that moment on everything really did change. Only a handful of people, that I knew of anyway, at my school actually went to university. My school cohort year apparently had the worst academic record for that school's history. Statistically, less than 3 per cent of people nationally at that time made it to university. Here was my teacher, who I thought hated me, telling me he believed in me. And that if I knuckled down, I too could get there.

This came as a revelation to me. Here was the second person who had recently told me that they had faith in me. Mr Hinds and now Mr Foster. These two people simply having confidence in me, a no-hoper (as I thought at that time), telling me that I could achieve something in my life and become a success, was completely new and alien to me. And so this changed everything for me. It was time to make new decisions and turn my life around.

I finally understood that if you want to do and achieve something you first have to push against yourself, to overcome yourself and your conditioned mind. I learned that you have to think differently to get different results.

Wake up and change to a new heading

To achieve anything, you have to overcome yourself and your own conditioning and fight and push against it. This is vital. To do this you first have to be inspired to change. Part of being inspired to do something else with our life is a necessary part of us. As you will understand later, we all deserve the right to make this transition and to be able to change our heading in life. When we wake up to the realisation that we have been unintentionally travelling along an unsuitable heading in life is often a light bulb moment. This revelation reconnects us to far deeper truths about who we are and the miracle of what we are really intended for. It is in itself a spiritual journey that leads to our true self. We all get glimmers of these inner truths as we live life.

The key is to be awake enough to become aware of them and then have the courage to pursue them. It takes bravery and tenacity to change course and take a new heading in our lives.

When we start to listen to our true selves, something profound shifts in reality. We get connected to a profoundly different set of underlying universal rules – I believe that discovering this is the difference between fate and destiny.

To pursue destiny requires us to awaken, or rather, more accurately, to reawaken. It is this reawakening and realisation that tells us that we have been off track in our life and that something needs to change for the better, to shunt us back onto the real heading we are meant to follow. This reawakening not only changes our attitude and mindset, it does other things too. Our imagination is awakened, and this is vitally important. It is our imagination that has the ability to change us, from the inside out. It is our imagination that begins to motivate and inspire us to pursue a purposeful and intended heading. When we set our sails and journey along this intentional new course then everything changes. Our purpose, our energy levels, our minds, our neurology, even our friendship circles. Our facial expressions change and reset into different configurations. People around us, especially those that know us well, will begin to become aware of such changes, certainly at an unconscious level and might even consciously notice these differences.

Once we are inspired to set our bearing to pursue a different heading, the internal changes create the necessary shift in life track. This in turn produces a completely different reality in the outside world for us. We become purposeful. We set goals to get the outcomes that we are seeking. In addition we discover that other people come alongside us to help us. Because we are inspired, our ability to influence others and bring them along with us becomes a part of our new reality. People will gladly help us to get what we are seeking and wanting to achieve. For example, people in authority, kind and interested people, will come along. Other people may have the wherewithal to help us, to open doors for us, and others still can grant us certain things.

So, to seek access to our true authentic selves requires us to reawaken from a dream world. It is our conditioning that creates this half awake dream world reality that leads us to accept a reality created from fate. Once we are awake we can overcome this conditioning. Each person's conditioning is like layers of untruth, created through life's difficulties that seek to protect us and to keep us safe. It is this conditioning that pulls the wool over our eyes, to convince us that we have no control at all and no power to change anything or do anything special in our lives. Overcoming our conditioning takes a little effort, as we have to do something in order to gain the right to set up a new reality – this is an immutable law.

This realisation allows us to reconnect to our true selves. It is our true authentic selves that have access to inexhaustible energy. This is utilised by our imagination. Our imagination, together with self-belief, is the most powerful conscious construct in the universe. Once in play, this powers and inspires us to achieve anything, and most importantly enables us to change to an intended new direction. This new life course in turn attracts our destiny. The tools to then change our heading are intrinsic. They are based on intention, purpose and self-belief. It is these tools that set us on a bearing – that of purpose, achievement, fulfilment and joy.

You have to work at it to get what you want

So that shift of course and change in heading in my own life track was the moment that I chose to turn my life around and pursue a purpose and head in a specific direction. I started to study at college. In fact I studied very hard. I thought to myself, if I am going to achieve anything then I need to be the very best I can be and prove this to myself.

This journey took a few years. I had to battle against my dyslexia. To my surprise, however, I found that with effort I could actually write legibly. In time my spelling got better and better, until it wasn't an issue any more. I was amazed to find that the harder I worked at this the better I got at overcoming the dyslexic issues that had plagued me during my school years.

The most startling revelation to me was that I started to get maths. After some private tutoring, I even started to enjoy it. I became proficient at algebra, and transposition in science became a 'doddle'… A whole new world of possibility was opening up to me. The feeling that I had when I started to put effort into overcoming my dyslexic tendencies gave me a tremendous sense of achievement and new found freedom.

To this day I believe that nothing, no disability or condition, or anything can hold you back. You merely need the tenacity and courage to overcome the false holds that your conditioning has over you. This is a deliberate and conscious choice. I also believe that its overcoming is a rite of passage that enables you to own the right to do something different and to have the choice to become the person you want to be and that you truly are. I learned that its power can be broken with effort. I found I could actually do formulae and equations and calculations.

I remembered back to what my head of year at school said to my parents. That I would never be able to pass English or maths. I was delighted to observe that this limiting prophecy was changing right in front of me. By changing my heading it was beginning to lead me to co-creating a new and different reality. With effort, I started getting good grades. These turned into top grades. Later I became one of the top students in my year group.

Over the years I served through my apprenticeship, I kept badgering my company's training manager, Mr Hinds, to send me away to study for a degree in engineering. I made sure that the company allowed me to go to a second day of day release to study additional engineering subjects that I needed to attain my goal. I also had to achieve merits and distinctions in all my grades to fulfil this ambition.

Eventually I got an interview with the man who was MD of my company at that time. He had the power to grant me my desires, and he needed to be convinced by me. I remember being scared stiff, as I'd never talked to him before. And he wanted to see me. I clearly remember being grilled about why I wanted to study for a degree. I promised him that I would get good grades. That conversation granted that door to open and everything changed. It was the beginning of many new things to come.

The beginning of better things to come

Four years later, in 1987, I was awarded my engineering degree. For me this was the culmination of all my determination and worth the effort and the eight years invested in this outcome. I was, and still am, extremely proud of this outcome. With this qualification, I was then able to advance my career to new levels, far beyond where I would have been able to without this. It enabled me to advance quickly and be at the top of the game in the world of engineering. Later this gave me the springboard to become a chartered engineer, which is considered to be the pinnacle of engineering excellence. This then opened other doors for promotion and betterment. It led me to doing a master's degree, and from there other pathways later paved the way for me to change careers, which carried me to eventually doing what I do now.

Looking back on my own story, there are some profound learnings about life. I learned about the vital importance of believing in yourself, planning ahead and building yourself up to achieve the outcomes that you want. This experience gave me a strategy or blueprint that I then utilised many times to achieve different and varied things from then on. The key is to be deter-mined to get what you want from life. To this day I look back on that time and believe that these are necessary attributes required by anyone wanting to do the same.

We can all overcome ourselves and get out of our own way. We have to push through and beyond our own conditioning of what we believe to be possible or impossible. When we do this a new world of prospects and potential opens up for us. I learned, too, about the power of qualifications and their capabilities to open up the doors of possibility in life. They are passports that give you the right to enter new levels. Each new level provides new and further potential opportunities in life.

So I hope that this story demonstrates some of the important practical factors that are required by anyone wanting to develop, improve, lead a better life and simply make change happen. The next section explores the key principles to believe in and focus on to make any personal change happen more easily. It took a long time for me firstly to discover and understand these as working principles, and then secondly to learn how to apply them. I believe that if you follow and apply the intrinsic wisdom behind these principles you will find that your own journey of personal change can be a lot smoother for you.

- Part 1 -

Universal principles of reality and freeing your mind

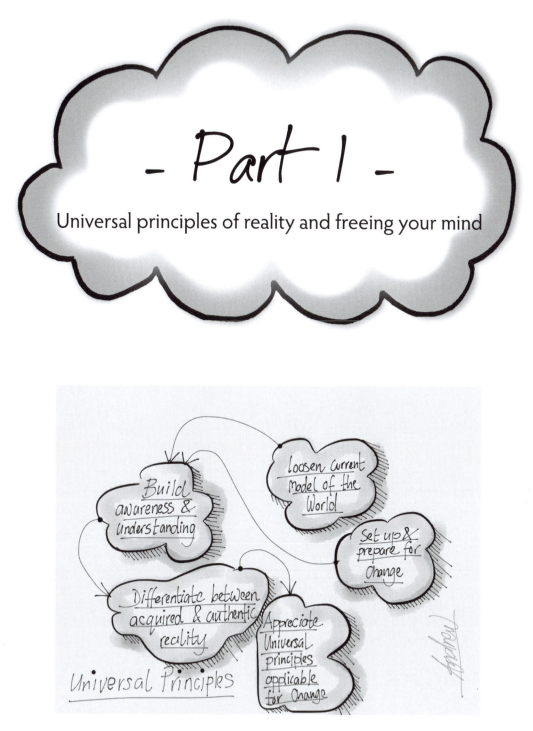

Figure 3: Universal principles applicable to personal change

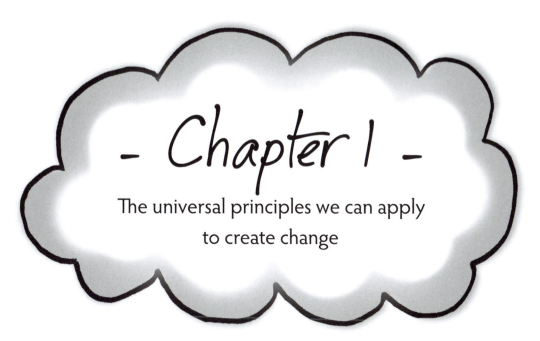

- Chapter 1 -

The universal principles we can apply to create change

Richard Bandler (cofounder of neurolinguistic programming (NLP) in the 1970s) once remarked (and I paraphrase) that all humankind are born as princes and princesses of this world. This is our authentic self. However, something in this world distorts that truth for all of us. And so we end up accepting and living the acquired lives of frogs instead, and not as the true and unique princes and princesses we are intended to be. In this way it seems that we spend our lives trying to return to becoming the authentic princes and princesses we were actually meant to be in the first place, and to shed our acquired 'frogness'.

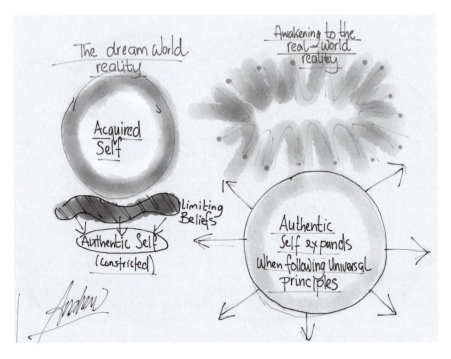

The dream world reality

Acquired Self

Limiting Beliefs

Authentic Self (constricted)

Awakening to the real-world reality

Authentic Self expands when following Universal Principles

Figure 4: Awakening to the expanding nature of the authentic self

By exploring the principles of universal reality, we can use our consciousness in smarter ways to honour and move increasingly closer to our unique and true authentic selves. When we apply these principles we therefore begin to awaken from the limiting effects of the dream world and expand ourselves. In this way we are able to obtain more of what we want, to grow and develop, and to live the lives that we desire and deserve.

The principles

Consciousness is eternal and is part of All That Is.
We create our reality through intention.
Natural grace and acceptance.
No frontiers, boundaries or limits.
The present moment has power and shifts the past and the future.
The law of importance, and the law of reverse effect.
Being joyful is our natural state.

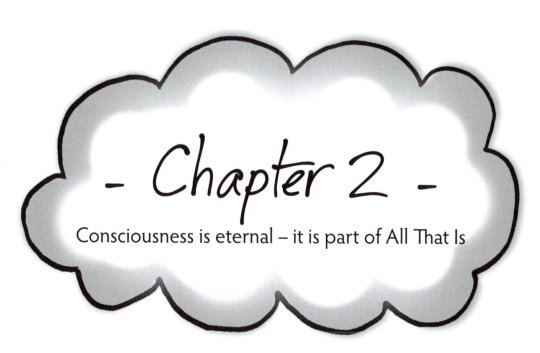

- Chapter 2 -

Consciousness is eternal – it is part of All That Is

The old tales about Aladdin and the genie in the bottle state that once the genie has attracted (conscious) attention from someone, such as the beggar boy, Aladdin, the genie in return (regardless to whom) always says, 'Your wish is my command', and whatever the wish is, it is magically manifested. No judgement is made by either party and what is asked for is simply accepted and delivered, every time, all the time. So it is with your thoughts and intentions.

Quantum science and the big picture about consciousness

Like many others, I have become intrigued by the alternative ways of thinking and looking at the universe that have been proposed by the study of quantum science.

This new scientific approach has, over the last 60 or so years, started to provide us with some very interesting and different ways of perceiving the universe of which we are a part. Quantum science starts with a number of baseline assumptions that form the core of studying the universe and the way it works. Many of these principles have been borrowed here in this book as a starting point for looking at our own personal lives.

For example, this is what quantum science suggests about the entire universe and consciousness:

That the universe is abundantly alive with consciousness. Consciousness is the ultimate creative force that drives All That Is. It is impossible to adequately describe. Consciousness is all around us, it is everywhere, present all the time in everything. It can't be held, seen, measured or touched. Consciousness just is. All consciousness is eternal. It never dies.

Consciousness is ever present. It makes up all things, humans and animals alike, from the largest mammal to the smallest microbe and virus. All organic matter, everything that grows has consciousness present within its form. Even inorganic materials and all matter, from the largest sun or planet, right down to each molecule and atom and particle is part of consciousness. All thoughts and ideas, too, are part of consciousness.

All things everywhere contain some form of consciousness

In this book I refer to the concept of God and spirit as *All That Is*. These words have been used interchangeably by mankind over the ages. I wonder perhaps if they might be an attempt to describe consciousness, in its largest sense. Many spiritual texts describe the spirit (of God) as unfathomable. It is the great I am, and is All That Is.

This phrase, All That Is, is one I first encountered in the manuscripts, research and writings of the late Jane Roberts (1929–1984; author of the Seth Books series). Jane established herself in the 1960s–1980s as a serious and pre-eminent figure in the study of extra sensory perception and paranormal phenomena. For many, even to this day, her work remains controversial, and perhaps way ahead of her time. However, in honour of her work, Yale University maintains a complete collection of her manuscripts and journals, which document her research and career.

Consciousness (like spiritual descriptions written in the ancient scriptures) is in time, and out of time, timeless and eternal. It is all that has been, all that is and all that will ever be. I believe that consciousness therefore doesn't begin and end with us as separate sentient beings. Perhaps it is not unreasonable to suggest that each individual awareness might be merely part of a bigger whole and that we are therefore all integrally part of All That Is.

With this as a starting principle, it is logical to assume that there are no boundaries of All That Is; it is universal, unknowable from our perspective. While we wrestle with what consciousness means as humans, there are even bigger aspects that go way beyond our own relationship with consciousness. Therefore this means that there could be infinite distinctions to consciousness.

From this viewpoint of consciousness we might say that consciousness is alive, it is life itself, it is self-structuring, self-organising and ever evolving. As we are assuming that all consciousness is connected to every other part of consciousness (in All That Is – as a concept) then quantum theory proposes that perhaps it is fair to suggest that all consciousness knows itself. That all other aspects of consciousness are intimately aware of all others at some level or another. It is apart and a part of itself and everything else. It is present in all forms: atoms, molecules, cells, organs, animals, plants, planets and so on. Quantum science uses the principle that all things have a consciousness of some kind, therefore each is a separate self, or fragment, while also being connected together as entities, the nature of which is currently a mystery and indescribable to us. However, our understanding is emerging as we are becoming more aware of it, its nature and its impact upon us and our reality.

In short, consciousness is big… huge… unfathomable and full of endless possibilities.

Human consciousness

Why is all this important? Why should it matter? What makes it significant?

Well, having an understanding of these principles is very useful, because understanding these principles enables us to apply them to ourselves and make them work for us as human beings. And why not? If these assumptions and principles turn out to be correct and we are a part of All That Is, then it stands to reason that we can then use these same principles as charts to guide our own direction.

As human beings, our consciousness has evolved into free will and is indeed very specialised, highly creative and complex. This consciousness is part of our true authentic self as we know it, and is intimately entwined with the ecosystem of our physical nature via our brain tissue, our biochemistry and our neurology – I call this the body whole. To allow us to interact with each other, our physical environment, as well as making sense of space and time constructs, our consciousness has evolved specifically around our unique external reality – the physical world. Our consciousness works effortlessly and symbiotically with both the conscious and the unconscious parts of our mind. As described later we have split brains that physically divide into two hemispheres, and create different ways of being, the interconnection of which creates the uniqueness of identity and our relationships with others and the world around us.

Our form of consciousness has organised and structured itself into distinct elements that are all part of the self (mind, brain, body and spirit), such as our psyche and ego, our imagination, memory and experiences as well as other elements. These interwoven interconnections between mind, body and spirit have uniquely evolved to enable us to experience the nature of this physical reality. At deeper levels our consciousnesses have intimate interconnections that we are only starting to superficially get to grips with. However, what is becoming scientifically clear is that we are not separate from other consciousnesses at all, perhaps they merely remain, as yet, undifferentiated.

Some aspects of consciousness are in our own awareness and other forms completely out of our awareness and comprehension. Its forms are endless and infinite. However, all reality is formed through these self-organising patterns of consciousness.

Consciousness is indeed a miracle and a profound wonder. It is not born nor does it die (including your own), it just is, and it is self-creating and the creative force for everything, everywhere, all the time. How our consciousness becomes part of the interplay of the mind, body and spirit that make up our physical being and reality is beyond the scope of this book.

But rest assured that you yourself are made up of a consciousness that is eternal. All your learnings and experiences here in this physical environment are important to your consciousness too and are never lost or destroyed, but will live on eternally.

How this operates and how to make sense of this is, as yet, way beyond our understanding.

Our form of consciousness is unique to this universe of physical and space and time-bound reality, and is what we are capable of being aware of, and what we make sense of, and can experience. As we evolve we differentiate and understand other subtler and interconnected realities (such as sub-atomic particles and electromagnetic realities, and even spiritual realities like afterlife and God, as a few examples). However, it may be possible that there are endless forms of other realities that exist, too, many of which might remain completely out of our range of awareness and experience, and that our senses might be unable to comprehend or even tune in to.

The principle that I'm adopting in this book is that all consciousness is interconnected and knows itself everywhere, always, all the time; therefore all consciousness follows the same indisputable, universal principles and laws. It is these rules that we can learn to understand, and therefore apply to our advantage.

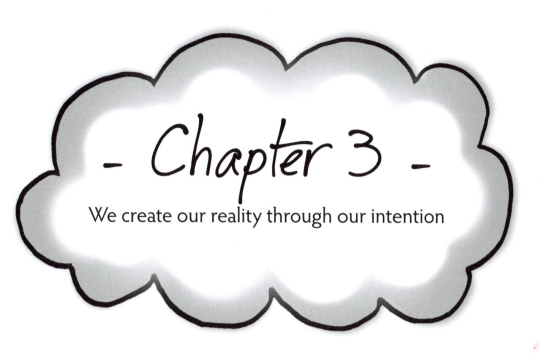

- Chapter 3 -

We create our reality through our intention

Intend what it is you want

All thoughts are conscious, energetic psychic constructs that provide the powerful means by which we as human beings constantly form, organise and hence create our reality every moment of our lives.

Intentions are a subject we will explore in detail later in this book. For now it is useful to understand that intentions are sophisticated, highly concentrated thought-forms, which, through the energy they collect and contain, naturally direct reality. They act as a vehicle that connects consciousness to All That Is. All That Is is highly attracted and tuned to correspond to the frequency of your intentional thought-form energy that we as human beings can direct. These then enable the necessary energy needed for your outcomes to be manifested into your external physical reality. This is in itself an effortless and graceful process that is continuously operating, everywhere, all the time, without fail.

An intention is consciously and deliberately formed by focusing and directing attention into the future, with purpose as to what it is that is really desired, what we love, what we like and what we want. Setting intentions is a process that only the true authentic self can do really very well indeed. Your awareness then watches out for the intention to unfold in external physical reality.

Interestingly, no information is required about 'how' it is to be manifested into reality.

So, we can also exploit this aspect of conscious creative forces to great effect, as we will see later in this book.

Pictures in your head and emotional states in your body

Whatever the intention you want to achieve, this element of conscious thought is able to enlist the support of your imagination (another conscious construct) and your internal resources unique to you. Your imagination is able to form representations (visually, aurally and kinaesthetically, using mind, body and spirit neurological connections) that project, in sensory terms, a probable prediction of what the experience will be like in advance. This then generates emotional body states that amplify the intention, to compare these projections with past recalled images to predict what might be manifested into external reality. Imagination also provides a large amplification of the psychic energy required to manifest whatever you intend into your external reality (more of how to do this in a later chapter).

So through our thoughts and intentions our mind–brain correspondingly represents these as pictures (and sounds) in our heads that are generated from emotional states in our body.

You get what you don't want

Counter-intuitively, however, intentions can be set 'unintentionally' too. In the same way, too much thought around what we don't want, what we fear, what we worry about, what we don't like and what we hate all eventually turn up, always, without fail every time. Positive or negative, wanted or unwanted – the process of converting intentional or unintentional thoughts into reality is one and the same. This is important to understand, especially how this sets up acquired cycles and patterns of grief for ourselves. We then end up living by these acquired constructs. Again we will look at this in some detail later on.

As briefly stated earlier, once a thought is intended, the conversion of that thought into reality takes over, and the transfer from our consciousness to All That Is is only tuned to the informational structure of 'what', rather than any 'how'. It is the 'what' that synchronistically gets worked and sorted into 'hows', in ways and means we do not comprehend. Left alone, the connection between any conscious thought or intention and All That Is will always sort out the 'how' to manifest the intended 'what' into reality by itself every time.

We are the artists and sculptors of our experience. We paint and sculpt our reality through the tools of our thoughts, desires and intentions. We therefore co-create our reality. We attract what we think, always, all the time, without fail.

- Chapter 4 -

Natural grace and acceptance

The universe and All That Is is self-governed by the principle of natural grace. This flows freely and abundantly in the universe. There is no effort required to use it, grace simply exists, and it is available and known by all consciousness. There is no right or wrong or good or evil in the natural universal order, grace simply abounds. So rather than become addicted to patterns of judgement and grief, if we simply accept the grace principle, then this will lead us instead to operate under different, more natural, universal paradigms.

Grace means undeserved favour, available freely. It is a complete acceptance of all events, thoughts and experiences, with no guilt, judgement or validation or justification required.

In the animal kingdom, for example, their consciousness is organised in such a way that grace and natural guilt are built in and instinctive. In this way they simply act.

Unlike their human counterparts, this is not differentiated in their awareness, as a choice. It simply exists, as a construct that operates automatically within their being. For example, both the prey and predator accept and understand when it's time to die when caught by a predator. There is no regret or remorse or guilt. It just is. That is grace in action.

For us as humans, our consciousness has developed the awareness of grace as the evolution of free will and choice. This has meant that grace, guilt and conscience have had to become a choice in themselves. We have as a consequence had to work out ways of applying these noble and universal constructs as ideas and notions into our own awareness. Grace principles can, however, be freely chosen to form part of our organised consciousness (more of this later).

In day-to-day life we consciously have to construct these within our human frameworks, for ourselves, with each other, and in our cultures and societies. Grace, guilt, acceptance, gratitude, judgement and conscience then become infinitely more complex in their nature for human consciousness.

As such, the natural idea of grace can be easily forgotten in the pursuit of our busyness, misused and misunderstood, or confused, or ignored completely or distorted in many ways. For example instead of choosing to live by the concept of grace, we can freely choose not to and instead adopt a more artificial form of survival, which is to accept cycles of grief and guilt. As a human race we do this really well, by the way.

We have the ability to fall out of natural grace from time to time and our authentic self becomes distorted through default and acquired constructs (limiting beliefs and bad habits etc.) in which other approaches are seemingly more important. An example might be defaulting to being judgemental or controlling, rather than being accepting. Hence the notions of good and evil emerge into our explanations of reality. However, at a much deeper level of consciousness, our authentic self knows all about the principles behind universal grace, and acceptance, how it works, and knows when it is present, and when it is not.

One notion of acquired constructs is that they are limiting beliefs we hold to be true about ourselves and the reality we perceive for ourselves. As we will see later, these are easily formed through association, socialisation, free will and choice, and sometimes even ignorance. Consequentially they are often fabricated distortions of reality that over time become progressively even more distorted, and as such we outwardly default to respond to them in correspondingly distorted ways. Limiting beliefs once formed become hidden away from view in our everyday conscious minds. These beliefs and attitudes eventually work their way into our entire being, adversely affecting both physical and mental reality.

In religious and faith contexts across our history this is often referred to and described in terms such as the human condition. That humankind is beset by original sin, and, being so, sets up beliefs around good versus evil in a fallen world. These can sometimes lead to accepting a fearful approach and this unintentional effect robs us of our connection to our true authentic self and All That Is – the very thing that such faith beliefs are supposed to connect to.

In contrast to this, as we have already described, many world religions have developed concepts around eternity, abundance, grace, acceptance and God as timeless, endless, never changing and all that has been, all that will be and All That Is. The interplay of spirit, mind, soul and body is grappled with in these various forms within all faiths.

In all cases, whether using grace and acceptance or not, we truly do create different realities.

- Chapter 5 -

No frontiers, boundaries or limits

As humans, we have physical form and so we can easily notice we are separate from others in obvious ways. So, that self ends at the outside of our skin is a logical viewpoint.

Other 'selfs' around us are the same. When we hold hands or touch we make connections. Even though our thoughts are our own, what we might not be so consciously aware of is that we constantly communicate our intrinsic thoughts through various channels, such as expression in body language for example. So I can seek to understand and am in turn understood. This for example is the basis of empathy, gut feeling and intuition.

Other less obvious organisations of separations and connections of self to other groups of self are made by colour, race, nationality, cultures, gangs, gender and so on. More subtle aspects of our personality separate us too, such as preferences, styles, likes and dislikes. So at one level we have the notion of separation and yet, at another, notions of connection.

Our own belief systems can separate us or connect us. Culturally learned beliefs pass amongst groups and become accepted, often without question or a passing thought. These define us as a collective and at the same time differentiate us from others.

So what is self? How do I define the me that I am and that am not? Where does me begin and end? Who am I really? What does it mean to be me, and not me? Am I defined by my personality, or gender, or learning and wisdom, or skills and capabilities?

You can choose to create and then hold a particular belief and then experience it manifested into your reality. If you don't like the results of this you have the flexibility, the power and authority to change your mind and adopt other beliefs instead. Subtly, though, you might not believe this to be true, or don't believe that you know how. We can all experience what we term as good, bad or evil things. As already mentioned, we have innate free will and choice. We can change our personalities, and our ego, although assumed to be fixed (like our personality), is flexible and adaptable if we so wish it to be. We can think big or be small-minded. All things are possible, always, every time. Even though our bodies have certain physical and mental capabilities (some more, some less than others), our consciousness is able to reach far beyond any of these constraints. Even in extreme cases of injury or disability.

The interplay of consciousness in mind, body and spirit that makes us human is multidimensional and highly individualised and of course unique. Our own consciousness constantly forms ever-changing and dynamic bridges and connections with itself and other aspects of reality, in and out of our awareness. It is a part and apart of this organised, physical, energetic mind and spiritual structure. It is also at the same time part and apart of All That Is in ways we simply can't comprehend.

Even though our physical body is finite, our consciousness is neither born nor dies in us nor through us, it simply is, has been from the beginning and will continue to be. Consciousness experiences and learns from being in this, that and any reality, and contributes to the collective shared experiences in All That Is.

So what are the boundaries to you and yourself and can we actually define them?

Self is part of your perception of your consciousness, your experiences, your learnings and your beliefs. What you believe is possible for you, and what is not possible for you. So self is ever flexible and adaptive and ever changing. Self is part of consciousness and, being part of it, cannot therefore be defined. So your true self cannot ever be defined. It simply is. It can be changed, you can change. Self is highly adaptive and is ever changing;

even in this reality it doesn't stay constant forever, unless you choose it to be so.

The universal principle at play here is that there are actually no frontiers, no boundaries and no limitations to self. Through your beliefs, you can define and control your own limits, or limitlessness, through your own beliefs playing out into and co-creating your reality. And so can I, and so can everybody else.

Through your beliefs, consciousness is able to express itself in infinite ways with endless potentialities and possibilities. Whatever you express through your belief constructs also directly affects the reality you will experience, every time, all the time, always. There simply are no frontiers, no boundaries or barriers and no limitations – apart from the ones that you create yourself. This applies to us all.

This is a theme that we will continue to develop.

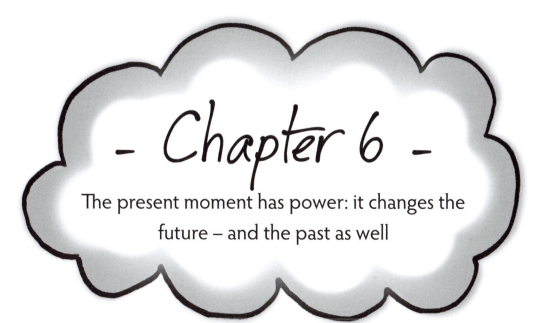

- Chapter 6 -

The present moment has power: it changes the future – and the past as well

For all of us, while we are experiencing our intimate connection with physical reality, through our consciousness being mind, body and spirit, this in turn creates the impression that there is a past, present and future in our reality. Sense of space and time are inextricably connected and entangled into the very fabric of our being.

However, our consciousness, while experiencing this, is also at the same juncture a part of All That Is too, and therefore out of time and not time bound.

Consciousness is timeless.

Human ideas of being have understandably been built around our notion of past, present and future. The beliefs that form our reality and make sense of the world around us tell us the past has gone and can't be changed. The future is perceived as being essentially unknown and unpredictable, and possibly influenced a little by planning ahead. With each moment just coming and going. So we all, through our beliefs, buy the idea that we have little or no control at all. This is far from the real and authentic truth.

The present moment has power, it is our choice point. Through the power of the present moment, we can choose to change our beliefs. As you will see in a later chapter, this then retunes, adjusts, alters and reorganises the patterns of our thoughts about the past as well. This in turn sets up new probabilities for the future.

So, by changing a belief in the present moment, its power is shifted to create a new reality. Both the past and the future are adjusted. New realities emerge. This is in itself phenomenal.

- Chapter 7 -

The law of importance and the law of reverse effect

Figure 5: The law of importance

Newton's third law states that every action has an equal and opposite reaction. This law applies as a universal principle too.

All things have balance; this includes the power of our thoughts and beliefs.

The law of importance implies that if we strain and push and 'yank' in pursuit of what we want in order to bring it into being, with unnecessary intense energy spent forcing and manipulating to achieve our desires, then the law of importance reacts in an opposing manner. The result is that the wanted outcome is then not manifested. This is because it is being over-powered by other negative thoughts instead. So our desires and wants can easily be confounded and frustrated by the law of opposing forces. These forces then correspondingly manifest nothing in return or, worse still, something unwanted and undesired instead. It is important for us to know that whatever is not wanted carries equal weight in universal principles.

It is a subtle take on you get what you want. Too much attention on what we want, or don't want, has a correspondingly negative effect. This is because our energy is spent on worrying about not having it, or wanting it too much, or wondering what happens if it goes wrong for me. What if I fail again? And so on.

We always get what we want, and we also get what we don't want. The same law equally applies to both statements. If we doubt an outcome, the thought behind it is what we are actually concentrating on and transmitting. Thoughts, good or bad, have power and in turn intend and drive reality. No intentional thoughts simply mean that you get blown from one reality to another, like living in a soap opera. This is the message that is actually literally being understood by our unconscious. So it is this that is then transmitted by and received from us by All That Is. Reality duly corresponds with matching manifested results (more on this later). Likewise, if we worry about whether it will be manifested, or not, then this translates to our unconscious mind as what is really required is worry or anxiety, and so that gets manifested into our reality.

If too much emotional energy is invested in any of our intentions, or there is a counter-limiting belief in play that is in conflict and opposes an intention, then it's literally translated in double quick time to big troubles being manifested in our reality.

Placing too much importance on any intention and desired outcome will mean that opposing forces will counter it. Therefore in the same way it is important to allow things to flow in your life and not oppose them. This is known as the law of reverse effect.

To apply this universal principle means that things that you hold loosely will come to you. Yield and you will not break. Go with the flow and what you seek will find you.

Don't try and flow outwards if the tide is in ebb. This means being tuned into the rhythm of all that is occurring to you and around you, and tuning into it while still desiring your intentions. In this way the law of importance is not activated and everything flows normally and intentions are met naturally and easily. It is in letting go and holding all things loosely that we are able to receive the gifts of intention.

For example, letting go of love gently (not holding it tightly in other words) allows love to remain and to constantly return to you.

In the stillness we can participate. In the silence we can hear and in the dark night, see. Empty yourself to be filled.

Choose to accept and not to judge, forgive not grudge.

Be graceful not spiteful.

Money and riches simply are not a desire in themselves, rather they come to you because of the help and benefit you give to others and for this you are rewarded.

If things go wrong, then accept this. Focus your attention on the patterns and potential learnings.

Let go of control. Let things shape up, the way they are meant to.

- Chapter 8 -

Being joyful is our natural state

Whenever I ask people, 'What do you want from life?', some answer by saying: 'I want to be rich, be successful or earn lots of money'. However, by far the majority simply say, 'To be happy'.

Despite this, according to the director of the film *Happy*, Roko Belic, paradoxically, traditional psychology has focused on unhappiness, misery and mental disorder – things that are wrong with us. Studies of happiness were considered lame and not taken seriously. This stream of thought has pervaded into modern culture too. It seems psychology has focused on measuring depression and disorder, but not happiness. However, since the 1990s positive psychology has grown exponentially and is beginning to change all of this. Neuroscience is now studying happiness seriously.

When happiness classes were put on at Harvard University in the 1990s these classes were attended by thousands of students wanting to learn more. Joyful states of mind are hugely resourceful. When you feel joy, you perform better and you are more effective in the whole of life. We have a better life when we are happy and experience joy. (Sourced from the film, *Happy*.)

Recent studies have since proven that once you have your baseline needs met, then more wealth does not increase your happiness. Joy is experienced from within. It is *intrinsic*, and comes through personal development and overcoming obstacles. It is not gained from outside us, through extrinsic means, such as a bigger house, more status, more success or more money etc. These are simply means to an end.

Happiness studies are now stating that when we firstly attend to our intrinsic happiness, then it makes it more likely for each of us that we will be able to also achieve what we want extrinsically too. Such as pursuing and reaching for goals and our dreams and desires. That we can attain more of what we want from life – success, money and other things, and reach our full potential.

Sonja Lyubomirsky, PhD, studied happiness and hypothesised that, through studies on twins for example, around 50 per cent of our happiness level is determined through our learned behaviour and through nature and nurture. Things that we have picked up from our parents. Over time this becomes our set point or range that we tend to return to as a baseline regardless of what happens to us, good or bad. Baseline states are discussed later in more detail.

Figure 6: We can choose to be joyful. (Idea adapted from the film, *Happy*.)

Interestingly the things that our schools, society and our cultures tend to tell us are that we should pursue the extrinsic material things. And through these extrinsic things we end up basing our intrinsic value upon. However, Lyubomirsky's research suggests this is not true but is a distorted viewpoint. Instead her theory concludes that only around 10 per cent of our happiness level is determined through extrinsic changes in life's circumstances.

She goes on to say that around 40 per cent is left for things that we can do to actively change our lives to consciously become happier. This 40 per cent is about the intentional choices we make, to intrinsically change ourselves from within, become more flexible, let go of control, and overcome our conditioning, and our learned behaviours.

It turns out that other studies on happiness demonstrate that joy is a kind of life-rhythm, enjoying a moment-by-moment flow. It provides a love for life. States of happiness and enjoyment diminishes your ego to its rightful place.

I believe when you take action, simply from intrinsic enjoyment, you access your true authentic self. By overcoming adversity and the conditioning that you acquire, you become more centred and more connected to happiness and the joy of being alive. And this then begins to become a baseline state.

So by using the power of your intentions it is entirely possible to choose to become happy in your life, and to centre your own thoughts around joy. As we will discover, part of the process of doing this is the need to overcome your acquired self and any obstacles in your way. To do this you have to make it your purpose and to enjoy doing this, until it is achieved.

Despite our propensity to react more strongly to aversion, we are all intended to seek joyfulness and to continue to return to it in our lives. When we do this we can truly return to our authentic self. All you need to do is to tune into it, and deliberately decide to set your course to find happiness. Whatever the circumstances, your life will change accordingly. And a new reality will begin to emerge. When we set our sails to seek joy, and pursue it relentlessly then it will find us along the way. As mentioned above, along the way, however, it is equally important to note that we may have to also face adversity and learn to overcome things. Paradoxically, it is through such tests in life that if we face them with the right approach and attitude, we discover our authentic self and deserve the right to truly feel alive, and strangely, out of life's struggles, we also find joy and happiness.

We pick this up in more detail later in Part 3.

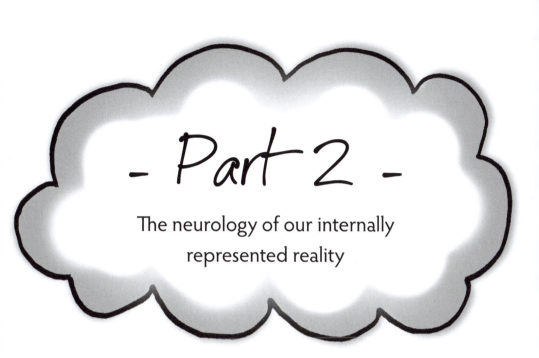

- Part 2 -

The neurology of our internally
represented reality

- Chapter 9 -

So what is consciousness and what does it do?

When we explore personal change and transformational development then it is important that we grasp a little of the way our neurology interacts with the reality we experience day to day. To do this, we need to appreciate how consciousness operates and how our mind and brain work and in what ways we attract and respond internally to external reality.

Recent advances in neuroscience and even in quantum science are starting to uncover some interesting findings that from the point of view of consciousness we somehow are not separate beings at all, as we once believed. That we are indeed somehow interconnected to each other and to everything around us. So consciousness and the mind–brain–body connection to greater things beyond our own body shell, as a working hypothesis, appears to be an inextricable part of our overall humanness. This cannot now be dismissed, as it has some considerable plausibility. However, this again is very dependent on who you choose to listen to, as the debate continues and neurological research discovers more about the way consciousness and its connection to our mind, brain and body operate. However, what is true is that we are more than we think.

So this second part of the book is about investigating some of the principles about how our consciousness and how our minds and brains operate.

From this context we can appreciate how our internal reality is shaped and how it can shift and cause our psyche to become out of balance, or return to a balanced baseline. From this, we can then begin to puzzle out how, as a consequence, consciousness can become distorted, through the very day-to-day experiences of our lives. As we will learn, this will then substantiate how we unwittingly end up choosing to move away from our authentic self, to form the conditioning of our acquired self instead. Finally we will consider how, through using the plasticity of our brains, we can learn to return ourselves back to equilibrium and our true authentic self.

Describing consciousness

Consciousness is in itself extremely complex and it is certainly true to say that neuroscientists are still trying to figure out what it is and how it works. My own interpretation of the latest research into consciousness, together with my own work and observations around personal change, is that consciousness is not merely a 'thing' that can be easily defined. It can't. It seems that consciousness has many aspects and facets.

I believe that consciousness can perhaps best be understood by considering it as being multidimensional and multifaceted and dynamic. The definition of consciousness therefore will depend very much from what perspective or viewpoint it is being considered. Because of this, one simple clear definition of consciousness is not, as yet, possible or indeed practical to express.

However, I feel that some sort of working definition or some agreed assumptions about consciousness are necessary in the context of this book. So, we will consider consciousness from the perspective of how consciousness relates to our internal reality, and how we therefore experience external reality. By doing this I feel we can get somewhere near to a useful understanding of what consciousness does, how our consciousness relates to our being and how it constructs and shapes our reality.

I believe that consciousness is intimately part of our mind, brain and body connection, as well as a connection to All That Is.

The conscious and unconscious mind

Research on consciousness points to its natural ability to directly organise itself through our mind and its deep connection with our brains as well as our physical bodies. Simplistically speaking, consciousness from a big picture perspective can be described as operating in two mind modalities – the conscious and the unconscious mind. Other brain research over recent decades supports the notion that the conscious mind has an inclination for more left-brain processes, while the unconscious mind has more of a preference for the resources that are in the right brain. As we will pick up later, left and right brain hemispheres have different takes on reality and each have different ways of perceiving and interacting with external reality. But together both our hemispheres and our conscious and unconscious minds operate as an integrated whole.

For example, some interesting research in 2010 discussed by Iain McGilchrist in his book, *The Master and his Emissary*, states that it is through these two worlds of consciousness that we experience, differentiate and shape our reality, in which we each uniquely exist. Accordingly, the organisation of our conscious and unconscious minds uniquely shapes our being independently, each from the other, and somehow these separate internal worlds then create a coherent whole that we experience as our understanding of reality.

McGilchrist suggests that rather than look at conscious and unconscious minds from a functional perspective, it is useful to look at them differently. His perspective is based on the viewpoint that the conscious and unconscious parts of our mind support us by seeking different outcomes, and therefore create completely different ways of being and relating to reality. We will examine this further when we investigate left and right hemisphere differences in more detail in the next chapter.

For now it is useful to first grasp that our reality is shaped entirely differently by the differing operations of our conscious and unconscious minds. The choices we make about the reality we experience alter, depending on the way we balance and combine, use and experience these aspects of consciousness in our lives.

McGilchrist also argues that, through history, our experiences are being increasingly influenced by favouring our left brain hemisphere and more conscious mind thinking styles based on knowing and familiarity constructs, perhaps to the detriment of our right hemisphere, which accesses the more adaptive elements associated with our unconscious mind and its style of being and becoming. He argues that modern life, with its conscious mind dominance and its unique way of being and its thinking style, is beginning to become a very real problem. What is meant to be a harmonious and delicate balance of integration of experience, from both our conscious and unconscious minds to shape our reality, is being gradually taken over more by reliance on consciousness mind thinking. This is one of the key, fundamental reasons for our human conditioning and the birth of the acquired self that is the topic of this book.

The story of the servant monkey and the master organ grinder serves to illustrate this notion very well. The servant monkey (representing the conscious mind) dresses up, looks cute and dances to a tune created by the master organ grinder (representing our unconscious mind). The monkey knows the dance and has honed the skills to do this well. Every time the monkey performs the monkey continues to receive all the attention, and is showered with applause from the watching crowd.

After so much continued adulation, the monkey quickly forgets he is in fact the servant of the master. He ignores, too, the contribution and efforts of the master and the organ the master is grinding to make the tune. Instead the monkey begins to create a distorted belief that it's all about him. As time goes by, this distorted viewpoint is repeatedly reinforced. After a little while this becomes part of the monkey's reality.

What the monkey, however, has failed to remember, and has, indeed, completely ignored, is the fact that he is the servant; he is dancing on top of an organ, which is a complex machine, that grinds out the tune. This machine was invented, designed and lovingly built by the master organ grinder. The tune the organ plays was written and composed by the organ grinder and built into the mechanics of the machine. It is also the master who turns the handle of the organ that allows the monkey the platform and tune to dance to and to show off. Furthermore the master gracefully knows and understands the pleasure of the monkey and the pleasure of the crowd. He knows and accepts the monkey and his distorted viewpoint. In return the master receives gifts from the crowd that sustain him, the monkey and their future. In this way they are designed to cooperate. But the organ grinder remains the master, and the monkey is really only the monkey.

As it is with the servant monkey and his distorted beliefs around reality, so it is with our conscious minds. In some cultures the conscious mind is termed the 'monkey brain'. However, it is our unconscious mind that is, in fact, the real master. Your unconscious mind controls the intimate connection between mind, body and spirit. It is your unconscious mind that creates all you are, all you have been and all that is possible that you can be. Your unconscious mind remains largely unexplored, unknown and undefined; however, it has access to the vast and infinite information field that makes up All That Is. As we will see it is a resource to be tapped.

These are important concepts, and the story above provides some of the context behind this book and why its message is so important.

Supporting perspective from psychology

Psychologist Carl Jung, a genius and way ahead of his time, published his ground-breaking research on personality types in the 1920s. Jung developed his personality difference hypothesis around personality being a delicate balance of differing mixtures of conscious and unconscious forces of personality.

Jung's work is complex; however, simply put he postulated that our personality is made up of several elements, or functions, and each is made up of opposite, paired, counter-balanced dispositions. Such as:

> *extrovertion* and *introvertion* for how we energetically relate to external reality;
> *sensing* and *intuition* for information gathering;
> *thinking* and *feeling* used for decision making.

He argued that one of each of these pairs would be preferred and therefore consciously developed, while its opposite would be a balancing force that was, for the majority of time, unconscious. Thereby the conscious mind is balanced with the unconscious mind to create stability and to be able to dynamically deal with different situations in different ways. He stated that part of healthy development is that we quickly learn to differentiate between all these opposite, elemental pairs of our personality. We each have and continue to develop a tendency, a leaning or an inclination toward using one of each of these elemental counter-balanced pairs more than the other. This weighting or leaning is then the basis for our personality in each of the above paired dimensions.

He developed his hypothesis further by stating that healthy development means that we still continue to use both ends of each of the paired functions of our personality at different times for different things, but never at the same time. That even though we differentiate one from the other in each of the paired functions of our personality as a preference, the other less used function becomes a counter-balancing force. This exquisite conscious and unconscious mind balance is integral to our personality remaining whole.

Jung's working hypothesis stated that either one of the sensing–intuition and either one of thinking–feeling paired mental functions develops consciously into the dominant function. The remaining one in each of the paired functions develops into the auxiliary supporting part of our conscious personality. Broadly speaking this differentiation occurs in the first half of life, when the dominant and auxiliary parts consciously balance each other, and together they form the core of our personality. Furthermore Jung believed that the dominant and auxiliary functions are in turn exquisitely counter-balanced by the remaining aspects of each of the undifferentiated type pairs of our personality, which develop mainly as unconscious balancing forces during the maturing phase in life and as such are, for the most part, out of awareness.

He also suggested that whilst our personality is innately part of each of us and will remain so throughout life, other sides of our character, however, continue to develop through our lives. He claimed, too, that the undifferentiated and normally unconscious aspects of our personality begin to develop and emerge as we grow through life, and so our views of reality shift as we go through the process of maturing. Jung believed this starts to happen around the mid-point of our lives. If this natural 'broadening' of our personalities does *not* occur (and this is often a deliberate choice, or because of trauma or stress when younger), then this may have consequences in the second half of our lives. Such as brittle and prickly and obstinate personalities, rather than rounded, mellow and flexible personalities. Jung's work is still current and highly regarded. Today it forms a key component of personality profiling used around the world.

I am highlighting this because Jung's observations underpin the premise of this book: that as we go through life we explore and add new and different parts of experience to our overall consciousness. He says that in our first half of life we develop and explore our preferences by differentiation and then by fine-tuning them. In the second half of life we begin to explore our balancing non-preferences next. This, then, in the longer term, creates the balanced personality.

In a similar vein, I argue that we seem by default to develop coping strategies based around conditioned responses, what I call the acquired self. These are analogous to conscious constructs that become distorted over time. These form what has already been described as our conditioning. We will develop the notion of conditioning much further later on. For now, as we mature and develop through life and our experiences, we begin to realise that these acquired strategies no longer serve us, and we need to learn how to return to our authentic self (more balanced conscious and unconscious ways of being).

I believe that we will all 'feel this internal calling' to do just this at some point in our lives, but it seems to me at least that many people don't know how to, and so in turn choose not to develop and broaden themselves. My desire and intent is that this book will provide hope, to you the reader, to take this journey, and will provide you with a guide to show you how to return to a balanced authentic self.

So just a passing thought that I'd like to share with you…

Similar to Jung's theory about personality, perhaps it might even turn out that the notion of the authentic self (that I describe in this book) might not be fully accessible and returned to, until the contrast of the acquired self (the other important notion explored within the pages of this book) has been initially experienced.

What is, however, more important to understand is that to live fulfilled lives, we must return to our authentic self during our life. If we don't do this then (just as Jung suggested) there are unavoidable consequences later in life.

The conscious mind, its make-up and its tendencies

For us to operate within the physical world and create our reality, our conscious mind has evolved and organised itself into a distinctive framework of hugely specialised parts, which are highly interconnected with our physical brains and bodies. The overall function of our conscious mind is to accept and perceive the outer physical world. It achieves this by acting as a window to our own outer experience and external reality. Our consciousness has ready access to our psychic energy to direct information to the various parts of consciousness contained within its framework.

It has ready access to unconscious material that includes mind, brain, body connections and, spiritually speaking, to All That Is as well. Our conscious mind develops as we grow and mature through life, and, as it evolves, it makes itself more and more aware of itself and its connection to unconscious sources become more understood. So the levels of conscious understandings are dynamic, ever changing and increasing.

Under healthy circumstances, the conscious mind plays a sophisticated director-type role and consists of many combined and differentiated parts of our psyche; these will be described shortly. It consists of highly organised and separate elements of consciousness that pay specific attention to our personality, and to different things happening in external physical reality.

As we will see later, the conscious mind has ready access to the language structures, logic and linguistic abilities that reside mainly in the left brain. Because of this ready access to topologically left brain biased functions it is our conscious minds that chatter away to us. This is often referred to as self-talk or inner mind chatter. The conscious mind also has ready access to all the inbuilt left brain tendencies that we will describe in the next chapter.

Below is a short description of some of the key elements that make up the organisation and structure of the conscious mind.

The ego...

The ego is a small and highly specialised part of consciousness, dealing primarily with personality and self in relation to the outer physical world or external reality.

The ego's job is multidimensional, in that it deals with projecting a stable personality that is perceived to be non-changing and constant. In fact this is not strictly true: in time our egos actually do gradually change and adapt, seemingly in cycles of between three and five years or in each passing decade. But from one moment to the next moment, the ego, for all intents and purposes, projects an appearance, at least, of steadiness. What the ego wants to do is to present particular observable and predictable patterns, based on situational and external factors. This is important, as the ego is the basis for interaction with others, dealing with factors external to us and creating a stable baseline against which we can detect changes and variations.

The (unschooled) ego is naturally judgemental and discriminatory. Balanced correctly, this is extremely important in creating consistency, stability, self-worth and personal power. It provides a sense of separation and differentiation from others in ever-changing external and internal situations. If left unchecked, however, the ego can grow in dominance and quickly become out of balance with other aspects of consciousness. While it may appear solid and robust, the ego can be susceptible to feeling fragile, hurt, lonely, of being got at, or even frightened and fearful.

In such circumstances the ego may invade, take over or run away with the conscious mind and its store of psychic energy. Under periods of duress or being unsettled, and when the mind and body consciousness is disturbed or out of balance with these inner workings, the ego can even become a 'petty tyrant' and 'control freak'. At this point it may feel threatened by unconscious balancing forces and, in its panic, start to refuse the balancing influences from the unconscious mind.

These distortions of the ego contribute to the workings of the acquired self becoming more dominant and restricting access to more of our unconscious resources. This point is taken up in more detail a little later on.

Internal representations... holograms of reality

A fuller description of internal representations is given in a later chapter. However, here is a short description. Consciousness, through your mind, brain and body connections, is able to organise, construct and internally form representations (re-presentations) of external reality. This ability is in itself a phenomenal miracle. This is a fantastically creative process that enables your consciousness to create a virtual copy of what's happening outside you at all moments instantly, in physical reality, in a sensory way. This ability to assemble such instant and detailed representations enables your mind, brain and body to reconstruct reality using visual, auditory and kinaesthetic building blocks of sensory information. These combine and are shared instantaneously, via mind, brain and body neurological connections, at all moments of your life. They form the communication between all conscious elements of what makes up you and your existence in this physical reality. Many of these internal representations are available and easily accessible to us through our conscious minds. In fact, it is through this mechanism that we can remember things, situations and events, that we can access the past and think about the future, and all the other elements that go to make up our daily functioning. These representational building blocks use many areas in our entire brain structure and some are thought to be stored as memories even in our nerves and body tissue. For example, musicians talk about finger memory. These representations combine to create our inner reality, by literally re-presenting, in internal somatic sensory terms, all external experience.

This process is going on all the time, at every instant. Every moment is captured using millions of instantly created complex representations. These are coded in such ways that are completely understood at all levels of consciousness within our mind, brain and body including our unconscious resources and access to All That Is. We will be looking at internal representations and their function in more detail just a little further on in the book.

Thoughts…

As mentioned earlier, our thoughts, too, are dynamic and living forms of psychic, energetic consciousness that constantly come and go. Your thoughts are very diverse and extremely wide-ranging and can be about you, others, facts, the environment, reality around us, the future, the past etc. Each and every thought-form produces energetic thought fields. All thoughts are entities of existence and, however brief, they instantly influence and rapidly communicate with your mind, brain and body consciousness. Thoughts are commonly augmented, supported and internally expressed by our inner mind chatter and self-talk. Thought-forms all inextricably work together at very deep levels with our biochemical body emotions and unconscious neurological communication levels through all parts of our body and brain. Thoughts also directly broadcast information to a cellular level. So each of your passing thoughts heavily influences your way of being at each moment, right down to your individual cells. As you will discover, in this book, your thought patterns also hugely influence your reality.

By way of the internal representations we described above, what is going on in your body and its emotional states are always being compared to baseline representational states stored by your mind, brain and body. These continuous comparisons automatically generate differences that communicate through your thought patterns to inform you about how you are feeling. So your thoughts include your feelings about yourself. As we will be seeing, these thoughts, along with all your other thoughts, all collaborate to co-create the reality you live in.

Memories, associations and dispositions

Our past memories and experiences are all built up from stored historical internal representations, which can be automatically brought back into consciousness, by means of our conscious mind. Any past memory and experience is stored in representational terms. Generally speaking, the more intense or significant the experience, the richer the representation. Natural triggers, such as similar experiences, emotions, thoughts and even certain words, can instantly trigger a past memory back into consciousness. So via internal representational constructs, any memory and experience can be revivified, relived and brought back to be re-experienced, again and again.

In addition to this, because of your innate ability to create internal representations, your mind and brain connection can associate any memory or experience to any other memory or event or situation or experience that your consciousness deems significant and relevant. As you will come to understand, these form important dispositional representations. They are special constructs that end up 'representing' your beliefs about yourself and about the reality you experience. Using these dispositional representations, your consciousness, behind the scenes, continually scans the reality unfolding in front of you at all moments to predict suitable responses that automatically trigger certain learned strategies in reaction to that unfolding reality. Much of our acquired self uses such mechanisms as a basis for default, automatic control, perceived survival or protection. However, as we will see, these learned (left-brain biased) responses are not always beneficial to us in our development and growth in the longer term.

Imagination...

Another psychic component within your conscious mind framework is the power of your imagination. This is a highly developed and sophisticated part of consciousness that has ready access to unlimited supplies of psychic energy from an infinite source of readily available energy. This is made possible via your unconscious mind and its connection to All That Is. By tapping into this infinite energy source, your imagination has huge potential to drive and motivate us, to achieve anything we desire.

Your imagination is the driving force allowing you to dream of and to desire what you want and to project learnings from your past and apply them to create potential benefit for you in the future. They allow you to become passionate about what's important to you, what drives you and what you enjoy doing. They allow each of us to form outcomes and plans for the future that we desire and want.

In spiritual terms imagination may also mean that you have an understanding of things and causes that are greater than you, enabling you to create what you are meant, or destined, to do.

Imagination is directly linked to your sense of purpose in life and why you are here. It helps you form the reality that you desire and want from your life. Importantly, imagination can be used by specific thought-forms called intentions. Intentions are highly concentrated thoughts, which when coupled to your imagination can start to manifest what you desire and want into the reality you are experiencing. We explore intentions again in detail a bit further on.

So what about the unconscious mind?

In stark contrast to the conscious mind, the unconscious mind is silent as it does not have access to linguistic structures. It forms ideas about reality based on what it is experiencing in the present moment. It is concerned about balance, flow and keeping in tune with reality. It innately understands and comprehends, and simply just knows.

Your unconscious controls all your bodily responses and internally regulates all the goings on that keeps you alive. It has a connection to your conscious mind and readily communicates all things it notices. The unconscious mind acts as a benevolent brother or sister to the conscious mind.

Under balanced conditions your conscious mind willingly cooperates with all the resources and all knowingness of the unconscious mind.

It is said that the unconscious mind is infinitely knowing, as it has ready access to vast amounts of your internal resources. Through quantum science it is believed that your unconscious mind has access to more than just you as a separate entity. Through its connection with All That Is, your unconscious mind seems to be able to access unlimited aspects of reality and consciousness as a whole. As we have already described, to the unconscious mind there may be no separation or boundaries between you and other conscious entities. It is at one with All That Is and, therefore, with everything all the time.

Your unconscious mind is intimately connected with your body at all times. It is extremely sensitive and instantly aware and empathetic to your emotional body state, which is largely processed through the limbic system of the emotional brain that resides in the lower part of the brain's make-up (the downstairs part of the brain). As we will see later, your body state is the internal reflection of what is being perceived in external reality. This information is vital to processing your internal reality and forms an important element to your internal representations. Higher up in the brain's upper layers, your conscious mind then uses these internal representations to form thoughts about your feelings and how you feel. Based on all these things your unconscious mind automatically makes necessary adjustments to all your internal organs to reflect whatever emotional body state is being processed.

It is the 'yin' to your conscious mind 'yang'.

So from a mind and body perspective, consciousness is a bit like a tree: its roots are present even at a cellular level and it is present in the branches of the nervous, limbic, body tissue and chemical systems. Finally, at the higher levels it is present in the crowning glory of the highly complex downstairs, upstairs and left and right parts of your brain.

Consciousness and the development of the acquired self

Although your conscious mind has ready access to information from its neighbouring unconscious mind resources, the conscious mind generally speaking, through the ego, if left unchecked, has a tendency to go and take matters into its own hands. Left to its own view of the world it can quickly become distorted, if it chooses to ignore the balancing forces of the unconscious mind which otherwise keep it in check. Over time it can become over-controlling with a disposition to go its own way. Through these inclinations, your conscious mind can then begin to ignore and negate, or disallow more and more 'balancing' information to influence it from your unconscious mind. Left unchecked for too long, this tendency starts to produce distortions that get progressively misaligned to the 'checks and balances' that should naturally occur between your conscious and unconscious minds.

These tendencies of the conscious mind then start to be displayed in our daily lives in myriad different ways. They are all representations of the acquired self. In other words, through these natural organisations of the conscious mind and its tendencies, it is this mechanism that your acquired self uses to gain a foothold and begin to take over and control your reactions to reality in various ways. This, as we have already described, is what I have termed as our conditioning.

Consciousness and the authentic self

I believe that your authentic self develops and matures very early on in life. Its purposes and destiny become clear to itself very quickly. It is more than fate, as it knows where it is meant to be, the purpose of your life and therefore the reality that you are meant to experience. Your authentic self knows you intimately and is always with you, everywhere. It never leaves you. It is aligned to your unconscious mind and under normal balanced circumstances this becomes readily known as you mature by your conscious mind.

As it is more unconsciously aligned, it whispers to you through the things that happen around you, you somehow know it to be, and yet… it is easily ignored and drowned out by the busyness of your conscious mind. To access it, you have to learn to harness it and this requires presence of mind, a gentleness and a grace.

Over time, if the conscious mind has run away with itself, and has formed different ways of being in the world, based on the reality it alone experiences, then the acquired self emerges and dominates your being through the mechanisms of conditioning. As a result, the authentic self is then squashed out of the way. However, it always waits patiently to be reinstated. It never gets hurt but gently waits for its return to prominence. The authentic self is the 'real master' that needs to subdue the powerful negative and limiting forces of the acquired self.

As you read this book you will learn how to restore the balancing forces necessary for your authentic self to return to you. As you do so, you will begin, step by step, to get the life that you desire and deserve. This is only possible when you align and restore conscious and unconscious mind balance. Only then can your authentic self return to its rightful place.

- Chapter 10 -

In two minds

Much neurological research over recent decades has helped us to understand more about how we think, feel and act and co-create our reality based on an interaction with the physical world around us. Like our evolving understanding of what consciousness actually is, neurological understanding is continually making headway about understanding how our mind and brain work in creating the human spirit, and the intimate connection with our bodies, each other and the world around us.

In 1981 Dr Roger Sperry was awarded the Nobel Prize for his discovery that the brain's two hemispheres process information in very different ways.

We know that our brains seem to be where consciousness (conscious and unconscious), our mind and our physical body meet to form our being. That the mind–brain is somehow a physical representation of consciousness and through our senses mirrors internally the external world and physical reality.

While the concept of definite left- and right-brain thinking styles and cognitive approaches has been highly popularised, and perhaps even over-simplified, and as a result has become somewhat polarised, these notions still contain significant truth. As we have already seen, each of the brain's two hemispheres really does process information differently and each seeks to fulfil different objectives and outcomes. These somehow end up as complementary versions of reality. That balance, differentiation and competing representations of reality are continually created by the division of our brain into these two separate hemispheres (a left and a right side). Much scientific research continues to enlighten us over their differing approaches and the ways each hemisphere co-creates meaning for us in seemingly different ways.

So neurological studies still point to our brain's amazing ability to create two different worlds of consciousness, two minds, two different ways of perceiving, choosing and living reality, and it seems that these choices are created through our left and right hemispheres. In very simple terms, science still supports the notion that our conscious mind has preferences and leanings to work alongside the processes that predominately are left-brain biased. Our unconscious mind seems to have inclinations towards the inner workings of more right-brain qualities. Yet, at the same time, the two hemispheres and our conscious and unconscious minds correspond with and harmonise well with one another. As we will discover later in this book, this delicate balance is crucial and can be only too easily and adversely disturbed by thought patterns and habits that interfere with or override normal functioning.

What we do now know from recent science research is that we are in a symbiotic relationship with the world around us, and that this co-creative relationship helps to direct our attention towards it. This also means that we bring something of ourselves to the 'process' of creating our 'vision' of the world.

As a generalised guide, the left hemisphere specialises in fine detail processing. It is involved in mastering skills. It examines the components and pieces of things and concepts, and precisely helps to distinguish each from the other. The left-brain hemisphere is able to access our precision in language to describe and categorise the world around us. It is involved in storing, recalling and using what is already known and understood.

The right-brain hemisphere specialises in being able to undertake to understand the bigger picture, it is more interested in a global view, larger chunks and principles. Where the left hemisphere is excellent at mastering learned skills, the right hemisphere in contrast is more aligned to picking out interconnections and relationships between objects and ideas and concepts. It is able to be more accepting and to perceive the whole, whereas the left is better at being critical and at breaking things down into component parts. The right hemisphere gets the essence and gist of things.

To summarise these differences, it's like seeing a forest through the right hemisphere and the trees via the left.

Two minds and two realities

For us as human beings there are two fundamentally opposed realities, two different modes of experience, and each is of ultimate importance in bringing about the recognisable world we live in and share. That difference is rooted in the bi-hemisphere structure of our brains. These hemispheres are involved in a sort of power struggle and this is particularly noticeable in our modern times and, in particular, in Western culture.

Past research on the two hemispheres has sought to describe what the differences are between each hemisphere from a function perspective. It seems that this way of describing the structural differences is not sufficient or adequate. As it turns out the functional relationship between them is more dynamic than originally conceived. Each hemisphere is involved and depends on the other hemisphere in constructing all human experience.

Our reality, however, shifts according to the stance we adopt, the type of attention we pay to it, the dispositions we hold in relation to it. This is important because the most fundamental difference between the hemispheres lies in the type of attention they (through our thoughts and actions) give to the world.

Although we can never fully know what reality actually is, some sort of 'out there' reality does exist apart from ourselves, but we play a vital part in bringing it into being.

An important theme of this book is the significance of our internally held dispositions. These can be termed the beliefs we hold about reality (the world around us and others) in forming what it is that we come to experience and relate to.

The working assumption from recent science research, and the one I have adopted, is that the kind of attention we pay to reality actually, and rather surprisingly, alters it. We attract what it is that we are paying attention to internally, to create what manifests externally. We are, literally, partners in co-creating reality. This then means we have a responsibility that exists apart from ourselves. Much of this reality is created through the choices we make and the way in which we view the world. This in turn is highly influenced by the way we have developed the cooperation or opposition of our left and right hemispheres and whether we over-rely on one (particularly the left hemisphere) to the detriment of the other.

Both hemispheres, it seems, cooperate in creating our reality on a constant basis. But each hemisphere has a fundamentally different set of values and, therefore, different priorities, which means that over the longer term they may, if we are not careful, prescribe the relationship we are shaping with our reality, and so create conflict. These differences can adversely influence us and contribute to the human condition. It seems that although each hemisphere needs the other for balance and integrity, through our conditioning they appear destined to pull away from each other.

Divided worlds that compete to co-create our reality

As we have already touched on, we know from research, scientific and psychological study that our minds are divided into conscious and unconscious parts. As we have highlighted, colloquially these are still often described as left and right hemisphere differences, and while this concept is perceived as a generalisation, it still seems to be pragmatically applicable, at least broadly speaking.

More to the point, over recent decades we have come to understand that the jobs of our left and right hemispheres are to process the meaning of reality in differing ways.

That our left side (our conscious mind) is about logic, impersonal analysis, sequence and language… That it develops strong representations about what it experiences. While our right hemisphere is believed to be more of a silent partner (the unconscious mind) that understands things intuitively and is empathetically tuned, and is more involved with newness and difference than is our left side. That the right deals in metaphor and story, music, rhythm…

However, it turns out from more recent research that such differences are really very subtle, and not so easily and cleanly divided hemispherically speaking. That both hemispheres are being stimulated in different ways all the time, when considering what was thought of as solely a left- or right-brain function. So current thinking suggests that simply dividing our minds into left- or right-based activities, tasks, jobs or functions is not the full story. What might be more accurate as a notion is that brain activity seen in both hemispheres is the product of a function that was driven by, and originated from, one particular hemispherical activity. That each hemisphere simply uses the services of the entire brain to meet its overall objectives.

What is emerging from research is that there are left and right hemisphere differences about the tendencies and inclinations each use to interpret meaning and reality. So hemisphere differences are not so easily divided into separate functions, but rather work together more symbiotically and the difference is about each hemisphere building different perspectives on reality in very different ways. In this way, each hemisphere helps us to relate to reality with different perspectives as to what is being sensed from external physical reality. Depending on the context and the activity, it is thought that one hemisphere may take the lead over the other.

So we literally do have two minds and these two minds strategically and subtly operate in different ways. When in balance, these in turn produce different learnings and responses, outlooks, results and outcomes. It is also known that the hemispheres are not symmetrical in physical size, or opera- tion. Each seems to work independently, and even in competing ways, so this produces asymmetrical results, with one hemisphere's approach or the other being selected as the better approach depending on the context. At the same time information transfer is known to bridge from right to left hemi- spheres. However, even though information passes across the hemispheres, current research seems to suggest that the left hemisphere is selective in what it allows in from the right hemisphere. It has a tendency to inhibit addi- tional information being passed to it from the right hemisphere.

Therefore, it follows, as a working hypothesis, that the way we interpret reality must also be influenced by inclining to bias, and that we lean or rely more acutely on one hemisphere over the other. This will depend on our thoughts, our choices and our experience.

Our minds have effectively learned to differentiate and hence develop preferences to think, feel, perceive and judge using particular patterns in our interaction with the world. These behavioural and thought patterns or strategies must then consequently have tendencies for one or the other hemisphere to dominate in particular contexts. Over time these build into generalised ways of being that in turn shape our choices and ultimately our reality. This also correlates with Jung's work on personality typing, which we described earlier.

Why do our left and right hemispheres each pull away from the other?

Well, one aspect of current neurological research stated that the two hemispheres, while having their own take on the reality they each experience, are constantly relaying or sharing this reality moment by moment (via the connecting bridge called the corpus callosum – a flat, wide bundle of interconnecting nerve fibres); however, as we have suggested above, these hemispherical understandings, if you like, are unlikely to be symmetrical in the way they are sharing these experiences. So the world we actually phenomenologically experience moment to moment means it is highly likely that one will predominate, thereby creating asymmetrical outcomes. This seems to be part of our prevailing culture too. For example a preference for more left-brain thinking and a more right-handed world.

Winner takes all...

At the same time, even small differences moment to moment will accumulate to create the tendency of one hemisphere to predominate over the other. The difference that makes all the difference, if you like. And it could be possible that this accumulated build-up creates a winner takes all concept for certain functions. And so one side may consistently trump the other, thereby creating bias to one side over the other. As this then is reflected in our society, culture and education, these differences build up and are amplified into expectation in the world at large and so the asymmetrical dominance of one hemisphere over the other is reinforced. As our society favours conformity, language and use of manipulating tools and so on, these all have left hemisphere bias. In addition to this, and as stated in an earlier paragraph, the left hemisphere has tendencies to inhibit and throttle back information being sent to it from the right hemisphere. So could it be that these small differences ultimately combine with cultural make-up to create bias towards left hemisphere dominance?

Also the value of the arts such as sculpture, painting, poetry and so on, which all have right hemisphere tendencies, are overtly discouraged as ways of earning a living and seen as not being useful or contributing to the social good.

In our Western and modern era it is this unique interplay of our imprint on the world and in turn the imprint of reality on us that creates this divide.

Our propensity towards left-brain thinking leaves its mark on the world, which in turn then re-impinges and rebounds on us, creating a spiralling effect of one affecting the other and each leaving its mark on the other.

This increasing reliance on left hemisphere thinking has, in the main, come about through industrialisation and the economic ages, and more latterly has been accelerated due to the technological society we have created for ourselves. This has inevitably led to an expansion in self-consciousness leading in turn to increasing difficulties in cooperation between the hemispheres. The resultant instability, I propose, creates alternations between more and more extreme positions of hemisphere separation and left hemisphere dominance, which creates pendulum swings that are going too far, to the extent that they are being further and further pulled to the gravitational force of the left hemisphere created reality. In time perhaps the pendulum will swing back the other way. Hopefully toward rebalance and not to the other extreme. As the left-brain reality becomes dominant then this in turn uses more acquired self constructs to cope with external reality and creates coping mechanisms that become our conditioning. The right-brain reality, however, has an entirely different approach to external reality as it is more tuned to dealing with adversity rather than controlling or avoiding it or protecting from it.

Thankfully, however, each of us uses our two hemispheres in distinctly different ways. This can be seen in degrees of left-handedness for instance. It is significant that this has not ever been genetically displaced but remains statistically constant (at 11 per cent). Five per cent of the population are also cross-lateralised (this means that some left hemisphere dominant functions are located on the opposite side and vice versa, for example). These left-handed and lateralisation anomalies are constant in our societies and infer that although statistically small they have never been bred out and are therefore relevant and important.

The observable universe has no profound symmetry either, but reflects an asymmetric manifestation in all forms of creation.

Above all, we need to unite the different ways of experiencing reality that are yielded by both hemispheres. Most important, however, is to find ways of letting go of the control and over-attention of the left hemisphere, and enabling the left to recognise the importance of balance and reintegration and reuniting of the right hemisphere with itself. Otherwise the left hemisphere will run away with itself and this is dangerous.

Left hemisphere control and dominance

Taking this further, there is increasing evidence from many neurological studies that hypothesise that the left hemisphere has a tendency to run away with itself and become a dominant preference. Because of its leaning towards clarity, and easy access to words, language and our egos it has a strong inclination to become 'sticky' and obstinate, and in so doing ignore other balancing information from our more unconscious right hemisphere.

It is often said that seeing is believing. Only when we see something will we be able to know it. This is a common enough saying. That what we say is true has to be seen first.

However, it has also been noted through research and science that our conscious mind (left hemisphere inclination) has a stronger tendency than our right hemisphere to lock onto and become captivated by certain things that we see in the world around us. That the left hemisphere seems to be more 'sticky'. This then starts to focus and narrow our attention. The current view from some neurological research is that this is little to do with choice. Even if it was due to choice, the world that it would be choosing from is in any case provided by the broader attention of the right hemisphere. Often what we notice and what engages the focus of our attention comes to us pre-consciously, and therefore bypasses any willed action.

So, in neurological terms, we know things first, then we are drawn to pay attention to them, so as to know more. Reality (the external world) comes to meet us and acts to attract our gaze.

Vitality, life and movement themselves draw the eye. The difficulty of the 'stickiness' of the left hemisphere, however, is that once we have decided what the world is going to reveal, we are unlikely to go beyond it – we can therefore become prisoners of expectation.

Neurologically, it seems that new experience, as it is first 'present', engages the right hemisphere, and as the experience becomes familiar, it gets 're-presented' by the left hemisphere. So it appears that the left hemisphere specialises in what is already familiar, and has a tendency to keep returning to what it already knows so it becomes familiar all too quickly. This tendency has implications for the kinds of knowledge that the left hemisphere can deal with. We know anecdotally that we don't like change and prefer the comfort of the familiar. This, it seems, is due to the 'sticking power' of the left hemisphere.

Also, our conscious mind can only really know something by bringing it into sharp focus, and to clearly see what it has re-presented itself; in this way things experienced are known and understood (pinned down) and are able to be used, through the application of practice and habit. All learning of skills and manipulating of tools are examples of left-brain preference learning. Therefore what is then *not* taken up and learned is what is perceived by the right hemisphere and present as a whole, but is not attended to by a more left-brain knowing conscious mind.

Below are some concepts that have come through recent research.

The stickiness of the left hemisphere

This means that if we over develop our left brain, we will have a tendency to miss or delete from our conscious attention anything that does not fit the frame we are currently working with. This inclination is so embodied and engrained that it makes it difficult to understand how we come to experience anything that is new and novel. In contrast the right brain is very engaged with what is new and unknown, so this experience can be missed.

The disposition to control...

Left disposition is that of utility and control. The right disposition is that the nature of its attention to the world is one of care, relationship, togetherness, and sharing, rather than control.

The left is ultimately dependent and reliant on the right, so each needs each other; however, through extreme left hemisphere over-reliance, it seems that the left completely ignores the right or, worse still perhaps, has little or no awareness of the right. The left extremes can be filled with an alarming sense of self-confidence. This then creates a struggle for left supremacy.

The world we have now created is one that is more a self-reflexive virtual and mechanistic world that is blocking off all the available exits. It's the reality created by a return to left and right balance that will provide us with the way out of this 'hall of mirrors'.

(paraphrasing Iain McGilchrist in *The Master and His Emissary*)

The side effects of this hall of mirrors create negative beliefs, ineffective behaviours with self and others, over-assertiveness and a drive to overachievement. These in turn spiral into deeper issues of disconnection, disorder, disharmony and, ultimately, if not checked, to disease via separation from others, lack of caring, obsessive–compulsive behaviours, illnesses and reactions to the world around us. Ultimately such a chain reaction creates extremes of the human condition and in the end we live behind a veil of inauthenticity that anaesthetises us from connection to the real world.

This reliance on the mechanistic virtual world created from an over-reliance on left hemisphere thinking has led us to dysfunction and a decontextualised world, marked by unwarranted optimism mixed with paranoia and a feeling of emptiness.

It is this story that we pick up in our journey toward an approach and framework that allows us to return to our real authentic selves, which are under severe threat from an over-reliance on and dominance of left hemisphere approaches. To do this we have to consciously make adjustments to our approach in our lives and the authentic reality we are meant to create. By taking the approach suggested in this book we rebalance and realign our left and right hemispheres to create the lives we desire and deserve.

Familiarity and attention...

Each hemisphere attends in a different way; and different ways of attending to the world produce different realities. For example:

Left hemisphere reality is emptied of meaning by being constantly re-presented.

Right hemisphere reality is enriched in meaning by being constantly present, lived with and actively incorporated into 'my life'.

The left-brain spirit of our modern times...

In the Western world we have advanced technologically, and invented machines and products to support and assist us. Social and political frameworks have been constructed to support modern ways of living, and bring us wealth and prosperity. Many eminent people believe that such processes and systems, while not intentionally doing so, are consequentially construing that society is becoming much more reliant on left hemisphere type dominant thinking patterns.

Philosophically and psychologically speaking, these may be beginning to have adverse effects on our society, on nations, on our natural world and the animal kingdom and the environment itself. If we are not careful, return to balance through left and right hemisphere realignments may become harder, if not impossible. I have much sympathy with these thoughts.

As a dire warning for all of mankind, I wonder, if this is taken too far and imbalance and harmony becomes further and further disturbed, whether it might be possible to end up with societies similar to that described in George Owell's infamous book *1984*. In some ways, perhaps fancifully, the reality of the fantasy film *The Matrix* might even subtly come to form around us without us noticing in the future…

Left and right brains use different memory constructs

The neural basis for memory is as yet unknown from a scientific point of view, but is well researched empirically, that is, through careful analytical observation. However, in the 1970s two scientists, E Tolving and RF Thompson, hypothesised that memory that helps us make decisions is based on two very different but highly complementary types of memory: episodic and semantic memory. Their theory, which still seems to hold today, suggests that, in general, episodic memory is more dependent on right hemisphere processing tendencies and semantic memory relies more on the left hemisphere.

Episodic memory

As we now appreciate, the right hemisphere is very adept at learning new and unfamiliar things. How this is achieved from a neurological perspective is that the right brain seems to access broad interconnections of different clusters of neurones that are topologically widely spaced across many areas of the brain cortex. In this way it seems to find connections to lots of helpful experiences and all sorts of other relevant and associative contexts that enrich the early learning process. In this way we can start to become familiar with and to make sense of what is unknown.

To help with this process, the right brain seems to favour using a specific type of memory specially designed to assist these more right-brain biased processes. It is called episodic or personal memory. This is associated with learning through inference, intuition, through story and metaphor and making wider connections to disparate themes. Episodic memory remembers the self in personal stories and situations, experiences and events at a certain time and place as well as any associations that might assist and in some way be useful in making sense of what is being currently learned. Episodic or personal memory is used when bringing back past memories, so that the whole story can be re-experienced. Episodic memory is therefore also very useful in revisiting past experiences to make better sense of them in hindsight, and therefore to learn from them in the future. This ability enables us to adapt and adopt new behaviours and strategies as we proceed through life. Episodic memory is also highly creative and generative; it forms a fundamental aspect of all the arts, writing and storytelling in all its creative forms.

An example of episodic memory might be travelling back in time to remember an event that took place at a particular time, such as your sixth birthday. When this memory is accessed then episodic memory will associate with all its detail, time, manner, place, emotion and behaviours and effectively retell the story.

Semantic memory

Once this learning has taken place, then typically the entire process is at some point handed over to the processes of the left hemisphere. The left hemisphere is a master at turning any learning into a honed skill. Typically this often is supported by cognitive or physical repetition and practice. As the left hemisphere is more specialised in rote learning and detailed breaking down of things into parts, then this hones the learning further. To support this, the left-brain processes seem to prefer using closely clustered and adjacent interrelated neurones in the brain cortex. This is a different neurone configuration from the circuits used by the more right-brain biased processes that were previously described. Here the learning is turned into known and specifically defined elements that eventually make up a learned skill. This type of memory refers to meaning, understandings and other concept-based knowledge. It underlies conscious recollection of factual information and general knowledge about the reality and world we experience.

Examples of this would be how to read and write, use grammar, add up and how to subtract, and the times tables. This is in contrast to episodic memory: remembering the situation of being taught these at school.

This type of memory is called semantic or impersonal memory. It is the opposite of episodic or personal memory in that it is best used to remember facts, figures, abstract and known logical information in an objective and singular form. Each element that is laid down in semantic memory exists in its own right and is not interconnected. This type of memory is skilled at deconstruction and forming things from parts. It forms the instructional part of the process of being able to write and speak language effortlessly, and to perform a skill that is constant and repeatable. Semantic memory defines things, and provides meaning and descriptions of objects and concepts in themselves. For example, facts that are learned about cities, our times tables etc.

Episodic memory and the return to the authentic self

It turns out that our brains have the ability to use both the hemispherical characteristics and memory forms described above. Well-balanced brains will naturally develop both instances of neurone configurations, which can then be called upon for right- and then left-brain processing at any time. Through nature, nurture or conditioning we will, however, tend to favour one or the other approach as a preference.

Under normal preferences, but balanced conditions, the authentic self can continue to develop normally and healthily through life's experiences. But too much left- or right-brain preference will create adverse consequences. For example, if left-brain approaches are indeed becoming more favoured in society as a whole, then we may perhaps be over-relying on decisions based solely on factual semantic thinking. Under such circumstances I believe that the subsequent reality that is then manifested is sterile and two dimensional. In which case this may mean that we might very well lose the ability to effectively use the advantages of being able to readily access the richness of episodic memory (at the expense of its semantic counterpart).

Furthermore, as I mentioned earlier, what I am witnessing is an increase in mental and psychosomatic symptoms that I believe are a consequence of over-control and dominance associated with overuse of left-brain tendencies. This then creates adverse conditioning that leads to the emergence of default coping strategies and protection or avoidance mechanisms. I call these forms of conditioning the acquired self.

As we will see later, the strategies of the acquired self then inhibit the natural formation, growth and development of the authentic self. This is because the acquired self squashes the authentic self out of the way. This is done by the acquired self distorting and hijacking left-brain abilities to capture and then divert the majority of available psychic energy to itself (we'll come on to this much later). This is because the acquired self seems to require huge amounts of nervous energy to operate and survive. And this is found more in the left brain and the constructs of the conscious mind. As a consequence the mind and body suffer in the longer term.

Use of episodic-based thinking to access imagination (visual imagery), our emotions and the narrative of our life story is intrinsic in the ability of the authentic self to re-emerge and return to its rightful place as part of our reality forming consciousness.

- Chapter 11 -

Mapping reality through internal representations

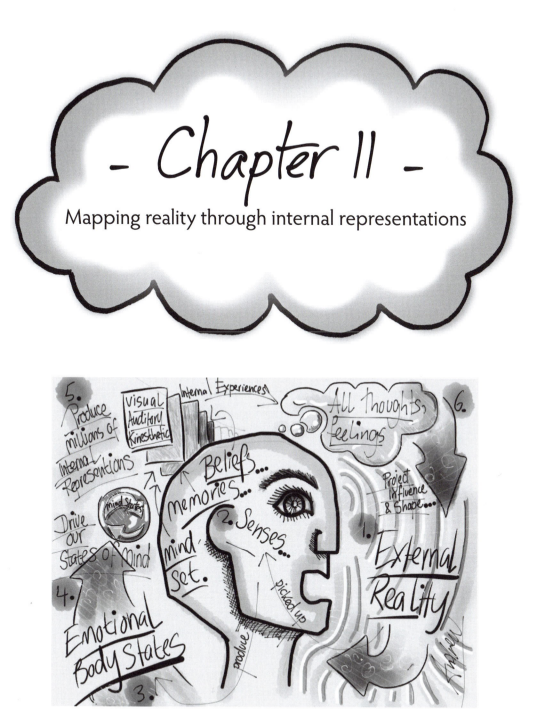

Figure 7: Mapping reality through internal representations

Our mind, body and spirit are intimately interconnected to our conscious-ness and the 'self' that creates life as we understand it. It is in itself a marvel to behold, a miracle in its complexity and beauty, and amazing in its pre-organised and entwined nature. This arrangement allows us to be intimately part of and experience the physical world around us. The most profound part of this compilation of integrated majesty is our innate ability to re-present external physical reality around us at every moment, recreating and mirror-ing this as an internal simulation, or facsimile. External physical reality as we experience it is literally recreated as an internal reality that is instantly and continually re-experienced within, by our mind, body and spirit. All this is happening in real time, all the time, by every living being on the planet.

How our mind, body and spirit construct does this is truly mind-blowing. Through neuroscience research over the last ten years researchers have begun to understand the mechanisms that achieve this. Analysis is reveal-ing that every moment, in every second of our lives, our consciousness has organised itself, via the mind, body and spirit connection, to instantly pro-duce millions upon millions of internal representations of what is happening to us in external reality. These are like maps that instruct our mind–brain–body connections that then use them to form our internal reality. Each internal representation in itself efficiently and effortlessly contains millions of pieces of data and information about the external world around us.

These informational maps or constructs use our five senses to assemble this data, to use our mind, body and spirit to instantly internally reconstruct a facsimile that is a representation of external reality – in other words, a map that internally represents externally experienced reality. In particular, our mind–brain–body construct uses visual imagery, auditory words and sounds, as well as kinaesthetic sensations from our bodies as the subjective struc-tures to capture this data and information to build these internal maps. Every representation is unique. Somehow our mind–brain–body uses neurological structures to achieve this internal map-making ability, as well as to sequence, make sense of, store and memorise and choose a response to these inter-nal representations. In addition, as we will learn shortly, these internal maps of reality can be influenced and coloured by our own interpretations, so the unconscious coding forms particular nuances, patterns and strategies we each use, based on our own personal experiences and attitudes, neuro-logical and physiological responses, reactions and choices about the external world and what we feel and think about it, which are unique to each of us as individuals. I don't know about you, but I find this breathtaking. Internal representations form the very subjective building blocks and reference structures that underpin our existence and experiences through our entire lives.

Construction of all internal representations that make up emotional mind–body states...

How this affects us, and how we can affect it for the good, is explored in more detail in Part 4.

Our consciousness entwined in our mind–brain–body automatically uses this map-making mechanism as a fundamental part of our day-to-day existence. Furthermore, our consciousness has gained the ability to also organise itself around producing different maps of our internal representations, based on different experiences, to make living and experiencing life efficient and effective. For example, your consciousness has adapted your mind–brain–body connection to use internal representational maps in highly sophisticated ways: as survival strategies; moving away from pain and loss; moving toward reward and pleasure; to form our past memories; learn and repeat skills; and as shortcuts to predicting responses in future moments.

As I will go on to describe, our positive or negative emotions, thoughts and feelings about events and situations happening in the external world, as well as our information-gathering abilities and decision-making processes and choices of responses and reactions, are all derived from the exploitation, manipulation and production of these neurologically produced maps (formed from internal representational information structures). All this is being enabled via your mind–brain–body connection. Our entire experiences and existence as beings is only possible through their production and their subsequent myriad uses.

So to make sense of all reality, external situations, events and interactions that you experience in the external physical world, they are re-experienced by interpretation and translation into internal maps. This is achieved through the organisation of our consciousness and the mechanics of our mind–brain–body connection. The construction and use of internal representations are the building blocks of our understanding of reality. It is therefore true to say that we all only know reality by representing it internally. As each of us do this in unique and particular ways, then we only have a distorted view of reality that we know is there by comparing how we each experience every moment and finding commonality and difference. Therefore we don't know first-hand what is true reality.

Many parts of our brain are required to organise and produce the internal representational maps (upstairs, downstairs, left and right hemispheres). However, the coding of internal representations are topologically assembled and instantly consolidated by consciousness through the mind–brain–body and from the body–brain–mind structures all operating in a symbiotic relationship to what might be best described as holographic information structures. These make up your internal maps of external reality. Each representational map is packed with millions of bits of information that combine to create a virtual mirrored instance of external reality. Consciousness is also able to reorganize, with a conscious command, past recalled or triggered whole sequences of internal representations, which can be reassembled and rebuilt in infinite varieties of combinations at will through association and cognitive thought at any time. So the past can be revivified and remembered. In addition, the self and our mind, body and spirit through the power of creative imagination (another conscious construct that is described in further detail later on) can also be applied to construct and generate endless possibilities, options and choices as well as new thoughts and ideas all around the structure of our innate ability to internally represent the reality we experience.

Acquired dispositional internal representations

Our mind–brain is highly associative to experience. We all have an innate and amazing ability to instantly and abundantly form connections from one event to another. Our mind–brain connection easily associates our experiences with other similar but separate relevant experiences in vast arrays of associations, and myriad different but related categories of all of our entire experiences. These are stored and act in exactly the same way as all other internal representations, but are marked in a special and unique way.

Once these specially marked internal representations are triggered they automatically alert a mind–body into emotional 'as if' responses. That is, any specific or particular dispositional representation can be triggered and instantly recalled at any moment by any circumstance in external reality that matches, or is similar to, the information stored in that particular dispositional representation. That recalled disposition is then reenacted and embodied by the whole mind–brain–body system.

Examples of these dispositional collections of particular categorised experiences are:

- Primary emotions: these are innate responses that essentially are responsible for triggering our stress-response fight, flight or freeze reactions to specific life-threatening dangers.
- Secondary emotions: these are more subtle variants built on the foundations of primary emotions.

They are recalled from our internal preference and belief systems such as our own unique attitudes about ourself and the world we have experienced. We explore this in a later section in this chapter.

I have assumed, too, that some of our habits and behavioural responses to certain situations are most likely also triggered by dispositional representations.

Apart from primary emotions, dispositional representations are acquired through your life, and are specifically unique to you. They are based on your particular neurology, disposition and attitude, to your set of unique experiences of external reality that you acquire throughout your life.

All dispositional internal representations are unconsciously created and represent fast shortcut predictors that aid our future responses to dealing with pain or pleasure, avoidance, protection or pursuit and reward reactions to our unique circumstances. Many are created when we are younger, in our formative years. They can be heavily influenced and learned or picked up from others – from our parents and significant others in our lives – as we grow up and mature and make sense of the world around us.

Overriding dispositional representations

It is important to state that while acquired dispositional representations are specially marked as such, on our behalf, by mechanisms generally out of our awareness, these default triggers can, in fact, be overridden.

While it may also be possible that some acquired dispositions around mindset, moods, attitudes and emotional responses etc. may have been initially acquired from some other family member, and then subsequently passed on through genetically inherited means, it is important to know, however, that any genetic disposition merely acts as a starting point in life. This does not mean that this then is a preset default for life for the next generation. Regardless of how we acquire dispositional representations they can be changed at any time (see Chapter 8 on research about happiness). We are therefore able to consciously choose to discard and reject any genetically inherited dispositions, or acquired dispositions for that matter, at any time and as we mature and proceed through life, that are not deemed useful to us at any time and at any point in life. More resourceful dispositions unique to you can be acquired by all of us based on what we choose to accept about what is experienced in external reality.

As we will learn in Chapter 15, the brain is very plastic: what has been learned and programmed, can be unlearned, relearned and reprogrammed by conscious choice and willpower.

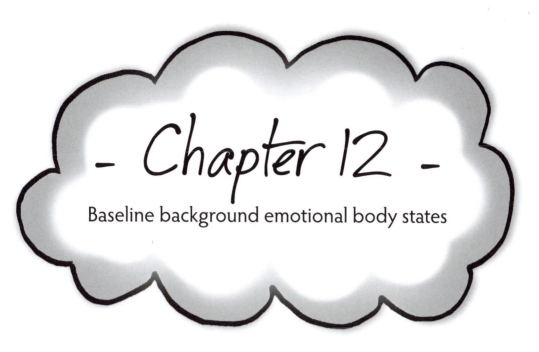

- Chapter 12 -

Baseline background emotional body states

Homeostasis

As we have already read, our mind–brain–body consciousness is continually monitoring and experiencing via our senses what is happening in external physical reality. As we now know, consciousness operating through our mind, body and spirit connection is able to constantly and instantly replicate and internally mirror an internally represented version of reality. This forms the physical and mental requirements for 'being'.

It is believed by neuroscientists that our representational mechanisms also embody a kind of background baseline version of our being – a model of the unique self, when we are operating effortlessly, at our optimum state. Perhaps this is best described as a neutral feeling or state that is possibly connected to a normal balanced background of no emotional secondary states affecting us negatively or positively, neither pleasantly nor unpleasantly. This neutral background state is termed 'homeostasis' by researchers. We all have a unique way of representing this homeostasis background state. Homeostasis, while consistent, is never a static state but dynamically changes, adjusts and modulates up and down within a predefined range.

Homeostasis can best be thought of as a general background sense of self and of well-being, feeling at one, and alive and content. Homeostasis is intended to be the state that we experience more of the time, rather than the emotional ones, which take us away from homeostasis. For normally adjusted people, this state can be easily described, and we often answer this when others enquire how we are doing, or how we are. Homeostasis states are very different from when we experience emotional states and their associated feelings, caused by events and situations that take us away from our balanced background and normally centred and baseline way of being state.

My knowledge from my own experience in working with people on their centred homeostasis baseline state is that it acts as an anchored state of the self, being at its best self when the self is at its most content and comfortable, and how we live with ourself and how we are in the world around us when things are right. So this baseline state acts as a representation of the very core of who we are. It has a critical role to play, in that it acts as a comparator when events and situations in the external world shift us away from our baseline state. Perhaps this may also be another reason why we tend to resist change so much – because at those times we get strong signals to tell us that we may have to move away from our baseline state.

However, the important aspect of our default comfort state is that we are able to tell the difference between when we feel, good, bad, okay or indifferent about what is occurring in external reality.

Under the conditions of our baseline state our mind–brain–body connections seem to be at their most content and that entire system operates at optimum condition. I have come to understand and believe that it properly represents our authentic self and our natural being state. The state we are meant to be living life through more of the time. We are meant to be able to return easily to this, our authentic self, once situations and events in external reality have changed or have been overcome. Our authentic self also represents our internal guide and compass to a physical and natural body image of our self, and when we experience our authentic self, we are able to optimise our psychic energy to easily pay attention to whatever and wherever we choose. In other words it is our internal compass that continues to point north towards our authentic self.

However, as conditions in external physical reality shift, we are meant to easily perceive this at conscious levels, as our mind, body and spirit state shifts away from this optimum authentic self state and we literally feel the difference and our available psychic energy bandwidth gets reduced as it is paying attention to what is happening inside ourselves instead. More specifically, if we experience some form of pain or pleasure, for example, then we know this because our internal reference structures and shifts in our body signals start to instantly inform us.

Artificially acquired baseline states

In my experience, I have often observed that, through the traumas, stresses and strains of life, people acquire all manner of pseudo baseline states. This is because people's acquired conditioning creates a kind of immunity or numbing. Under these conditions it is then easy to lose the reference that points back to the baseline and authentic 'north'.

This acquired conditioning is artificially created by our attitudes. They seem to gain prominence and eventually dominate the more natural and authentic homeostasis balanced state. These acquired artificial states eventually tend to override our naturally intended homeostasis baseline comparator. It is almost as if the authentic self becomes temporarily lost or hidden as the more active acquired and inauthentic self pushes the natural homeostasis authentic baseline self out of the way. It absorbs the available psychic energy and takes over. It is a bit like having a young cuckoo in the nest, who takes the major share of food from the adult parents, starving the other bona fide chick.

Addiction to or attitudinal habits formed from a desire to control and judge outcomes and experiences also tend to develop into an artificial baseline state. Control and judgement are discussed in more detail in Part 4. For now, however, such states, along with worry and anxiety, have an adverse affect on your mental and physical being if sustained over the longer term. Associated emotional body states of 'tightening up', tension and rigidity are inclined to be a by-product of over-control and excessive judgement. Highly effective and detailed solutions to these are worked out cognitively later on in Part 4, and more advanced holistic approaches, using relaxation techniques and strategies, are described in Part 5.

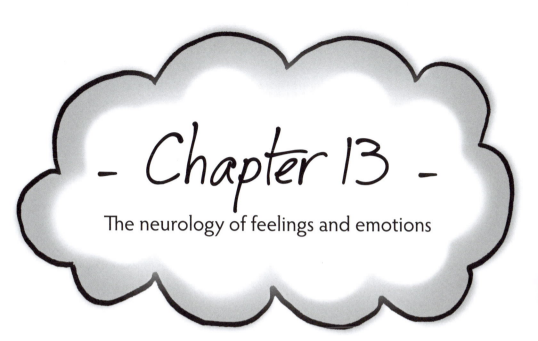

- Chapter 13 -

The neurology of feelings and emotions

Consciousness through our mind, body and spirit connection is wired up to experience and respond to our emotional states. It is these emotional constructs that allow us to perceive external physical reality through our physical bodies. The body is able to interpret what is occurring in the external world and use many aspects of itself to generate and amplify emotional responses that can be picked up through mind–brain–body channels.

Feelings and emotions are words often used interchangeably; however, some neuroscience experts and researchers have recently started to differentiate between these, and I find the distinction useful and will use it from now on in this book. It is useful to separate our feelings from our emotions as they have different processes.

Emotions are automatic internal responses, constructed through our mind–body that amplify matching and mirroring of external physical reality into internal structures that can be understood by our mind, body and spirit.

Feelings are cognitive processes that help us to become aware of our emotions and consciously make sense of them. They help us to learn, and provide us with useful knowledge that builds from our experiences to enable us to make more informed predictions in future similar events. Therefore, the ability to 'feel' our emotional states caused by external events, situations and circumstances provides us with an additional level of cognitive conscious information. This enables us further flexibility, possibilities and options to act and respond, based on particular past learnings, and how we responded to similar previous events and interactions in external reality.

Primary emotions

Areas of the downstairs part of our brains that are unconscious, such as the amygdala, act as sentinels to incoming sensory and somatic data and are able to trigger dispositional, or inherent, inborn internal representations, and the enactment of an appropriate body state, characteristic of an innate primary emotion. Primary emotions such as fear, anger, disgust, surprise and happiness are innately present in all humans. The coding of these cognitive emotional processes are pre-organised and pre-wired body responses that automatically enact this state of mind when they match the triggered dispositional internal representation. This auto-wired ability is often referred to as our stress-response mechanism, when we react instantly without having to think about it. These automatic responses are triggered without having the full sensory data. This is because they utilise a special set of innate pre-organised dispositional internal representations. These automatically create the mind–body state without waiting for the full sensory information to be present, which in normal circumstances would be required to build the emotional response. Hence the fight or flight responses that occur in highly charged situations.

These pre-organised dispositional internal representations are stored solutions to certain events as they are perceived. If 'x' situation or similar is perceived, then react with 'y' state of mind and body response. So, if you like, these act like 'as if' shortcuts, developed through evolution as ready-built, prescribed reactions to certain stimuli that are happening in the external physical reality. In this way these mechanisms are able to assist and instantly predict the best body and mind state reaction to a given situation. As such, these built-in states have been developed to predict the probability of imminent future danger and instigate an associated and appropriate mind–body response, which acts as a reactive survival mechanism and strategy to help us pre-empt danger or threat.

In addition, once the innate body–mind state reaction has been triggered the conscious cognitive processes then catch up with the primary emotion reaction and begin to evaluate the feeling of the emotion in connection with whatever triggered it in external reality. This ability to consciously process our feelings about emotions helps us to build strategies to pre-empt, avoid or tackle them in future.

Secondary emotions

Primary emotions are a specific set of foundational, innate, emotional responses that are preprogrammed. They depend on limbic circuitry and downstairs parts of the brain (principally the amygdala). Through our development and learning through life experience, the primary emotions are built upon and followed by the broader, more developed and subtle mechanisms of secondary emotions. These are developed as we learn and gain experience of our feelings about the external world with which we are surrounded. Through such development and learning we begin to form systematic categorisations, associations and connections between events and our feelings.

While primary emotions rely on limbic systems, the network supporting secondary emotions requires more processing power, which is found in the prefrontal lobes of the upstairs part of our mind–brain connections as well as other parts of our rational and thinking areas.

Whenever we experience an external event that produces an emotion, such as a reunion with a best friend we haven't seen in a while, or responding to some bad news, then our body reacts in specific ways:

- viscerally (heart, lungs, gut and skin etc.);
- skeletal muscles change;
- endocrine glands (pituitary and adrenal etc.) secrete specific chemical reactions;
- furthermore, a number of peptides are released at the same time, from the brain into the bloodstream and regulate the body, as well as constrict or dilate blood vessels.

All these mind–brain–body responses and modifications happen instantly as reactions sensed in external physical reality. Consequently these sets of specific and pre-organised alterations produce corresponding internal representations that move away from the mind, body and spirit normal baseline homeostasis balanced and centred state.

Any emotional state caused by the above-mentioned examples creates a rapid departure from our homeostasis and balanced state, and, as such, shifts our neurology and state of mind in the following ways:

1. Your mind, brain and body via your senses produces millions of internal representations that are instantly brought into consciousness, and are recalled through conscious thought. These internal representations will have myriad aspects and contexts of your associated relationships, reflections and consequences of past events that are similar to what is being currently experienced. These internal representations are built from highly associated responses to certain experiences and some will be made up of verbal, internal dialogue (calling up associated names, places etc.), while others will be associated with remembered visual imagery. All these collections of internal representations are instantly reconstituted topographically from many areas of the brain and neurological structure. These widely distributed constructs are organised as holographic information, containing vast amounts of associated past details that make up our memories in many modalities. These all come together instantly and form a tapestry of information held in that instant within your mind–brain. A phenomenal feat of nature. These representations will also be filtered through another special set of 'dispositional representations'. These, as we have already seen, represent information about your previously experienced secondary emotions and may also trigger and set into motion other dispositional internal representations about your own beliefs and attitudes about yourself and your relationship with the external world around you. As previously described, they act as sentinels that filter all external experience and contain huge amounts of pre-organised detailed information that set up prescribed specific body, mindset and emotional responses that can be recalled, enacted and rebuilt instantly once triggered.

2. At an unconscious level your mind–brain unconsciously reacts to these triggered dispositional representations that embody your past experiences, past choices and strategies about how similar situations have been associated and connected with your secondary emotional responses in your personal experience. So dispositional representations simulate acquired past emotional experiences similar to that being experienced presently and rebuild that same mind–brain–body reaction. These

constructs have the advantage of instantly predicting the next moment and selecting and generating a pre-prepared response that has the advantage of speed and efficiency. Unlike primary emotions, which are innate and provide instant reactions to danger or threat, secondary emotions are acquired uniquely through life experience. These experiences are yours alone, but they can be learned and picked up from others around you. Secondary emotions, however, do perturb an associated underlying primary emotion in which to express the secondary emotion. However, secondary emotions are subtle variants of primary emotions and do not trigger a stress response or survival reaction.

3. Responses to triggered dispositional internal representations are signalled unconsciously to the downstairs part of the brain (again primarily the amygdala). These automatically simultaneously activate the following responses:

    a) The autonomic nervous system signals to the body to place the viscera (all body organs including the skin) in a state associated and encoded within the particular dispositional internal representation.
    b) Signals are dispatched to the skeletal muscle and motor systems to adjust and alter posture and facial expressions as well as other skeletal muscle groups.
    c) Chemical reactions also take place in the body via endocrine hormones and peptide systems whose chemistry alters mind–brain–body states to match the associated informational coding described within the dispositional internal representation that has been triggered.
    d) Brain stem and basal forebrain in the downstairs part of the brain release their chemical messages to adjust body regulation.

All this is instantly achieved by consciousness within your mind–brain–body construct – an astonishing feat of organised coordination that seems miraculous.

Changes in a), b) and c) above create an emotional body state and then signal back to the limbic system, and kinaesthetic sensations are also produced that are sufficiently amplified to enable you to then consciously 'feel' the emotional state cognitively and therefore have thoughts about it. Signal changes in d) that occur in the brain stem structures that secrete chemicals in the brain to regulate the body as a whole system also help to send signals to the prefrontal lobes to assist and impact cognition. So the differentiation of your emotional body state caused by a), b) and c) and the parallel route of signals to d) enable you to literally think about how you 'feel' as a result of this experience. This evolution therefore allows you to choose to avoid, react or take action in a prescribed way, based on past experiences, or to purposefully override and act on the new situation in a different way based on your thinking about the feeling of the emotional body state. We will look at this again later.

Nature has enabled us to use a set of structures, constructs and channels in the mind–brain–body that are used to support our existence, to express primary and secondary emotions, as well as other dispositions, such as our beliefs and attitudes about ourselves and the reality we perceive around us. In this way we therefore literally co-create our reality, both internally and externally, through the choices and ways we respond to the external physical world around each and every one of us.

So, in essence, our emotions are a collection of automatic changes in the mind–brain–body system that are united through the complex structure of our mind–brain which is automatically responding to the context of our consciousness as well as additional cognitive thought processes that interrelate our being with external reality by allowing us to think about how we feel about our emotional states. As we have seen, these constructs are highly influenced by our acquired dispositional representations that are specially marked and that we hold within the same mind–brain structure about past dealings with specific instances of external reality that we experience. In this way our mind, body and spirit has pre-organised itself in specific ways related to the information encoded within our dispositions. Therefore emotion is a unique combination of mental evaluative processes that can be in part actuated and recreated into predictable responses in an attempt to match external reality in the next moment.

Feelings of emotions

All emotions generate feelings. Say for example you are meeting up with an old friend you haven't seen for a while, or receiving some bad news, naturally you will have different emotions and feelings (thoughts about emotions) for each of these examples.

All such events and situations and internal changes are continuously being signalled to your mind–brain–body via your nervous system. It is the return journey (body–brain–mind) back to the upstairs thinking part of your brain (the prefrontal lobes) that receives data about what is being mirrored and simulated by the body as an emotional state that is responding to external physical reality moment by moment.

These upper brain thinking structures are organised in such a way, by another part of consciousness, to get a dissociated view of the ever-changing emotional states being produced in your body. This allows us to think about our emotions and these are termed feelings. So I am making a distinction between emotions and feelings here. All thinking structures also instantly produce millions of additional internal representational maps that are unique to each thought and to its context. Like all internal representations these are equally dynamic and newly made every moment. These representations are created to respond to the representations about your emotional body state. So they are thought representations specially generated to think about the emotionally produced representations. These are combined with other informational sources from chemical changes in the body via the bloodstream. These all form internal representations. In this way you become conscious of the existence of your body emotions and sensations and through this mechanism you are able to reflect and think through what is happening to you as things unfold in real time and offline too.

In other words you are able to process and experience cognitive thoughts, which you become aware of as feelings about what is unfolding in external physical reality as your body experiences it emotionally.

Therefore, in this context emotions are about what you are experiencing as sensations that are amplified to you by your whole body. The essence of these internal experiences is at the same time being perceived as feelings that your thoughts can grasp and act upon. Both use your mind–brain, the body's miraculous ability to structure such subjective experience as millions of instant and simultaneous internal representations every moment of the life you are experiencing.

How we feel a feeling

Scientific research is providing some interesting knowledge about comparing positive and negative body states.

Negative secondary emotions (such as depression, worry and anxiety etc.) tend to produce slower moving body responses that also generate slower and more deliberate cognitive reactions and sedated reasoning abilities. So processing negative things that happen to us literally takes longer. In addition, their associated internally represented coding provides output that is limited, with a smaller diversity of choice, and available options are also severally constricted. These end up becoming more loop like and repetitive in nature, often creating trance like mind, body and spirit states.

In contrast, positive emotions (such as joy and laughter etc.) generate rapid body states and faster responses that create the rapid production of more internal representations, which in turn provide more choice and diversity of potential options.

Faster reasoning abilities are also combined with these states. In such instances we seem to operate with easier and more relaxed movements, and things literally seem to flow. Thoughts are freer, more wide-ranging and varied.

These body and thought states are correlated and compared with neural representations of the current self as well as the baseline balanced self (homeostasis) state that then engenders a perceived feeling.

Universal innate feeling states are based on the primary emotions of joy, sadness, anger, disgust and fear. When these states are generated our attention is more focused on our body and body landscape via innate stress response mechanisms.

Secondary emotions are more subtle variants of the primary emotions. For example, excitement or ecstasy are more subtle versions of joy; melancholy and wistfulness are expressions of sadness; shyness and panic might be expressions of fear. When secondary emotions are generated, attentional psychic energy has the capacity to be used by our prefrontal lobes to think about how we feel about these secondary emotions.

It is the subtle connection between these intricate combinations of feeling, cognitive content, baseline state comparisons and variations of pre-organised emotional body state profiles that allows us to experience such a richness and variety of internal experiences.

So our feelings are just as cognitive as any other perceptual thought process. Feelings allow us to make sense and act upon our body states. They literally allow us to 'mind' our body attentively. This can be done via the body state live, as it is occurring in real time, or from re-broadcasted, recalled internal representations or dispensations as they are triggered into consciousness and once again revivified as 'as if' states by the mind–brain–body to match similar conditions that are occurring in that moment in external physical reality. In this way this combined experience enables us to predict efficiently and effectively the next future response to the external world.

The danger of not adapting

However, these same structured mechanisms of representing reality might also get in our way, preventing us from learning how to be more resourceful and adaptive to overcome and resolve issues and problems. For example, if we are feeling angry we can merely end up reacting to our internally generated representations about the emotional state of being angry. And so we simply feel anger and our thoughts could easily become consumed by this state. Our thoughts and feelings about being angry can then perpetuate the corresponding emotional state for as long as we want. Another example could be that someone may be consumed by worry about a past situation that continues to haunt them and they can't stop thinking about. In this case the emotional state of worry simply keeps cycling around and around. Yet another person may be continuously anxious about something that is coming up in the future and they too continue to generate the emotional state of anxiety simply by continuing to think about it. However, we all have choices to think about different feelings instead. When we choose to be proactive and purposefully and deliberately change our thoughts to more resourceful ways of feeling instead, then we will correspondingly build different representations that in turn automatically generate different emotional states – such as happiness or joy for instance.

So if we rely on reactive default approaches to situations and events, issues and problems that we face then we may also miss out on feeling the richness of other experiences and end up not developing and growing – which is part of our design as human beings. Putting this another way, if we do not use our reasoning and thinking abilities to evaluate whether or not our tried and tested dispositional response mechanisms are still actually giving us the best results, then we might not be getting the best outcomes for ourselves in the longer term.

It is therefore important that, as we go through life and gain more experience, we also spend time evaluating and challenging our preprogrammed approaches to situations. If we don't do this, we risk getting ourselves stuck and not maturing and experiencing the whole of life. If you always do the same things you will always get the same results. We are not meant to lead our lives that way. Instead we have been designed to continually experience, feel and learn, to grow and to develop as we mature. We are not meant to stay rooted to past and set ways of doing things and handling reality in the same way all the time using set preprogrammed ways. Because if we do, all we are doing is setting up our future reality to continue to correspond to our internal reality of feeling bad, for example. However, if we shift our thinking, and we can, to more proactive thoughts instead, like feeling good, then the same internal mechanisms will shift to a different happier reality instead.

In my experience, I have noticed that many people start to get stuck at some point in life and in their development, as they grow and mature. This in itself is a natural juncture in life, where we all notice that things are somehow no longer working in the same way as they did earlier on in our life. That certain patterns may end up controlling our responses in unresourceful ways and how we respond to something that needs overcoming is now getting in our way.

These feelings are often associated with the limiting dispositions (beliefs) that we have acquired through life experience, but are now for whatever reason no longer working for us in the way that they once did. Usually at this point it is because uniquely formed protective mechanisms, once designed to keep you safe, are now no longer necessary. However, through habit these dispositions are still being triggered by external circumstance. At this point it is important to take stock and re-evaluate better more proactive responses and learn to take on new ways of being in the world. These then create different pathways and dispositions are replaced. These are the subject of the chapters ahead.

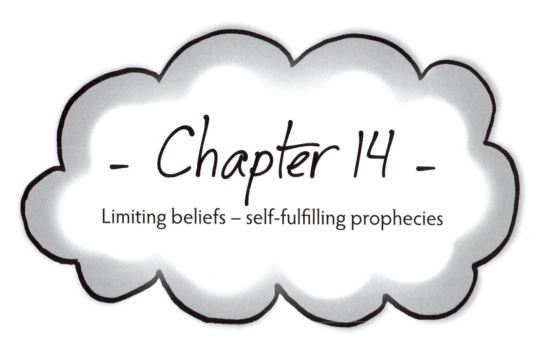

- Chapter 14 -

Limiting beliefs – self-fulfilling prophecies

Proactive and reactive choice points...

Imagine for a moment a young boy being continually abusively name-called and, on occasion, physically attacked by his peers at playtime and after school. A recurring event of this nature is obviously perceived as being highly threatening to the young boy. His mind, body and spirit consciousness begins actively exploring strategies to deal with these repeating experiences.

In these situations we all make subtle choices about how to deal with such information. Some choices may be more resourceful than others.

Some people may see such events in relatively proactive ways: simply as a test of skill, or a game to be played that somehow can be overcome.

Other possibilities may involve gaining back power by employing humour, or fighting back in some way. Perhaps by meeting the aggression with equal force. All such proactive choices tend to rapidly gain back personal power and are supported by strong inner understandings of being worthy. Personal power defuses and collapses the threatening situation or event (in the young boy's case, those picking on him). The issue then simply vanishes, and any possibility of repetition quickly subsides. The event, by all parties, is rapidly forgotten.

The person with such strategies therefore learns in healthy ways that risky, adverse and threatening events like these can be overcome with purpose, intention and perhaps some effort. Subtle understandings of acceptance and the nature of their authentic self are in this way learned, absorbed and folded into mind, body and spirit consciousness to become part of their internal and external reality. In cases such as this, no belief is actually formed. What is formed instead, however, is innate awareness and understanding of the use of personal power and of the nature of our authentic self that takes care of us in the world. It is then these attitudes that get further reinforcement.

However, in contrast, other more reactive choices can be made to the threatening experience. Such reactive choices may instead emerge by attending to different forms of information. For example, from intensely negative feelings of being unworthy, powerless, fearful, guilt or in denial. These sorts of choices utilise differing neurological mechanisms to form reactive strategies that quickly develop into dealing with such issues in more limiting and conditioned ways.

Reactive choices or strategies are inclined to be built through, fear, denial, avoidance, etc. and tend to lead to limitations being artificially imposed on the mind, body and spirit consciousness.

These sorts of ideas and thoughts start to create very different constructs, called limiting beliefs. Such strategies find ways around coping with the issues being experienced, which fast track into certain reactions and behaviours. Limiting beliefs, then, are an attempt to artificially find ways to avoid threatening situations being experienced. However, despite intentions designed to protect from future harm, threat or danger, their very existence in internal reality means that they continually attract corresponding and similar events happening in external reality. These then become self-fulfilling prophecies.

From my own experience I have formed the idea that internal workings that empower us create different responses in us, and operate with completely different types of neurological mind–brain mechanics and structures from those that activate our limiting beliefs. We will explore this in detail shortly.

What is a limiting belief?

We are born with the biological machinery present within our mind–brain–body neurology to develop and organise aspects of consciousness in ways that help us to build sophisticated coping strategies and responses to whatever is manifesting in external reality. Our belief structures form part of this machinery. They act as generalised filters that seem to be able to monitor everything that is occurring in external physical reality. Specific subsets of dispositional internal representations that we have also acquired about ourselves and the world around us are automatically triggered within the make-up of the belief system and activate it.

When a particular belief is activated its intention is to control the mind–body to act as 'as if' shortcuts to predict our response to the next moment. Therefore the belief purpose is to attempt to head us off as quickly as possible from potentially difficult situations that we prefer to avoid, and where perceived pain, loss and fear etc. are manifesting in physical reality.

As human beings, achieving survival is an innate preprogrammed ability and our brain–body defaults to programmes and strategies that reduce or avoid unpleasant emotional body states, and instead drive towards a return to our baseline homeostasis neutral state that provides balance and harmony as quickly and efficiently as possible. So our beliefs share in this overall mind–body strategy.

When certain external situations are perceived, our belief systems interact with and have direct access to the mind–brain–body's ability to produce millions of instant internal representations that are generated in real time every moment, in the ways previously described. More specifically, a belief is constructed from clusters of many different types of interrelated internal dispositional information representations that may be relevant about ourselves to deal with and handle myriad specific situations and experiences in external physical reality. Together this cluster of dispositional representations jointly combines into a (uneasy) cohesive cohabitation or working alliance, and operates under the umbrella of a limiting belief. Examples of dispositional information it contains are our internal and unique preferences to our attitudes, fears, threats and dangers, moods, emotional responses and ways of behavior.

Their purpose, as already stated, is to act as a default automatic survival and protection mechanism to a particular perceived aspect of external reality. All limiting beliefs will directly have an impact upon your external reality. Every time. Always, without fail.

Limiting belief systems

You may have noticed with your own beliefs that they are confusing and hard to pin down and there may be more than one limiting belief in operation at any time.

This is because people may hold many beliefs, each one designed and intended to be triggered for specific instances and circumstances that we perceive as a threat in the outside world. However, each separate limiting belief commonly shares similar dispositions that are relevant to a number of external circumstances and so beliefs tend to operate and survive within interrelated clusters – I call these clusters limiting belief systems. So our limiting belief systems are inherently predisposed and designed to avoid pain or loss.

From where do your limiting beliefs derive?

Generally, limiting beliefs start to form in childhood and adolescence; however, they can continue to develop and form throughout life and from social experiences and learnings.

More specifically, limited beliefs are acquired and adapted by our unique experiences and perceptions about the world around us. Beliefs form into personal control mechanisms. They are artificially adapted and acquired. They are not innate. Beliefs are highly personal, situational and complex in nature. They are artificially shaped and acquired by our internal preferences and circumstances that are unique to each of us. We each develop internal preferences that are governed by individual factors, unique circumstances and to the personal reactions to commonly occurring external situations and particular events we face through life. They are also formed through social conventions and cultural rules, family traits and customs that are learned or imposed.

Beliefs can be created at any time in our lives. Some are even created instantly as one-time learnings – these are how phobias (which are in themselves highly intensified belief constructs) are instantly formed.

Scientific research and anecdotal literature points to many of our foundational beliefs being generally created in our much younger and formative years, somewhere between three and seven years old. This is when we are more impressionable, while our brain is developing and is in its more plastic stage, before we have formed our own independent thinking.

Belief constructs are mainly formed through repetition of ideas and events that have occurred in our early lives, as we try to make sense of the world around us. During our formative imprint years, we are heavily influenced by our parents, significant others, such as our teachers, and our peer groups around us.

It is believed that the original intention of these constructs are the mind–brain–body's way of acquiring the means of dealing with difficult situations when we are young and have not yet developed sufficiently robust thinking and rational evaluative parts of our brain (these develop more in our late teenage years). The theory is that they are brought into existence by choice, in that the beliefs are formed to protect us and keep us safe in our formative years. Whether this is true or not, the reality is that, left unchecked, they continue to operate but often outlive their original purpose.

As we will discover later, once these artificial belief constructs are acquired, limiting belief systems want to survive and cling onto their existence and go to extreme lengths to protect themselves from change and eradication. If exposed, or challenged, they seem to be able to defend themselves in clever and intelligent ways. This may be because they are built for survival and protection first. For example, they can convincingly call upon other parts of consciousness (such as verbal reasoning) that forcefully project information justifying why any change is completely unnecessary, painful and difficult, if not impossible. Beliefs can also have contagious effects in that they have the tendency to be passed on and 'jump' from one generation to the next. This applies to all groups and cultures. This has cultural and social survival benefits, though.

Scientific research tells us that by the age of 12 years old or so, many of our limiting beliefs are so well formed that they begin to be polished into repeating looping routine strategies. Left unchecked, these self-perpetuating loops then play out into our lives from then on, as they cycle around and around. Beliefs have power to act when perceived circumstances manifest in external reality and as such have the power to create self-fulfilling prophecies.

Generally speaking, left unchecked and unchallenged, they become hidden from everyday awareness, and so we only occasionally have passing and fleeting glimmers of their existence. As such they remain largely un-policed by our minds, and continue to operate and remain highly active and controlling and limit our adult lives.

The inner workings of limiting beliefs

Now, in general terms, beliefs act in similar ways to intentions, but in more specific ways: they are highly specialised and concentrated, and produce specific results.

Once acquired, they quickly form into self-organising conscious entities and intelligently adapt themselves to the inner workings of our mind, in very structured ways. Put simply, limiting beliefs are a controlling construct that are specifically designed to intensely focus and narrow our attention to concentrate on a specific pre-organised solution or response to what is being perceived in our external experience. The consequence of our conscious attentional energy being constricted and narrowed is that other potential choices are limited. So while the benefit is a programmed response that is instantly available and conscious attention is acutely focused, its downside is that it tends to limit us to that particular response strategy. This is because attentional energy is not available to consider other options and potential learnings. We therefore end up either limiting and filtering out and closing down negative or positive choices or other possibilities, or not.

Some examples of limiting beliefs:

- If you believe that you can do something, this filters out it not occurring to you that it can't be done. Or if you focus on not being able to do something, it thereby limits thoughts that say you can do it.
- A belief that change is possible, thereby it never occurring to you that change might be impossible in this instance, and vice versa.
- That things never work out for you filters out that things work out for the best for you, instead. Or the other way around: that things always work out for you, thereby it never occurring to you that things might not work out for you this time (and so limits other creative options from being explored).
- Believing things will succeed implies little thought given to learning from failure and mistakes. Conversely, beliefs that things always fail for you, imply no, or less, attention given to your successes.

- Believing in the idea that you always seem to have problems filters out the possibility that you can find solutions and outcomes and, conversely, an outcome orientation may filter out a problem focused mentality that might be useful from time to time.
- You might believe that you have to always fight for what you want in this life, so no thought is given to the times when the world cares for you in some way. A belief that the world cares for you might mean that it is less likely that you ever have to fight for your place and rights, and so on.
- Judgement filters out acceptance, and so a paradigm of acceptance will therefore eliminate judgmental attitudes.

The language of limiting beliefs

As you may have noticed from the examples above, beliefs have access to our language structures within our mind–brain. They use this ability to readily create endless amounts of often negative and highly limiting inner mind chatter that form into cohesive repetitive patterns of internal statements. Inner mind chatter is an extensive subject in its own right and we will explore this in more detail again very shortly.

For now, some typical examples of internalised reactive and limiting statements that easily work themselves out into consciousness, could be one or more, or clusters of the following…

People don't like me.
I'm not like others.
I'm not good enough.
I am too different from others.
I can't wait to grow up, so this stuff won't happen any more.
I wish it had never happened to me, and would all go away.
I will pretend it never happened.
I will avoid them by being ill.
I want them to feel sorry for me, and then they will leave me alone.
I'm never brave enough to stand up for myself.
It's never my fault; it's always other people that pick on me.
I'm always weak and frightened.
I'm always being bullied.
I'm never worthy.

Never attract attention and you will never be noticed.
And so on…

The controlling nature of limiting beliefs

Once acquired, limiting beliefs justify their right to exist in a number of ways.

Firstly, by their very nature limiting beliefs are built from and express themselves in extremely generalised (linguistic) and simplistic terms. This means their actions can be applied to all experience, anytime, anywhere, any place as we will see in more detail in the later section on inner mind chatter.

Secondly, they have a highly filtering nature. By doing so, they are able to monitor and compare all external reality experiences, and internal information, against the specific pattern of each belief. In this way, limiting beliefs operate rather like a software program, with coded instructions. Only information that matches the belief's internal code or pattern will be accepted into the conscious mind, and its supporting brain structures. As already mentioned, once in play the limiting belief filters out of immediate awareness all counter-information, possibilities and options. So as all attentional energy is engaged and focused through the belief and its mind–brain–body response, then other more resourceful, probable and existing solutions will most likely be out of awareness of other parts of consciousness.

Thirdly, the limiting belief artificially controls what is perceived as reality. This is because each limiting belief is constantly comparing itself to external reality and is then able to call upon attentional energy to fulfil its purpose. In this way beliefs seem to be able to justify their own existence through these comparisons to the mind, body and spirit consciousness. Together with copious amounts of constant and unceasing limiting inner mind chatter it sets up a 'I told you so… You see, I am here to protect you and keep you safe' paradigm. As the belief construct is in itself a sort of conscious entity, whose sole purpose is all about survival, it stands to reason that perhaps beliefs might also have abilities to protect their own survival too, from the threat of being superfluous.

Furthermore, its easy access to and manipulation of linguistic abilities are so prolific that they quickly literally hypnotise the mind, body and spirit consciousness at the attentional and cognitive level into being convinced of its importance and necessity, and that its way is the most efficient approach to predict and protect from the future moment. In this way its survival remains viable. Inner mind chatter is unceasingly used as a vehicle to waste and drain away attentional bandwidth from being used elsewhere. So the limiting belief distracts and occupies the mind, body and spirit consciousness.

A few examples of limiting beliefs and their effects

- A belief system built around the premise that 'all people are dangerous' will continue to manifest into external reality as ongoing streams of difficult situations involving people perceived as being dangerous.
- A belief system based around the idea that 'life is a nightmare, and my life is a soap opera' will create continuous streams of drama and counter-productive events that match these statements in external reality.
- Believing that 'I have to fight for my right to exist' will manifest aggressive life situations, which need to be continuously fought and overcome to validate their right to exist. Attitudes to other peoples' situations will be dealt with in a similar manner.
- Beliefs constructed around being bullied, treated badly and victimised will correspondingly create these types of situations and people to turn up in that person's life. Self-fulfilling prophecies are thus created and the victim sets up a 'poor me' or 'why me' submissive strategy.
- Good and bad, rich and poor, sickness and health, lucky and unlucky, happy and sad are all set up in this way. Whatever is the predominant intention is translated into reality via the principles of attraction.

The effect of limiting beliefs on our authentic self

It seems evident to me that limiting beliefs, in time, tend to gain an over-prominence in their role as guardians of our survival, and if left unchecked overplay keeping us safe and protecting us. In my experience helping people to develop and move away from their limiting beliefs allows them to make resourceful changes to their lives and become highly effective on a personal basis. Personally, I have been testing out the idea that, as we mature, we often grow out of our need for limiting beliefs. Instead, we can begin to turn our attention to our authentic self, to take us into a new paradigm of self-actualisation. However, to do this we have to wean ourselves away from the 'addictive' controlling nature of our limiting beliefs and turn our attention to the more subtle approach we can gain by developing attention to rely more on our authentic self.

However, this is easier said than done. As limiting beliefs seem to work in clusters and systems (probably as another level of self-preservation and subtle control), then their demand on attentional energy is amplified. In this way belief systems are able to take large amounts of attentional energy bandwidth from being used by other resources and strategies that are used by our authentic self. Our over-acceptance and automatic reliance on our default belief systems to look out for us means we fall into a less awake state and become numbed and lethargic.

In contrast to the mechanisms of our limiting belief systems, the authentic self doesn't rely on representational knowledge, but works with whatever is in the present situation as well as wisdom attained from vast information fields that our unconscious minds seem to have ready access to and draw from life in each and every moment. So its approach is much more adaptive, flexible and spontaneous than limiting belief systems that use conscious mind constructs of the past to control future outcomes. Effectiveness is the mandate of unconscious mind approaches, whereas efficiency through structure is the quest of the conscious mind. Both are opposing approaches. As our authentic self emerges we become more awake and alert in the newness and magic of the current moment and its 'nowness'.

Looking for a moment at the evolution of our two hemisphere mind–brain topology for another source of information, the competing nature of the conscious mind allows it to favour and trust its own domain, over its opposite hemisphere, where the unconscious mind rules charitably and trustingly. The unconscious mind manages itself in more subtle ways and does not vie or tussle for control, but waits benevolently to be asked, and, perhaps for those reasons, the conscious mind often seems to deeply distrust it. As already mentioned, it may turn out that our competing two-brain approach to human life means that a sort of 'winner takes all' approach might be at play here, and so the efficiency of conscious mind constructs, such as our limiting belief systems and their controlling nature, tend to win out over potentially more effective but less controlling ones that could be used by the authentic self, which resides in our unconscious mind. As the authentic self does not assert itself, perhaps it falls back into the unconscious mind, always patiently ready to be invited through. So in the meantime we lose awareness of and pay no attention to the existence of our dormant authentic self. Perhaps too, limiting belief systems are based on what has been learned and known and are accordingly laid down as neural brain maps – this is what makes them so efficient, they are just called up by automatic default. The other more right-brain approaches, which work by learning different and new concepts, means that new maps have to be formed for these and need to compete for 'brain real estate' over their established limiting belief counterparts. See the later chapter on neural plasticity.

So instead, as the mind, body and spirit consciousness grows, and matures, the artificial, or acquired, belief control structure remains, without ever adapting. If left unattended, out of everyday awareness it will continue to operate in the way it always has. No new learning is allowed to superimpose on it, as this will mean the limiting belief's deletion. However, without any conscious remodification or updating, then in time other trouble can begin and most likely will get worse.

Let's now turn our attention to the ways limiting beliefs use to create reality in their own image.

The seduction of mind, body and spirit consciousness

The conscious mind is a part of the overall mind, body and spirit consciousness, and is organised to achieve certain things on its behalf. It is, for example, the constant watcher of external experience. The conscious mind also acts as a director of psychic energy that allows mind, body and spirit consciousness to respond to what is being sensed from external reality. Left to its own devices, without interference from artificial constructs such as limiting beliefs, it carries out this function very proficiently. Seamlessly comparing what it senses in external reality, it provides balance and harmony via checks and balances with the unconscious mind, using informational flows between the conscious and unconscious minds. The balance of these two elements of mind, body and spirit consciousness highly influences and co-creates our reality, both internally and externally. Operating together in this way they are joint masters of creation. When artificial limiting beliefs exist, then their operation significantly corrupts and distorts this harmonious process.

By means of the ego construct, the conscious mind is able to judge and compare external reality to other information from itself as well as from unconscious origins. If artificial limiting belief systems are operating, then the ego directs its flow of psychic conscious energy towards the depositional representations contained within the limiting belief system. The belief system uses the ego's function to judge and compare, to constantly monitor and filter reality against its own dispositional encodings. Information that supports the conditional rules contained in the limiting belief construct are then allowed to pass into the conscious mind, with the rest being effectively ignored.

The belief system calls upon, and engages the services of, the imagination as a supporting agency, and exploits its access to the source of unlimited energy from the psyche. Energy is then diverted to fuel the intentions encoded within the belief system. Furthermore, filtered informational commands from the belief system also use the services of the imagination to gain access to the function producing internal representations within consciousness. In turn, a constant stream of internal (dispositional) representations are instantly and accordingly constantly produced or rerun. These represent the filtered, corrupted and distorted information originated by the limiting belief system.

The parts of consciousness responsible for accessing internal representations also has direct access to the storehouse of all past memories of mind, body and spirit consciousness. Associations to all relevant past memories are then automatically added to further reinforce the belief system's orders. In addition, current information from the senses about external reality also produce further dynamic internal representations. All these internal representations of current experiences and past memories are being continuously and instantly compared, sifted and translated into highly complex informational instructions. All these representations are highly influenced, coloured and tainted by the original commands of the limited belief system. These are then automatically broadcast, understood and acted upon by deeper functions of the mind, body and spirit consciousness through various channels.

In this way, the belief system parasitically exploits these complex organisations of consciousness to broadcast its version of reality to the entire mind, body and spirit conscious structure.

Overcoming our limiting beliefs is possible

I have developed considerable experience and expertise in helping people to do just that for changing dispositions around limiting beliefs. Later in this book I describe the processes in more detail. However, for now the important thing is helping people to learn to understand and become aware of these limiting beliefs, their circumstantial and situational associations, and their triggers. This exposes these belief constructs and their contexts and we can then learn to do something about them.

After this, the next thing is to develop ways and choices to challenge them, and then to create more useful new mindset approaches and beliefs to enable you to respond differently to certain situations instead. This process interrupts the original programming and instead enables new, more resourcefully acquired neurological choices that in themselves become dispositional triggers and then actually replace the less resourceful default dispositions. We will discover how to do this practically later on.

Whenever we make changes in this way, there is often some sort of inherent resistance to consciously changing any dispositional belief that has been laid down through unconscious learning. This is part of the territory of changing dispositional belief patterns.

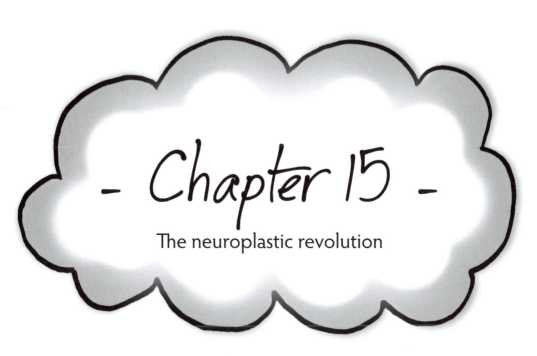

Chapter 15

The neuroplastic revolution

Running our brains

I remember feeling a huge sense of sadness and utter disappointment when an experienced psychologist (and at the time a human resource manager) once told me that research in psychology has proved that our brains are fixed constructs. This was in the late 1990s and her statement was a reflection of what she had been taught during her psychology education in the 1980s. This was certainly the prevailing view of that time, and 20–30 years later still largely remains the prevailing thoughts that have been seeded into our culture for many decades. She went on to state that once the brain had built up its neural pathways in response to our experiences in life that they then become fixed and set in that pattern. She went on to say that our resultant behavioural responses are then predictable. She said that because of this, we can ask questions relating to how people dealt with past events to accurately determine and predict future responses and therefore select appropriate people for new roles and promotion etc. When I heard this viewpoint, I felt hope completely drain away from me. I wonder how it makes you feel? However, my reflection about this viewpoint at that time was one of disbelief, and I still hold that today. I simply refused to allow myself to believe this, or accept this principle.

My own personal development journey told me a very different story of hope – that this viewpoint was most definitely wrong. My model of the world has taught me that if you are sufficiently motivated and desire and want to, you can change any habit, behaviour or belief as long as you are prepared to work at it. Empirically I still believe this viewpoint is correct, as I often observe people making such changes when I work with individuals. People can make changes, and think, act and believe differently if they really want to. And if we do want to then we have to gain and deserve the right to attain the freedom we desire. This comes through effort. That doesn't mean it's difficult or will take a long time; what it means is that if we want change then we can but we have to pay a price. That price is that change takes effort, and the motivator behind this is hope. Hope to find release from the curse of our conditioning.

According to Dr Norman Doidge, a psychiatrist and author, in his book, *The Brain That Changes Itself*, he interviewed a number of top scientists at the forefront of brain science. From this he stated that in the beginning of modern day science the belief was that the brain, and with it human nature, once fully developed was static and was not able to change or alter its structure (this was called localisation). This was evidenced by studies of the mental limitations, of people with sustained brain damage, that mental exercise around thinking differently was given a wide birth and unscientific approaches of positive thinking etc. and other such theories were shunned for many decades. The psychology of the day worked from an underlying premise that we are all in some way deficient. That mental illness was just further advancement of that deficiency and once developed could only be controlled, never improved or recovered from. The viewpoint at the time considered the brain like a clockwork machine and once built did not change. In addition inadequate and unsophisticated measuring instruments considerably slowed down research. Therefore advancement of new ideas and hypotheses were not possible, simply because the technology was not sufficiently advanced. All of these ideas have spread throughout culture, stunting our overall perception of human nature and growth: that all these things are unalterable.

More recent research, thanks to persistent scientists fighting against decades of localisation theory and the invention of sophisticated machines, has altered mindsets. Today we are beginning to appreciate that our brains are more soft-wired than hardwired. That the neuro-machinery and specialised functions of the brain can work together to allow change to occur to human nature. And, more fundamentally, that research is now proving that beyond a doubt our thoughts significantly influence and drive these changes to occur. We now know that the brain is malleable, pliable and plastic. It is true that children as well as mature adults can shift away from the mental disabilities they were born with; that mental trauma can, with the right interventions be recovered from; that mental disorders around learning can be understood, and eventually remediated. We know, too, that by changing our thinking we can influence and even change our gene structures. That inherited or learned behaviours can in fact be changed.

Doidge proceeds to describe one of the most interesting discoveries of the dynamic nature of the neurone structure in our brains by a neuroscientist called Merzenich. He noticed while brain mapping finger movements that neurones develop strong connections with one another when they are activated at the same moment in time. He concluded that neurones that fire together, wire together. And he observed that these brain maps could dynamically change location in the brain. For example, if a middle finger is removed (don't ask), then the brain map for that finger gets quickly taken over by the index and third finger. No brain 'real estate' is wasted. Merzenich also proved that if a part of the brain is damaged through a stroke, say, then whatever function is affected can be relearned, and the brain maps this in a new and different undamaged location. Merzenich showed beyond doubt, through his scientific demonstrations, that there is competition in the brain for cortical 'real estate', and that the brain is able to dynamically allocate its resources according to the principle of use it or lose it.

Doidge goes on to suggest from Merzenich's work that this competitive plasticity also explains why our bad habits are so difficult to break or unlearn. Our brains are not containers of learnings. So learning something new is not a matter of putting something new into the brain. Instead as we learn a bad habit, a limiting belief for example, then it creates its own brain map, and each time it is repeated it claims more control of that brain map, and therefore prevents that space being used for a good habit. So the bad habit has to be unlearned and replaced by a good habit. And during this process the brain's real estate is being competed for and has to dynamically make a change to facilitate this unlearning and relearning. This is perhaps then why it is often a lot harder than first time learning. In my own experience, I have often observed this competitive battle for brain real estate going on every time people start to shift their limiting beliefs. A process of relearning has to happen. The importance of the above research is that the brain is purpose built as an ever-changing dynamic and adaptive living machine to support our changing lives and our changing thoughts, desires and wishes.

So Doidge rightly believes that there is reason to hope that people born with problems in brain map processing areas, people with all sorts of learning problems or psychological issues, strokes or brain injuries might be able to form new maps if they could be helped to form new neuronal connections, by getting their healthy neurones to fire together and therefore wire together. Merzenich saw that neuroplasticity had all sorts of potential implications for therapeutics, for neuropathology and psychiatry.

Today, thankfully, neuroscience is providing us with a different picture – one of hope. As outlined already, it turns out that the brain is infinitely more flexible than was first assumed. The brain has a plasticity that enables it to take on different ways of reacting and different beliefs, and these are supported by our brains building different neurological pathways that enable us to respond and learn from our experiences in infinitely different ways. This is the neuroplastic revolution, says Dr Norman Doidge, which directly impacts our interrelationships, love, sex life, grief, misery, happiness, and includes psychotherapeutic change. And that all these aspects of human nature are 'self-changeable'.

Good news, bad news

All of this sounds like great stuff, and it is; however, there is a flip side to neuroplasticity too. It is not all good news. If we can make positive changes to our brain, via our mindset, then it is entirely possible that our mind–brain–body connection can, by means of the same plasticity, be more vulnerable to external influences. That is the conditioning that we have been talking about.

According to Dr Doidge, neuroplasticity has the power to produce both more flexible and more rigid behaviours. He calls this the 'plastic paradox'. A nice phrase. He goes on to state that, ironically, some of our most stubborn habits and disorders are products of our plasticity. Once a particular 'plastic' change occurs in our brain, and becomes well established, it can deter and prevent other, perhaps more resourceful, changes from then occurring, taking hold and replacing it.

By understanding that both positive and negative changes are possible, only then can we truly understand the powerful extent of our humanness and its ability to change, both in its ability to take on negative conditioning, and then in the way it can overcome this. To overcome such conditioning is the challenge, and we have to work purposefully to make such changes and relearn so we can return to more beneficial ways of running our brains and living our lives. This is the purpose of this book and the next chapters.

The beginnings of change

I believe spending some time initially talking to people I work with about the aspects outlined in Part 2 of this book is very important. Particularly aspects of how our mind–brain–body operates neurologically, about how limiting beliefs are formed and the plasticity of our brains. I spend time emphasising how neurological patterns and pathways can be adapted and can be permanently changed and changed again. That if something isn't working then do something else instead. That nothing in our brains is fixed. That the brain is highly capable of learning to flex and change habitual pathways, and that learning to do this occurs relatively quickly.

Why do I do this? I do this because by starting change conversations in this way provides people with hope as well as research knowledge about the potential of personal change. It also provides the first subtle shifts in beliefs and peoples' neurology: that we can change. This is in itself a change. Paradoxically the first change was that person choosing to learn and acquire a particular pattern and form of conditioning. So setting up change in this way is important, because it gives hope, and that in itself is a great starting point.

Once people start to believe in the hope that change is possible, they are then more ready to move on to exploring what the actual problem is, and developing an inventory of current patterns of conditioning and their consequences.

As I am writing this book, I am beginning to realise that the above fundamentally became my own motivation and inspiration to do the work that I do with the people that I work with: from executives, through to management and teams, directors and leaders, in all kinds of large, small and global organisations. It is this purpose that inspired this book, so that anyone, anywhere, can find the principles and tools to make changes for themselves and apply these changes for the benefit of others.

The next parts of this book look at how we begin to loosen and break the hold of our conditioning and our acquired self, and then at strategies to return to balance through our authentic self. Read on.

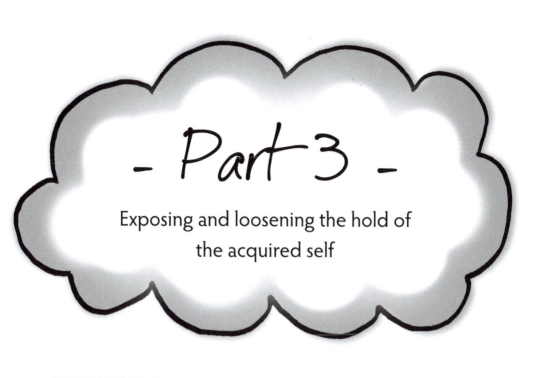

- Part 3 -

Exposing and loosening the hold of the acquired self

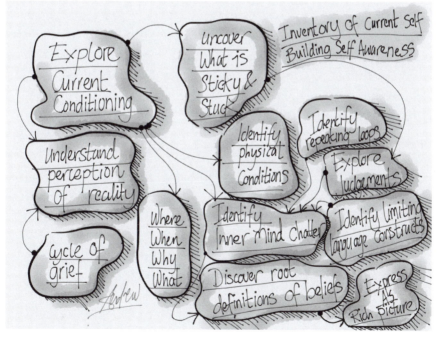

Figure 8: Inventory of the current self

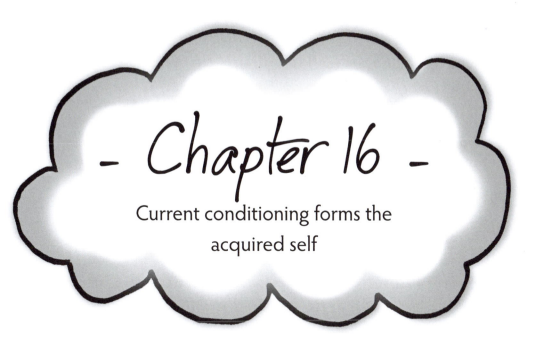

- Chapter 16 -

Current conditioning forms the acquired self

You can change, you just need to want to

The following chapters deal with exposing and loosening the hold of your acquired self. Much ancient Buddhist wisdom suggests that to attain enlightenment we need to go on a journey to seek it. All great missions appear to start you on some sort of a journey of discovery. En route, the journey ultimately leads you to returning to who you truly are, but seeing this from a new and mature perspective, through new eyes and new insights that you gained and developed along your way.

In this part I will outline a series of practical step-by-step approaches that build on each other. I have successfully developed, tested and honed this programmed approach over many years of trial, error and experience, to help people to re-pattern aspects of life that were not working for them and becoming limitations or interferences that they needed to overcome. I believe that by following the spirit and essence of the changes outlined in the following chapters, you too can make similar choices to achieve this for yourself so that you can lead the life you desire.

As a whole these approaches form a comprehensive programme to achieve exactly this. These changes are ultimately and absolutely possible by using the infinite power and flexible nature of your own mind–brain plasticity to program any change to work simply and effortlessly.

From having read Part 2 I hope that you are starting to get the idea that changing your mind is certainly possible and that change can happen at an individual and personal level. As we have seen, this is because our mind–brain–body connection has an infinite plasticity. So it is certain that we have the capacity to change the neurological structures and mechanisms that forge our habitual patterns. This belief is in itself the first level of change and is very subtle. By having faith and hope in this, it means that personal internal controls, and resistances and limitations can be broken and changed to new ways of being. This is because such hope and faith start to change our internal perceptions of ourselves and about personal change and development. When our perceptions begin changing, then at a neurological level this changes the pictures, images and internal representations that we form in our heads.

When we believe that we are fixed and forever as we are, with no chance of changing our habits and behaviours, then our internal representations will match these perceptions. If you like, one could say that this is now, neurologically speaking, an outdated mindset and way of thinking. However, if we hold this sceptical view, then this will be the reality we create.

As has been described, the essential building blocks of our experience that ultimately drive the mechanics of our mind–brain–body is its ability to instantly construct millions of internal images or representations of every single moment of our physical existence – waking and sleeping. Not only are these produced in every moment, the same mechanisms are also used to recall previous experiences. This is so we can better predict the future. Many of these are acquired and used as defaults. As we have also already discussed, our perceptions match our dispositional internal representations, which are triggered by certain things occurring in external reality that fire off a chain reaction of automatic brain–body responses. These dispositions are encoded within limiting belief systems. So one drives the other, and vice versa.

So it follows that our attitudes also produce and trigger internal mind–brain–body representations. So, when we change our attitudes or opinions and begin to open up our mind to other possibilities and options, then these opinions also produce, drive and deliver entirely different sets of internal representations associated with being open-minded and open to change. Simply moving away from self-judgement, self-guilt etc. to being more self-accepting and less serious about ourselves and our situations will do the same. This is also true when we change our inner mind chatter – see later for more detail on this vitally important area of change. So changing our attitudes and our thoughts about what we are thinking, changes our states of mind. As I have outlined, internal reality is driven by our states of mind, and this in turn sets up what happens to us in external reality. And one reality effects the other. They are co-related.

I believe that you, or anyone, can change any reactions and responses to any part of life. You can do this simply by desiring it and following a few principles outlined in this book. That any negative or unresourceful, limiting, accommodating, avoiding or constraining reactions that you may be currently experiencing can be overcome. That if you are habitually feeling bad about yourself, or constantly sad, pessimistic, negative, angry, fearful or anxious, or any prolonged and regular negative or unresourceful feeling, this can be replaced and changed for different and more resourceful ways of being and living in the world. If only we make the effort to make the change, then it is possible. Any perception of limiting and constraining situations or circumstances being lived through can be changed. You do have the choice to change your mind.

> So it's really important that you begin to feel good about yourself and make this a habit.

Such personal change from what you no longer want can be simple. It doesn't have to be complicated at all or take a long time. I believe that such personal developmental change can be practical and straight-forward. While such change needs to be adapted and suited to you to match you and you only, there are principles that need to be followed and applied. The rest of this book provides you with these principles, guidelines and frameworks.

Following these is not necessarily difficult, but neither is it easy. It simply takes effort and willpower and motivation to work at changing your mind. I will guarantee, however, that if you stick to and follow these principles you will change your mind. Changing the responses and reactions that happen in your mind will mean that the brain and body reactions and responses also will follow and change. So if you apply these principles to your own unique experience this will be true for you too.

So it is vitally important to allow yourself to be aware of what is in your current psyche and make-up. This is a crucial step. It is also important for you to take a little time to understand what, where, why and how your ways of being, your interferences and limitations and your reactions and responses to these have been acquired, learned and habitualised, as default responses. In the following sections I will pick up on these principles that form a bridge towards change in more detail. Other more specific approaches will be tackled in Parts 4 and 5.

Acquired self versus authentic self

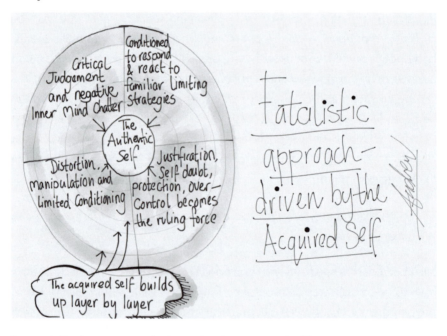

Figure 9: Fatalistic approach driven by the acquired self

As you might have noticed by now, I use the expression 'the acquired self' as a general term to describe all conditioned reactions and responses as a whole. This is because they are acquired by us through circumstances and their presence seems to build up over time, layer by layer.

Each acquired layer overlays on another, layer by layer and they manifest in our general psyche as a general narrowing of attentional focus, and overall limitation that actually affects the whole self. This notion of an artificial self stands in stark contrast to the true or real self, which I call the authentic self.

When it comes to personal development, I work from a high level principle: that to get back to the authentic self we have to teach ourselves new ways to overcome the limitations that become imposed by the acquired self. This is a critical factor to achieve success.

Each acquired layer creates another way of coping and accommodating the world in set ways. These acquired strategies take us further and further away from the real, true and authentic self. These, if you like, are automatic default coping strategies acquired by parts of the self that wish to protect us and are based on more instinctive primary fight, flight or freeze innate drives. I have already outlined these in some detail in Part 2. They intentionally provide quick and efficient protection and avoidance mechanisms. They are mainly left-brain, conscious mind biased, quick fix solutions.

However, I have discovered that, if left unchecked and unchanged, in time they become hindrances to personal growth and development. As we have seen already, this is because I believe that as we grow and mature, these set responses become less relevant but fire anyway because our thought processes are conditioned to trigger them through learned patterns that have formed grooved and well-trodden neurological reactions by our brains as default protective mechanisms.

The acquired self uses conditioning to form default approaches to life's issues and circumstances. So these collective strategies form strategies based on what is known and what is internally re-represented to the mind–brain–body. So the acquired self uses conscious mind principles to narrow and limit attentional focus on dispositionally represented knowledge as a basis for predicting suitable future responses.

The true authentic self, on the other hand, is more attuned to the unconscious mind and is therefore focused on what can be discovered based on what is being currently experienced and what is happening right now. It is more open-minded as a consequence. It does not rely on previously stored knowledge, dispositions or internally re-represented reality. Instead it forms solutions based on the moment, what can be connected to, what can be learned. It has a wider interest than just the self. Unlike the acquired self, its focus is not narrowed, but broadened in the depth of current experience, and is more sensitive to things greater than the self that are outside the self.

Before I move on, let me describe the concept of acquired self versus the authentic self in another way to you using metaphor:

When we are born, we acquire clothing to suit our babyhood. We are dressed in what is given to us. As we grow older, we acquire more clothing and our wardrobe continues to expand. We acquire different clothes suitable to be worn on different given occasions. So we wear what is expected of us and conform to convention. However, it is perhaps not difficult to imagine that these layers of clothing can become a dress or mask to represent who we think we ought to be to suit the circumstance. The real self therefore gets hidden underneath layers of different clothing, fearful perhaps of being exposed. It is through what we are wearing that we then act and become conditioned to behave in certain default ways that others expect of us. However, there is, underneath all these layers, something or somebody else too. Underneath the layers of clothing that represent expectations, accommodations and fears, lie ways of being accepted, being exposed, avoiding ridicule and perhaps even excuses for not becoming who we are meant to be. So much so that the outline of our authentic beauty and original intended and unique shape is hidden from view. So in order for us to return and transform to our true authentic self, we first have to take off the many layers of what has been acquired to conform, so we are no longer governed by our many acquired habits.

Purposefulness and joy

I understand that not everyone is driven by personal ambition, achievement or fired up by ultimate purpose, desire to thrust forward or to carve a particular destiny through life. Many people are very happy to have a more relaxed and easy-going approach to living life, and if you are more of this persuasion then that is a perfectly acceptable principle to adopt and live by. Others may have a deeply driven desire to not accept fate, but believe in some form of ultimate destiny that is uniquely theirs to follow. These two approaches to life are perhaps at either end of a spectrum of many different ways of being. All approaches to life are there to be experienced by each of us in different ways. So however you have chosen to live your life, I am firmly of the opinion that humankind at the very least is not meant to stay confined to the past but is instead intended to purposefully flourish, grow and change as we mature through life. Ultimately from a mind–brain–body perspective we are not designed to experience misery, angst or for that matter permanently suffer in this life. That doesn't mean it doesn't happen. In life there is room for all experiences, tragedy and suffering included. Why such tragedy and suffering exist in the world is a mystery to us. I also know that through free choice some people make suffering and misery happen to others as well, and this is in itself a tragedy too. So while all experience is valid, I simply believe that we are not designed to be forced to accept this in our lives.

As we have already covered in Part 1, we are ultimately designed to achieve joy and happiness in this life, and in this case we have a right to move consciously away from pain, angst and misery etc. We don't have to put up with it if we find that we are continually experiencing these through acquired learnings. These occurrences are therefore not what we want or desire. We simply haven't learned yet how to overcome them to change our mind and our thoughts to match what we desire instead. We may have to learn to live through it though to make the effort to get away from our defaults and therefore deserve the right to ultimately get what we want. Also as any experience (good or bad) is valid (though, to be clear, I don't mean acceptable in every case), we may purposefully decide and choose other pathways that have different consequences for us – that, however, becomes a conscious and very purposeful choice.

Therefore we have all the right and authority to return to pathways that enable our true authentic self to ultimately shine out so that we can become the person we are meant to be. Perhaps this is life's mission for all of us: to overcome the struggle with ourselves, with life, with adversity and adversaries as well as overcome our conditioning; to find a personal pathway to generate our own freedom, and reach our own meaning of joy and wonder in this life. This is true for you, too, and me, and all of us. Regardless of whether or not you think you have an ultimate destiny to achieve in this life, now or later in another (spiritual) life, we all have been given a unique, true and authentic self that ultimately has some sort of drive that shapes us.

This principle, I believe, is a fundamental hope that we all share. We all have a right to experience this uniquely, personally and individually through all sorts of ways and infinite means that generate endless possibilities. Surely this is then the hope and gift of life given to each of us to spend in ways that are right for us. We do, however, each of us, have to discover what that means to us as individuals. That then perhaps is the journey through this life – the ultimate ride.

The chapters that follow in this part are about strategies for how to expose the nature of the acquired self and how to loosen its hold on us.

Once we understand how our acquired self uniquely operates, we can then work on creating change, so we can return to our authentic self. This is covered in more detail later on in Parts 4 and 5.

In Part 2, we learned that any personal development change starts by giving ourselves permission to develop and change. In Part 3, we show that it is important to explore and discover what is currently being experienced; how the acquired self operates; and in what ways it then constrains change and prevents us from being our true authentic self.

I highlight in the following chapters a number of principles and factors that I have found to be crucial to expose, lever out, and develop and build change strategies. Each chapter focuses on a particular aspect of what to look out for, and how to expose those elements taken on by the acquired self. The acquired self in itself has many parts that manifest in different and various ways but collectively affects the whole person. While each individual's conditioning is remarkably different, I have learned that the principles below are generally common even though present in unique ways.

This, if you like, is a self-learning inventory and takes into account perspectives from your past, present and future.

- Chapter 17 -

Opening your mind to change: the authentic self and spirituality

In my experience, at some point in our lives we all have fleeting moments or a passing glimmer of a suspicion that life seems somehow caught up in some sort of limitation pattern. Perhaps you may have noticed that the same sorts of patterns, circumstances and things seem to keep happening, albeit at different times and in different situations. We may see these more readily in other people, or we may generalise this by saying to ourselves: 'Well we're all in the same boat in some way or another, we all have our issues and this is the way it is.' I believe that we all get such glimpses, out of the corner of our eye, from time to time, that we don't need to put up with our patterns of conditioning and briefly experience what could be instead.

At such times, for a short moment, we become aware of and perceive our authentic self, which stands in stark contrast to what we have been conditioned to through our acquired self. At that moment our authentic self breaks through the condition of the acquired self, and for that brief moment we realise that something could somehow be better, or different, and that the reality we are living through could perhaps change and improve.

And yet that fleeting glimmer passes as quickly as it came, and we return to accepting the control of our conditioning. And from time to time we may still wonder, what if… But ultimately this train of thought is put off as a topic for some other day. I have heard this called *someday island*. A pipe dream that would be very nice, but never comes nearer than 'some day'.

With this in mind…

Do you do anything about it, or simply make an excuse for it (some day island)?

Do you spend time reflecting deeply about what is happening to you and why this or that happens?

Perhaps you may want or desire something different to what you are getting?

For those that do consider these rhetorical questions then these glimmers turn into realisations, and these manifest themselves into consciousness and a more concrete desire to change emerges. Thoughts of…

… Something has to change; something has to give; I must be able to do better for myself than this; or…

… Surely life has more to offer me than what I am currently getting from it?

And this is the first step. The step to realisation, and taking this first step then opens your eyes to developing your own self-awareness.

People of all ages seek change. This seems especially true for many people between the ages of early-to-mid thirties up to their mid-50s (some younger or older people too). During this time period we all seem to begin to seek more self-awareness, about ourselves, our personal circumstances, our limitations and beliefs etc., and seek to develop ourselves, and desire to make adjustments to our lives.

Moving on from religious viewpoints

When it comes to hope, the great religions and spiritual wisdom over the past millennia often point to hope and human happiness either now or in the future through faith connected to paradise in an afterlife. Buddhist enlightenment principles, for example, teach about seeking bliss or happiness and to avoid pain. In the Jewish Torah and New Testament of the Christian Bible much is said about the human struggle. St Paul classifies this in the Letters to the Apostles in the New Testament as being the human condition. Many of the letters in the New Testament argue that this can only be resolved by turning to God. That it is only in the afterlife that we truly experience freedom from the human condition. To be clear, I don't hold with this exclusive view. You don't have to believe in any particular religious system to become enlightened.

As I said earlier, as far as this book is concerned, I have no contention with a belief in God, or faith or a hope in paradise or an afterlife. In my own walk with faith, and understanding of religion, I have come to understand that faith comes in many variations, which exist along a spectrum, and that religious understanding holds people to have certain views and beliefs along this spectrum. At one extreme you have the religious idea that a faithful and loving God intimately cares about all individuals and desires a personal relationship with each of us. Who understands how and why we are the way we are and cares about wanting to give each of us the gift of life at its very best. To each individual the gift of grace and mercy is also freely applied when we get things out of perspective. At the other extreme you have a more judging, socially adapted and organised religion. These state that to belong and be loved by God you have to conform to culturally acceptable ways that hold people in more controlled ways for the good of society now and in the future. By doing so, your life will be judged and rewarded accordingly in heaven, or eternal paradise. This extreme end of the spectrum means that if you don't conform then you will not be accepted either within the religious culture you belong to or later by God. Many people who have a religious faith seem to learn to somehow come to terms with and find some middle ground between these extremes. They accept this as a tension that needs to be lived with.

As I have said, I have no issue with religion or faith in God. But the point I would like to put forward is not to get confused between religion and the human condition. They are separate and different. That personal change and changes to your past conditioning does not need to be a prerequisite of a hope and faith or in belonging to any religion. That personal change is entirely possible with or without spiritual belief. They are not co-dependent. I also want to make the point that change and development are part of the 'here and now'. They can be grasped in your own life, by you and you alone. They are not elsewhere, or 'out there', on some heavenly plane, or to only be found in the next life. Instead they are to be found inside you, internal to you and your make-up and you alone and your choices. They don't depend on any set of religious rules or principles. That doesn't exclude anyone from faith or religious belief, however. Both religion and personal change are very able to happily co-exist. In other words, change can be embraced by you either way. You don't have to believe in God or spirituality to make personal change: they are not mutually exclusive. That doesn't mean that religious belief does not offer you something else or something more either. It does for billions of people on this planet.

However, the internal changes I am talking about are practical and solely reliant on you and what you want. Personal change from your acquired conditioning and returning to your true authentic self is about changes to your mind–brain–body and are firmly rooted in neurological change that is made internally by you, by shifting your mindset. These then allow brain and body patterns, responses and reactions to occur because of new thinking, new perspectives and new outlooks.

So I am saying to you that you have the freedom to choose change for yourself. You can overcome your acquired conditioning and return to your true authentic self. If that leads you on a journey of spiritual discovery or to find a connection to God along the way then that experience is equally open to you. There is quite possibly profound spiritual connection and wisdom to be found from experiencing such beliefs and following 'Godly' principles, but this is not what this book is about.

I want to take a moment to take this point a little further, as I believe it to be important to understand. Just because I have separated religion and religious belief from personal change I am not suggesting that anybody should dismiss the concept of spiritual connection to something greater than humankind. While I am stating that personal change has its basis in neurological change and should therefore not be confused with religion or religious belief, it is possible that a return to our true authentic self can also invoke a spiritual discovery at the same time. There is room for all experience.

Remember, in the above section I said that the authentic self is interested in widening and broadening attention to take in greater meanings of experience. This is in contrast to the acquired self, whose strategy it is to narrow and limit experience to focus attention. So don't be surprised, as you develop a greater sense of your authentic self, and as it grows and matures, that some of your thoughts may well become more open-minded to the concept of spirituality. This is only natural and an indication that you are more open in your approach to life. You still don't have to believe in anything you don't want to believe in.

It is also very true that conversion experiences, like St Paul famously had along the Damascus Road, are still commonplace today for ordinary people in all walks of life, just as they were 2000 years ago. Unexplainable miracles continue to happen to many people living their lives today, all over the planet. Near-death experiences, too, can invoke a complete turnaround in peoples' lives and they turn to God. People trapped in unholy or selfish lives, for example, suddenly turn to God for repentance and forgiveness, or convert to a particular religious persuasion that makes sense to them. So it's important not to be dismissive, or judgemental, but instead become tolerant and perhaps more open-minded to different ways, and different philosophies; this is indeed the road to true enlightenment.

Many millions of people continue to dedicate their lives to causes greater than themselves, religious or not. That doesn't mean you have to, or need to. But it is important to understand that these experiences are just as valid. Again this open-mindedness is also found along the road to enlightenment.

I do know that conversion experiences seem to connect people to their authentic self very suddenly. I think this is because conversion experiences are phenomena that are extremely profound. Neurologically, however, I believe this occurs due to a rapid shift of psychic energy and attention that is suddenly reassigned and acutely focused on, releasing the hold of our acquired conditioning. This enables us to choose unconscious mechanisms to take over and allow the authentic self to come through and take prominence, where the strategies of our acquired self once dominated. This provides the impetus for the sudden switch. This sudden switch can be such a profound experience that it seems miraculous and so perhaps an understandable explanation could be attributed entirely to God's grace. Despite this, it may not in all cases, however, mean that through conversion the acquired self has been totally tamed. In time these old, unresolved issues may slowly re-emerge and as such will still need to be dealt with at some future point.

What we can learn from such turnarounds is that change can happen rapidly, even instantly. It doesn't necessarily always follow that it has to take effort or be painful. It is the motivation and imagination that enables the psychic energy to become available.

This principle is equally true for the power of limiting forces such as phobias: we have the capacity to instantly form a phobia, for example, based on a one-off traumatic experience, which from then on is powerfully instantly triggered into re-enactment again whenever similar circumstances are re-experienced.

However, unlike the above experiences one-time learnings like phobias do not form from authentic self-mechanisms, but rather fall into the acquired category using the built-in mechanics of our innate fight or flight structures.

Other examples of rapid change strategies are used by witch doctors using voodoo to cure a health issue, or people that practise 'black magic' to curse. These examples most likely are using the above principle in more subtle ways, applying some sort of facsimile to create a cure or a curse in an artificial way that suddenly interrupts or provokes our psychic energy through terror or innate fear connected to belief systems that instantly associate, latch on to or take hold of and acquire the required change out of compliance, or fear, due to the nature of the invoked ritual. However, again I am doubtful whether its success is based on principles that return us to our authentic selves.

Hope, along with faith, peace, love and forgiveness is also a central theme of many of the principal religions. We'll get to ways of looking at these principles from more practical personal perspectives later, as these concepts are not solely owned by religious practice.

- Chapter 18 -

Exploring the make-up of your conditioning

Taking an inventory of the current self

The main part of exposing the strategies behind the acquired self is to conduct an inventory of what is currently being experienced by you. This is an important and fundamental step in making personal change. This is because by doing this, it makes you more acutely self-aware of what needs to change for you as an individual.

Spending time here allows you to learn from your own unique circumstances and issues, as well as your chosen responses to these. I call this process 'taking an inventory of yourself and your current conditioning'.

I help the people I work with to do this for themselves, and my approach is detailed in the following sections for you to do it for yourself on your own. It simply requires you to spend some time alone. Your inventory is unique to you as an individual. It will include your past and current circumstances and history, and could be about your future too. This part of the change process identifies these aspects by building self-awareness. These next few sections describe various aspects in more detail.

One option that I would recommend is that you get yourself a working journal so that you can make notes and write down your answers to the questions as you go along. This will allow you to set aside and take time and a little effort in working through your self-inventory based on the aspects mentioned in this book. Soon I intend to produce an accompanying manual that will provide you with a ready-made structure and detailed tool that can be a framework or blueprint approach to carry out this exploration of current conditioning in a systematic way for yourself. This will be my next book. In the meantime, as I mentioned above, get yourself a journal to start this process now for yourself. This will work equally as well.

Uncovering what is sticky or stuck

Working on your own, the first practical step is to take some time to carefully consider and answer the following statements (write them down in your journal)…

- What do you want to change about the way you deal with what happens to you in life?
- What seems to be happening to you at the moment? How is this linked to other similar occurrences in the past? What kinds of patterns keep repeating themselves?
- What are your problems, issues, interferences or self-fulfilling limitations that you notice might be getting in your way?
- What aspects of life are you experiencing problems with? How long have you been this way? What do you notice about how these affect you and your life?
- What kinds of things are you aware of that are sticky, you can't seem to shake off, that perhaps don't seem to go away, or that get you stuck?
- Do you have any repeating patterns or situations that seem to recur or that you seem to continually bump into?
- Do you notice any limiting beliefs that you might possess and, if so, can you name them and how do these affect you?

The answers to these questions start to provide a picture of your internal reality and external reality and your patterns of responses. These types of questions are not commonly asked in everyday life, but they have been intentionally designed for the specific purpose of building up your self-awareness about yourself, your acquired patterns, interferences and limiting beliefs. By allowing your internal attention to focus on what you have noticed about yourself and your response patterns, it helps you to bring this internal reality more into your consciousness. Having done so allows you then to pay attention to this information. As this information begins to be attended to by you, you can evaluate and think about it, and process it. By doing this, it allows self-change to begin to naturally occur internally for you. In effect you are learning to see things objectively, and subtly this creates a layer of change in itself based on moving away from self-degradation and judgement to learning as a first step to simply just accept these as things that have occurred. As you do this you will begin to see them as happening to you, rather than becoming overly and emotionally involved. This is because you are learning to consciously think about how you feel about these patterns, reactions and responses. The more you do this step by step, the more you will naturally be able to become adept at acting as if you are an objective and neutral observer, just looking from a detached point of view. You are merely evaluating your internal patterns as information. This first simple step has surprising power in itself and you will learn from it and become aware of new things. In this step you are learning to engage the resources of your right brain to see from new perspectives.

Whereas before your attention was focused on *feeling* the emotional response acting on you, now, in contrast, you are helping yourself to begin *thinking* from a 'meta' position about your past responses and patterns, and how these make you feel from this perspective. As I have said already, the subtle purpose of this inventory and subsequent evaluation is in itself setting up the potential for creating personal change. I have discovered that change happens at every step in these processes.

As you may have noticed already and will now, no doubt, continue to notice, my approach is to create lots of small, simple opportunities, by way of layers of subtle cumulative interventions that continue to make change happen for you as an individual. My working hypothesis in operating in this manner is that I have discovered (through much trial and error) that the more subtle and natural the change interventions are, then the more successful you will be at achieving them. These subtle adjustments and alterations each provide unique opportunities both at conscious and, more importantly, at unconscious levels at the same time. And so rebalancing and realigning is occurring as you move through each of these chapters.

Little steps and step-by-step approaches mean that acceptance of them is easier for you, because they are easy and you learn that it's not hard to progress by making simple and small adjustments. In this way you begin to open your mind to changing the way you desire to live and start to believe and trust in yourself. You are also beginning to loosen the hold of left-brain biased thinking by subtly engaging right-brain approaches.

Therefore you actually end up changing bigger aspects of yourself that you might have originally thought impossible to even dare to think. These have not been forced on you by me or someone else, either. The thing is, that by being subtle with yourself in this way you are your own Michelangelo, forming and sculpting yourself from your own raw material. The presupposition here is that 'everyone has the ability to change what they don't like to what they want, and that all the resources are available to you, you simply have to access them'. You simply have to reawaken them and trust in yourself. Now we can move on to other aspects of opening your mind to change and loosening the hold of your conditioning.

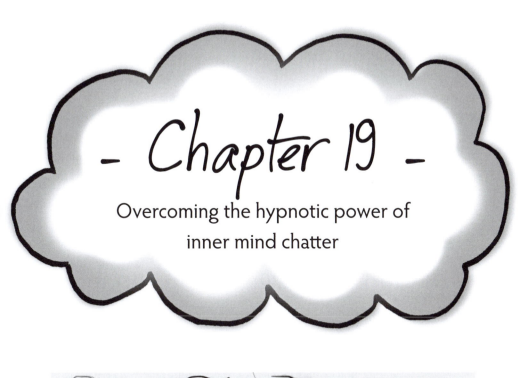

- Chapter 19 -

Overcoming the hypnotic power of inner mind chatter

Figure 10: General examples of everyday inner mind chatter

Linguistic expressions of limiting belief systems…

We all have inner mind chatter; however, for some this gets way out of control and for those people it is being exclusively driven by acquired strategies. Acquired or limiting belief systems express themselves linguistically via self-talk that goes on (and on) in the conscious mind. For the most part, this self-talk is internal, said to oneself. My theory here is that topologically the linguistic structures are readily available to other parts of the conscious mind, which layer by layer, if left unchecked, unwittingly creates the acquired self.

However, back to inner mind chatter. As you may have discovered already, the verbose nature of inner mind chatter means that it can readily leak out of you as externalised, spoken expressions. These just seem to pop out, sometimes unbidden or in the background of your awareness. Either way inner mind chatter is expressed consciously.

For many people it can become extremely active and perniciously verbose, to the point where it seems uncontrollably profuse. Often people get convinced into believing it cannot be controlled and is unstoppable. Or that it is part of their identity or who they really are. Often, however, most people just become desensitised to it, and just ignore it as internal background noise. It is not true that your inner mind chatter is part of your identity. Inner mind chatter is merely an expression associated with your acquired self. Inner mind chatter has many terms: self-talk, internal dialogue or inner self-talk are other descriptions.

As already mentioned, this sort of internal monologue (if left unchecked) often spills out into our external verbal communications. Often people are not fully aware of this entrained dialogue being actively expressed or leaking out into their conversations with others.

Whether completely silent and internal, or being voiced externally, inner mind chatter is for some people profuse and unceasing in its expression.

Certain situations can frequently aggravate bouts of increased inner mind chatter. For example, this seems especially to be the case when you are facing difficulties, a challenge, or overcoming negative forces and issues, or perhaps when you are in the grip of an emotional body reaction that has been triggered by a limiting belief. In addition, working towards achieving something important in your life, such as a new goal, or undergoing a significant life or career change can often have the same effect. So expect that for a while at least your inner mind chatter might increase as you begin to make changes. The advantage, however, is that you are beginning to become aware of it and noting its distortions.

Overcoming habits and compulsions also have tendencies to throw up increasing amounts of inner mind chatter. The same goes for times when you are faced with temptation in whatever form.

Inner mind chatter is the window to our belief systems…

In all cases, however, inner mind chatter is always an accompanying feature, a hallmark of acquired limiting belief systems in play. It is the conscious linguistic outward manifestation of limiting belief systems. So, inner mind chatter can also be used as a tell-tale sign and overt evidence of an underlying limiting belief system operating. Despite its verbosity, most people are oblivious or only peripherally aware of its ongoing activity. No real time is spent evaluating it or considering challenging inner mind chatter. Or simply consciously making the choice to modify it.

I often use the expression that inner mind chatter is the window to our belief systems. These are the outworkings of your inner acquired contrivances.

Some very simple typical examples of inner mind chatter are given below. Perhaps you might recognise one or two of these…

- It's not fair.
- It's never fair.
- I'm always hard done by.
- I am always the victim.
- Typical, why does this always happen to me?
- I'm always completely useless.
- I'm never any good at this or that.
- I've always been rubbish at this.
- I'm never good enough.
- I always doubt myself.
- I always fall short; I am never as good as others.
- I am always the worst at this or that.
- I never deserve anything other than what I get.
- I'm never good enough.

- I'm stupid and thick.
- I'm not worthy of that.
- I can't do that, I never have been able to do things.
- That's impossible for me.
- I am a control freak; I have to be in control.
- It has to be right otherwise it will never be good enough.
- People always laugh at me and that always tells me I'm rubbish.
- I must pretend I am strong.
- If people know I'm weak, I won't have control.

In your self-inventory journal take some time to note down your own inner mind chatter examples.

Despite inner mind chatter often being silent to the external world, its expression, even in the mind, is highly limiting to you because of its existence, verbal or not. Its expression is often very negative and self-depreciating. This internal dialogue, like the underlying belief clusters it represents, and by which it conveys itself, has a tendency to form into a series of contextually similar statements that become well-trodden pathways that form into habitual and repetitive cycles.

These, if you are inclined to lots of inner mind chatter, persistently go around and around in your mind. Interestingly, even though inner mind chatter statements are in conscious awareness, on the whole, they largely go unnoticed, ignored and unattended to, and so to a great extent go unpoliced in your head.

Some further more complex and real examples of typical recursive inner mind chatter statements. You might spot some that are near to your own inner talk...

- People hate me. The universe hates me. No one likes me. Everyone hates me.
- All people are dangerous. No one can be trusted. I've never been loved by anyone ever. I am flawed.
- I have to fight for my right to exist. Life is a fight for what you want. My life's a soap opera. Everything is a drama all the time; it always has been. Things never change, it's always the same.
- Nothing works out for me. I'm always unlucky. If I don't stick up for

myself then I'll be taken advantage of. Everyone always takes advantage of me. I always get taken advantage of.

- Typical. This always happens to me. I never get things right. I always get things wrong. I'm stupid, I'm dumb. I'm always awkward. No one ever listens to me.
- I never get taken seriously. What I say never counts. Everyone always ignores me. I am no good; I've never been good at anything.
- I'm useless. I've always been a complete failure. I'm an idiot. I always make an idiot of myself. I'm always embarrassing. I'm always rubbish at everything.
- I can't do that. I can never do things right. I'm never good enough. I'm not good enough. I'll never be able to do that; I will be found out. I've never been good at anything really. I'm a fraud.
- I'm never worthy. I always feel guilty about everything I ever do. It's always my fault. I never get anything right. I never deserve anything ever.
- I always get blamed for everything. I always blame myself for everything that goes wrong. Things always go wrong for me. It's always me that gets everything wrong all the time. Why me? Why does everything always go wrong for me all the time? I never get anything right. Why do bad things always happen to me?
- Hit me. Poor little old me. Blame me. Everyone always blames me all the time every time. It's never fair.
- It's not my fault. Blame somebody else. Why should I take any of the blame?
- It's always other people. People never do what they should do.
- I can never accept myself. I always judge myself. I am and always will be a failure. I must always be hard on myself.
- Never say anything, and no one will notice me. Perhaps I will get found out, so I need to keep quiet. It's wrong to tell people you are good at anything. Be perfect. I must please others. People never understand me. I always get hurt.
- It's wrong to please yourself. Always be strong, never show weakness. Never admit you are in the wrong: that is weak.
- I will never forgive them for what they have done to me. I will never forget that.
- They will always be my enemy. I will always hate them. They are scum.

- I'm never appreciated. I try so hard and no one ever appreciates it. I never get thanked. I always get overlooked by everybody. It's never me that gets any praise, ever. I work so hard and no one ever thanks me, or appreciates me.
- It's always been this way. Things will never change.
- I must prove I am better than everyone else, otherwise they will see that I am not as good as I need to be. I always have to be seen to be better than everyone else.

Spend a little time making further notes in your self-inventory journal of the internal statements that go around your head in this way.

Typical patterns and make-up...

By studying these statements in more depth you might notice certain patterns. For a start they are all limiting in nature and have negative connotations. They operate in clusters too. Also words and phrases like 'don't', 'can't', 'won't', 'ought', 'should', 'must', 'need to', 'have to', etc. act as modal operators of limitation and result in a lack of perceived choice and, seemingly, other possibilities and options are therefore unavailable.

Secondly, they are generally self-depreciating and self-effacing. These point to, and are aimed directly at, the individual themselves. In this you are thinking: Me! Me! Me! In simple terms, most of your internal dialogue statements are implied judgements and put-downs of one type or another. If they are not you, they will be about the effect of others and their faults and how that impacts on you. In other words, the judging of others applied to you, or you to them. Self-based chatter that leaks out externally is a definite clue that can be picked up by receivers if people take the time to tune into this type of indirect communication. As you start to become aware of your own inner mind chatter, you might also notice that you become more aware of others' self-talk that leaks out during conversation, or when people idly talk to themselves out loud.

Thirdly, your inner mind chatter language is often extremely simple, short, brief and compact. On average most inner mind chatter expresses itself in four words or less.

Linked to its brevity, these statements are highly generalised in construction as well. Generalisations such as always, never, everywhere, ever, everyone, no one, all the time, every time, etc. are used. Both these points are significant, as this means that your internal self-talk can be applied to any situation, at any time, always.

Next, inner mind chatter is always a type of judgment or put-down (which is really doubt or fear) of some type or another, and is an emotional outward expression of an underlying acquired limiting belief in play. These judgments, even said in your mind, can be loaded with intonations of certain key words and marked with more emphasis than others.

As we have already been through, what is said in the mind, or verbally expressed with emotion, acts as a trigger for the body to produce associated emotional states. When the body produces such corresponding emotional states, this in turn amplifies further negative self-talk. More inner talk sustains more negative emotional states being produced in the body. As you begin to become more aware of the feelings caused by these emotional states in your body, your mind–brain–body automatically diverts even more of your attention and psychic energy to them. This then triggers more energy to be diverted to thinking about how you feel about the emotional body state you have inadvertently triggered and produced. And so the cycle continues.

As such, your attention becomes increasingly narrowly focused, the more you attend to it. So the more you reinforce it, the more you waste further energy feeling bad because of it. And so the spiral downwards goes on.

The more you become tuned into your own inner mind chatter, the more easily noticeable and distinguishable the emotional emphasis becomes and how this is linked to and associated with your subsequent emotional body state (both mentally and physiologically). You can then begin to more objectively learn from it and understand how it affects you.

Keeping an ongoing self-inventory journal of this type of awareness is an extremely useful way of loosening the hold of these constructs. Regularly noting this type of activity allows you to expose it and therefore view it very differently, as it allows you to develop a dissociated objectivity. This is important, as it will quickly give you more self-awareness and control. This will eventually lead to a loosening of the control these structures have over you, which will rapidly allow you to make better choices. For example, by maintaining your self-inventory journal activity you can start to monitor and evaluate what you are incessantly chattering about and begin to interrupt or neutralise this cycle, simply by tuning into it, noticing the emotional body and mind thought reactions, and then selecting a different language in your mind to counter these habitual statements instead. Within a short period through your objective learning you will begin to notice how you can take charge and control your own emotional body state reactions, simply because you are reframing your inner mind chatter as you go along.

Neurologically you are starting to build new brain maps, and reduce reliance on old pattern brain maps. Remember applying the principles we learned from Chapter 15 on neural plasticity, what fires together, wires together, and also what you don't use you lose. The earlier self-inventory journal activity was to carry out an inventory of your current mind chatter as it stood. The purpose of this was to make you aware of it, and learn to see it from an objective viewpoint. This creates a subtle layer of change in itself. Now, adding the above learning into the next step, see if you can reframe or out-frame each one of your inner mind chatter statements. Even if you find yourself resisting these at this time, it is a good exercise to do and to keep these in your mind by reviewing them and taking note of them regularly. Again the strategy is to loosen the hold of these inner mind chatter controls. This objective reviewing and reframing allows you to make subtle changes at both conscious and, more importantly, unconscious levels.

The more you do this, the more you break the hold of their original format. It's akin to the belief that the more you practise a skill, the more it becomes part of you and after a short while of practice you suddenly notice you are doing it more easily as new pathways and patterns are being formed.

Another tell-tale sign is non-verbal body language. This always accompanies inner mind chatter when it is in play. Hand movements, shrugs of the shoulders, arms and hands are often giveaway signals of inner mind chatter leaking out into behaviours and physiology. Eye movements, looking up, down, away, looking sly, sheepish, eyes to the side, corner or rolling of the eyes are other signals. As are eyebrow raises, furrows, frowns. Facial features, such as blushing, tightening of the muscles around the eyes, lips, thinning and pursing of lips etc. are all subtle giveaway features of inner mind chatter in play. As are feet shuffles, leg shakes, foot tapping. Postures and body positions are also tells. As are tonal shifts, coughing, muffling words and silence.

Exaggerated blank facial expressions and stifled body language are other giveaways.

These are all clues that can be picked up easily when observing others, but most people pay little attention to them. However, these are much harder to self-attend to, but if you are very body aware then you will be better at monitoring this. If it's too hard for you to spot your own body movements, then just be aware that all inner mind chatter can be exposed in this way.

Using your self-inventory journal you can note these, too, as you become aware of them. Learning to shift and use your body and gestures in different ways will help you to further loosen and therefore change and reframe associated inner mind chatter. This is because if you interrupt an unresourceful body posture or gesture, and physically alter your body to be more resourceful then your emotional body state will follow the body accordingly. So intentionally changing body language will also start to automatically produce different states that result in the mind selecting different thoughts. Ultimately this awareness and interruption helps to loosen the hold of default mind chatter responses.

Doing this won't feel natural by the way, but that's okay, as you are simply becoming aware of your inner mind chatter, its association with acquired beliefs and how they manifest physically. This awareness in itself will boost your ability to challenge your thoughts and so the process of interrupting and loosening default responses is underway. So it doesn't matter if it feels awkward or hard. The mere act of doing this again creates another layer of subtle change. As these accumulate then permanent positive change will replace those acquired defaults and it will happen in a more natural way.

Furthermore, limiting belief systems incessantly broadcast inner mind chatter, and this gives the impression of an applied defensive tactic. Constant internal dialogue will mean that conscious attention is being continually diverted away from challenging the limiting belief system itself. At the same time, inner mind chatter drains and wastes significant amounts of our psychic energy, reducing the available bandwidth that could have otherwise been made available to the authentic self and by more resourceful purposes and intentional activity. The presence of inner mind chatter ultimately limits access to our authentic self. All these manifestations of inner mind chatter expressions significantly contribute to the profoundly powerful hold that your underlying acquired limiting belief systems are able to bring to bear and exert. In your self-inventory journal it may also be handy to monitor how much energy you perceive you waste on a day-to-day basis on your limiting beliefs. You will be surprised what you notice, as many people report that once they have become aware of their limiting beliefs in play, that a lot of their attention and thus internal energy was wasted by them. This once wasted energy now becomes freely available to help you to overcome your conditioning.

Limiting beliefs cluster together

The limiting belief system in itself may be made up of a number of other like beliefs.

These seem to naturally organise themselves into clusters that form root definitions.

These root definitions are internal statements that become the outward face of the clusters of beliefs, which I term limiting belief systems. As these 'clusters of limiting beliefs' form and gather, often one main belief acts as the root and central core, with the others being a subset that are associated, interlinked, subordinated or lower ranking. Together they form into a collective alliance, a league or stronghold (safety in numbers). This increases their power and hold. Their combined energy creates a dissonant cacophony effect of prevailing inner mind chatter. The limiting belief system then has more psychic bandwidth to thoroughly occupy you and overshadows the true nature of the authentic self.

Using your self-inventory journal it is beneficial to note as many interconnections of any acquired limiting beliefs that you begin to become aware of. Many people report that their limiting beliefs, once they perceive them in this way, also become aware of their connectedness with one another and represent or draw these like spiders' webs. Others note that they become aware of their beliefs in a clustered form, with one acting as a core, supported or linked to all the others.

The petty tyrant of extreme and enforced limited reality

The persistence and repetitiousness of inner mind chatter directs your conscious behaviour and, over time, may appear to have a tendency to take on even more control of your mindset and resources. In extreme circumstances this can begin to become almost like a 'petty tyrant'. In these conditions, the underlying belief system can behave as a spokesperson for you. If this occurs, and is left unattended to or ignored, we seem to become deceived into believing that this inner voice is actually our identity and our actual self. Convincing as it might be, this is simply not true.

Believing our limitations to be real reinforces and self-justifies their effect.

Acquired limiting belief systems have the ability to hijack us using inner mind chatter as a 'mouthpiece' to channel and broadcast their limiting propaganda far and wide in our internal and external reality. Extreme inner mind chatter is insidious and, left unchecked, is able to create unholy alliances, built around self-survival and self-protection of themselves. As such, this action constantly hypnotises the person into believing this is who they are and that whatever they believe is absolutely true and so deny any possible better solution as being impossible. By its very nature, it absorbs, diverts and concentrates attention and conscious psychic energy.

So belief systems using inner mind chatter become self-justifying and distort inner dialogue. Over time we can gradually become immune to other more resourceful choices and ideas. The yak, yak, yak babbling nature of reinforcing hypnotically induced limiting self-talk eventually creates an addictive and intoxicating effect on the person. In the end, if left unchecked, the person then becomes completely seduced into believing its message, and swallows these false messages whole as the final truth. These simply get worse over time.

Fighting against the grain of limiting beliefs

If the belief system's controlling hold is in any way threatened, by glimmers of realisation from the awakening mind–brain–body consciousness for example, provoked by the authentic self, inner mind chatter can subsequently be substantially increased as a first line of defence by any acquired limiting belief system. This reaction is highly convincing to our conscious mind. Under such attack, you can easily slip back into the comfort of the status quo. In this way, any questioning of the belief by the authentic self and other parts of consciousness is immediately rebuffed and refuted – we go into a state of denial.

Such is the strength and power of a limiting belief and its association with inner mind chatter.

Consequently, it can become harder and harder to muster up any counter-challenge as being too demanding and so the individual gives up and concedes. As a consequence, dominated by the limiting belief system, people can live in a sort of anaesthetised twilight. A sleepwalking state if you like. The zest for life correspondingly becomes a glimmer of what was, or a passing flicker of what might have been. Access to the counter-balancing authentic self seems ever just out of reach, and not quite attainable. Put simply, apathy sets in and any ideas of loosening or freeing and breaking through choices are ignored. The prevailing attitude is succumbing to the limiting beliefs' actions, and our self-identity falsely believes that this is all there is, this is who I am, and nothing can be done to change this.

If in your own personal inventory journal you too have suddenly realised that this extreme position has actually developed and now exists, then it is an important wake-up call for you to do something about it.

Language forms pictures in your head

As already mentioned, the words we use in language have a profound effect on our neurology. At the deepest levels of our psyche and our mind–brain structures, consciousness represents every experience, event, situation, thought and feeling by instantly building millions of representations of internal information every moment.

These are kind of 'holographic' in nature as they represent millions of pieces of data from our senses. For example information from our words, which automatically associate with and generate emotional body states and cognitive feelings, external information (visual and auditory), our somatic sensations (kinaesthetic) and hormones all combine to create complex informational internal representations of the reality we are experiencing. In simple form these are like pictures in our heads.

This is consciousness acting in all its magnificence. Our bodies, organs and every single cell within them are miraculously constantly sharing and exchanging these, and all our entire internal physical sense contributes information to these real time constructs, all the time. These form the basis of physical and mental recall, and memory too. In effect, it is through this dynamic and complex consciousness system or mechanism that these representations are able to create our internal reality; all of our memories and our attitudes, thoughts and feelings about the external physical world are all re-presented internally. So what is happening on the outside of us is converted via consciousness to our reactions and responses. More importantly, however, it is what is recalled (good or bad) inside of us that shapes the reality of what then happens outside of us.

So the words we use drive our states of mind. These directly contribute to the way we in turn represent ourselves. These internal re-presentations constantly form our reality. Ultimately this then directly affects the reality we experience externally. As we will see later, it is the internal world that ultimately shapes the external world. So our limiting beliefs access dispositional internal representations and also powerfully create correspondingly limiting internal representations at every moment the belief is in play.

This is why the self-inventory journal is such a useful and powerful tool. Because as you start to become aware of the words you use to describe yourself and the world around you, you begin to see the direct consequences for yourself: passing on limiting beliefs to others…

As mentioned earlier, inner mind chatter can and does externally express itself.

Often this chatter simply leaks or 'slips out'. This can commonly occur during emotive conversations with others. This external verbalisation on the whole goes largely unnoticed by most people. Such simple inner mind statements, as already given above, therefore fall out into general conversations. Typically, verbalised inner mind chatter seems to just drop in at the end of sentences almost as disconnected tag-ons. They seem like fill-ins during conversational gaps and interludes and said under one's breath. They are not necessarily intended to form part of the overall conversation, but slip out, unawares, as appendages, and seemingly superfluous to the content being discussed. These statements are often repeated in similar patterns and tend to come out in similar unconnected circumstances. If this is the case then they are usually the by-product of a limiting belief system in play.

And so, expressed mind chatter, on the whole, goes by unnoticed, not being picked up, within the conversation, and not commented upon, and therefore simply ignored by the majority of participants. It's as if two conversations are going on. There is the main conversation about the actual subject being discussed and attended to, underscored by the other more subtle broadcast, by the belief's ideas and reactions about the subject. However, despite these going by, being largely ignored, these externalised expressions act like poker tells: tell-tale signs of the presence of a belief in play. If you tune into this subtext carefully you can easily become aware of it and uncover people's beliefs in action, as well as becoming aware of when your own beliefs are in play.

As well as being a by-product of a belief system in play, there may be another more surreptitious nature of this phenomena occurring. Through such conversational channels, it is entirely possible that limiting beliefs are passed on from one person to another. This is perhaps what happens in family dynamics for example. Although such beliefs are out of immediate conscious attention, it is the content of inner mind chatter that transfers its limiting statements on to others. These are picked up and communicated at subliminal or unconsciousness levels. Human beings are incredibly sensitive receivers of such information: we readily pick up subtle subliminal changes in intonations, expressions and body language. So despite such expressions being typically out of general conversational and conscious awareness, the raw material is present, and is always being picked up at deeper uncon-scious levels. This is because your conscious mind (left brain hemisphere) is attending to content and familiarity and what's known and understood, while your unconscious mind (right brain hemisphere) attends to subtleties and new goings-on that occur dynamically in the moment. This means that, through the tell-tale outward aspects (verbal and non-verbal cues and clues) of inner mind chatter, acquired beliefs are being broadcast to others all the time. Because of their make-up and psychic influence, they are, therefore, in themselves contagious constructs. This holds true for any emotion, belief or feeling that we generate. The properties of these can be communicated through the network of open systems created through human interconnec-tion. We are not closed, but open circuits of such conscious information exchange. Psychologists call this process 'projection'. It is also the same mechanism for building rapport with each other. Daniel Goleman and col-leagues, in their book *New Leaders*, used a term 'lymbic soup' to describe these open human interaction systems.

In these ways our beliefs, via our inner mind chatter, can easily have negative effects on others around us. Their properties make them able to 'sit within' the conversational circle, often unnoticed by our conscious minds. Therefore, the sentiment of the emotional body and feeling context within these broadcasts is sufficiently strong to make others feel instantly as negative, or as bad or as hopeless as the person who introduced these sorts of thought-forms into a conversation. The reverse is also true: that positive emotions also make others feel good about themselves. In this way, any of our ideas, suggestions and thoughts can be contagious and transferred. Good hypnotists work with this concept too.

Even when inane mind chatter goes unnoticed, or unchallenged, its hypnotic power is still being unconsciously transmitted to others during conversations. If left unchallenged, the sentiment of inner mind chatter may linger within the conversation circle. So we all can effect each other very easily, even without saying anything. In this way, you can easily 'catch' beliefs from others. Such is the power of hypnotic suggestion. This is how beliefs jump from one generation to another. People in leadership or authority can pass on their beliefs to others, with their authority and influence acting as a strong convincer that they must be right and we need to be like them. There are, however, built-in safeguards and counter-balances to any exchange of ideas and suggestions at thought, feeling, emotional or belief levels. The receiver of such information always has a choice of acceptance or rejection. You do have to be consciously wide awake and aware in the attentional sense though. This is important as nothing can be exchanged or accepted without a choice. We either choose to accept to take on other people's beliefs, or not. This choice is always a conscious one; however, the choice made may not always be immediately understood in immediate awareness, or later by recall.

But there is always a conscious choice made, even if it dawns on you later. No matter how subtle, we can either accept or reject any idea or belief transmitted by another person.

So another question to ask yourself in your self-inventory journal is: Where did my belief or beliefs come from? Did I construct them and, if not, from whom have I picked them up? If you remember, we looked at how limiting beliefs are formed when we are young, and how the major influencers in our lives can transfer their beliefs to us. Knowing this then at least helps you to know where the belief came from and when. This then leads you to understand why you behave and respond in particular defined ways in certain instances.

But the key question perhaps should always be: what do you want to do instead? Or what do you want to do now? These questions can create a more profound shift for you. We will explore this shortly, and look at ways of replacing negative inner mind chatter with positive language.

- Chapter 20 -

The cycle of control and grief

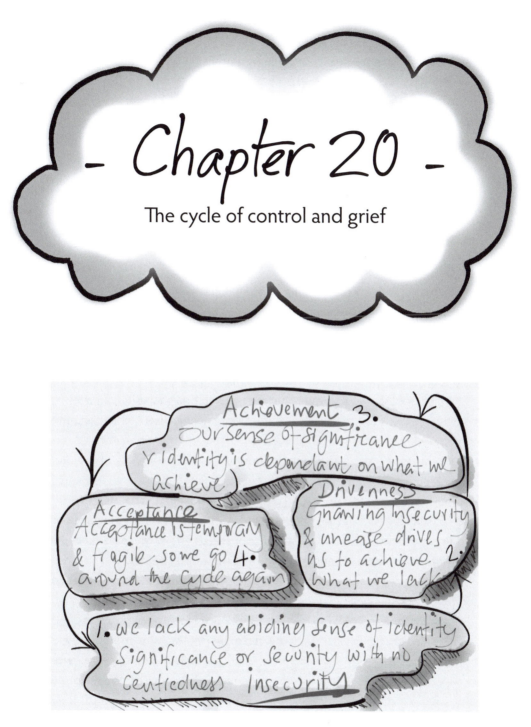

Figure 11: The cycle of grief (Source: James Lawrence)

In the previous chapters we have started to build up your awareness of how your conditioning creates your acquired self. In so doing this sets up a corresponding limited reality that we end up living under and even being controlled by.

When we become conditioned to operate from our acquired self, then this can take away an abiding sense of identity and we can lose sight of who we truly are. That is our authentic self, and the feeling of a loss of identity is a tell-tale sign that the connection to the authentic self has been lost. I often hear people that I work with telling me about their work and in particular about their perceived lack of identity.

For example I frequently hear people say:

'I don't know who I am, and what I stand for, and what I am as a person.'
Or
'I struggle with my identity, and who I am in what I am doing.'

I believe that it is becoming a commonplace issue amongst people of all ages. A consistent theme in such cases is that someone's identity becomes wrapped up in the significance of their work, and in their significant achievements, or worse still a sense of a lack of significance.

When our identify is in question, this leads to other aspects of ourselves coming into question, too, such as self-esteem, significance and our security in who we are.

All this starts to become uncertain and, at the extreme, 'wobbly and shaky'. Some understanding is being sought of questions, such as who am I, why am I who I am, and what am I desiring to become, what is my purpose and why do I feel so insecure at times? These are all important aspects of our authentic identity and our natural consciousness's efforts to come through, often as an unconscious counter-balance to this feeling of loss.

The author James Lawrence, in his book *Growing Leaders*, created a model called 'the cycle of grief' that succinctly describes how we end up losing our identity and its marked consequences for us. It is our acquired conditioning that gradually starts the cycle of grief. Anguish and guilt seem to keep repeating and returning. The same problems seem to keep coming up, coping patterns ensue as the acquired self dominates, as previously described. As these beliefs and subsequent emotions take hold of us they control and recur through our lives in this way. We feel a gnawing sense of insecurity that something could be better. This is an oblique awareness of the fact that our acquired self is dominating and our true authentic self is being overruled. To compensate we throw ourselves into a compulsion to achieve. This is so we can attempt to feel better about ourselves. Eventually achievement turns out to be the only way we can prove our identity, and this self-acceptance therefore is very fragile and temporary. This is because it is reliant only on what we have achieved and what status or self-significance we have earned for ourselves in the process of achievement. And so the grief cycle goes on.

Round and around it goes.

And it incessantly drives and controls us on and on.

This cycle of grief represents the ultimate consequences of the outward workings of the acquired self and its limiting affects on us. Feeling good about ourselves only comes through our achievements, and not by deeply understanding that we can be accepted purely for who we are and not through what we achieve. This can seem impossibly simple to people caught up in the cycle of grief.

> If you recognise this cycle and it is something that you are presently caught up in, then there is hope. Again, the mere realisation of its effect on you personally brings you out of its control and provides you with the impetus to seek something different. Ultimately this 'something different' is based on a return to your authentic self. It may be worth noting now in your journal any thoughts you have based on how the cycle of grief manifests in your life.

We begin to explore an antidote cycle to this in the next chapter. This antidote or alternative cycle builds up your identity as it relies on the presence of your authentic self being honoured instead. It is called the cycle of grace. Before we get to this I want you to understand that a change of direction needs to be desired first. You need to want and desire to make a change and choose to chart a new course. By taking a new bearing you allow yourself to purposefully choose new neurological pathways in your mind–brain to be constructed behind the scenes. This is all part of you taking this journey that is uniquely defined by you and which explores returning you to your authentic self.

- Chapter 21 -

Drawing out conditioning into rich pictures

'Rich pictures' is a term originally coined by Peter Checkland and used in his methodology, soft systems thinking. Part of that process was about drawing out learnings gleaned from rich pictures. These provide a mechanism for learning about complex or ill-defined problems by drawing ('rich') representations of them. The purpose of rich pictures is to deliberately create a story describing the issue, situation or circumstance being explored. It uses visual modalities to create a big picture that tells a whole story. The old adage of a picture telling a thousand words holds true.

I have used rich pictures in many different circumstances to learn about complex and dynamic problems and issues. I have found them extremely powerful as a method of self-expression to describe one's own past conditioning and the consequences of conditioning on subsequent ways of being, and associated responses, repeating patterns and behaviours etc. As such, I find it very helpful to use them in this early part of the change process to expose and loosen the hold of such conditioning patterns. When people express themselves using rich pictures, I find that they can access their emotional side much easier. I believe this is for two reasons. Firstly rich pictures access the more intuitive and creative parts of our brains, because they are more attuned to right-brain modalities. Secondly, the right brain seems to also topologically access episodic or personal memory, which is an adept master at being able to construct a big picture story. Interestingly, some people are initially uncomfortable about drawing pictures. My own theory as to why some people are more reluctant often correlates with people that are more used to using left-brain approaches and impersonal semantic memory. They are therefore not used to or discourage themselves from expanding their thinking by using their more creative and intuitive abilities.

Typically, rich pictures follow no common format. They are free flow sketches describing the context of how acquired conditioning affects an individual. There are no set rules. As a guideline, they usually consist of symbols, sketches or 'doodles' or are 'cartoon-like' and can contain as much (pictorial) information as is deemed necessary by the individual. The finished picture is of value and benefit as the process readily articulates the overall effect of that person's issue and readily describes acquired conditioning. It often captures many different facets of a person's unique life situation, and the subsequent circumstances and reality this creates for that person. The real importance and value of this technique is the way it helps the creator to think deeply about their situation, issues and consequences and therefore to understand it well enough to express it pictorially and then to learn from it (a process I term 'action learning').

Rich pictures are a diagrammatic and sketch-like way of relating the story of your own experiences and perceptions to your unique problem or situation by identifying and linking various contexts and issues. The creation of a rich picture provides a way in which to think about your unique situation and your responses to a given situation.

So, rich pictures are a part of the enriching, recording, understanding and learning process that help you to expose and loosen the hold of your own acquired conditioning. Metaphor in rich pictures is also useful as a change agent.

People often start out using rich pictures to literally draw out their past experiences and issues and tendencies. These past issues often form the context of what is also occurring currently as well as how they perceive their limitations are holding them back.

Using the same picture, or sometimes drawing a second rich picture, I ask people that I work with to spend some time on not just the problem but to also express what they desire. So in effect the rich picture process captures the past, present problems and future desires, intentions and goals in a format that is free flowing, rich with metaphor and unique to each individual.

Here is an example from one of my own clients…

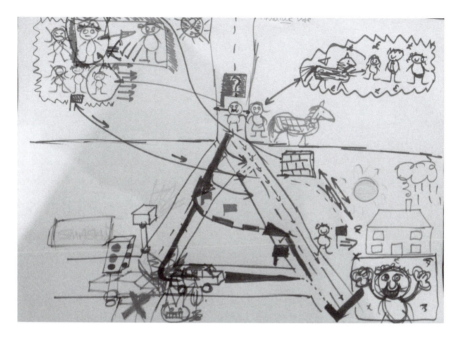

Figure 12: Example of a rich picture

The specific explanation of these rich pictures is not important; they are unique to the individual so every rich picture is different. The reason I have included them is to show you an example. Note the use of metaphor, puzzle pieces, roads, journeys, stick people, no-go signs, crashes, vehicles, ticks and crosses, happy and unhappy faces, and the use of colour etc. This person also drew a professional and personal life representation, as well as a depiction of their past and present.

This is a very powerful way of being able to represent and describe your own situational context, and summarising in a rich picture format all that you have experienced with regard to your acquired conditioning and also what you want instead. As already mentioned, a picture is indeed worth a thousand words. I have found that this process really helps to start to articulate how a person is feeling and what they want. More subtly, it begins to nudge towards a mindset shift that breaks past assumptions that change is not possible. It also starts to create the awareness and motivation and energy to enrich thinking towards new future paradigms of potential that look to a more desirable future.

- Part 4 -

Breaking the patterns of the acquired self

Figure 13: Challenging your acquired self

Chapter 22

Overcoming your conditioning

Impossible is just a big word thrown around by small men who find it easier to live in the world they've been given than to explore the power they have to change it.
Impossible is not a fact. It's an opinion.
Impossible is not a declaration. It's a dare.
Impossible is potential.
Impossible is temporary.
Impossible is nothing.

(Muhammad Ali, http://www.goodreads.com/quotes/121663-
impossible-is-just-a-big-word-thrown-around-by-small)

Can I make changes for myself, or do I need help?

Have you ever wondered why it is that you seem to keep having the same relationships?

Why is it that you keep having the same type of negative experiences over and over again?

And why is it that you repeatedly create the same sort of reality for yourself?

Have you ever wondered if it might be possible to change the things that seem to keep happening to you?

Or have you found yourself saying, 'It's just impossible to change'?

Many forms of belief and habitual pattern change techniques are used in various therapy approaches, such as cognitive behavioural therapy, NLP, hypnosis and many interventions. These often involve specialised techniques that have evolved as part of a particular, specific therapy. For this reason, they do require practised skill and should be applied within a professional therapeutic or coaching relationship for best results. This is not just because of the skills required, but also because the relationship that develops during such interventions can in itself be a useful part of the change process.

However, this book is intended to give you tools and techniques that you can apply for yourself that will help you to make your own changes. That doesn't mean that you can't use this book while also getting professional help. For example, simply reading this book will provide you with new understandings and insight about change and about yourself, and about what you want moving forward. That's important, as it provides you with the responsibility for your own changes. You might also feel that, having read this book, it gives you the impetus to work with a professional to help you get closer to your goals.

Again, this is a perfectly good plan.

So if you want to work on your own, or undertake some parts individually, while additionally working with a professional, or in reading this book you feel that you would work best with a professional who uses specialised approaches that might suit you and your preferences or circumstances to help you to get what you desire, all these ways are open to you. Remember that you are in charge of your own changes however you prefer to work. The process in this book can be used as an alternative approach or in collaboration and conjunction with other interventions. It may also be that you the reader might be a professional practitioner of a particular discipline and you are interested in using this book to augment your own skills and practice. Whatever your reason for reading and working with the techniques, ideas and approaches described within these pages, the contents are for you to freely use and apply.

You will notice significant differences and changes as you become more aware that you are, in fact, more than you think.

Also, it is not a prerequisite that you have to work with a professional or use any formal intervention for a particular problem. This book is intended to open your mind to the prospect that personal change is possible by you with application. You are in charge of your change and your level of freedom and therefore this should not and is not intended to be prescriptive. This book aims to provide you with the principles to make personal change, to enable you to find ways of achieving freedom from your conditioning. They are easy to follow and to be readily applied by you. If you apply this approach along your own journey, you will open your mind and change. You will have ways to overcome your conditioning and by applying them find the freedom you deserve.

Proactive responses to external physical reality

In Part 3 you began to develop your own self-awareness. You may have also started your self-learning inventory. This is designed to help you to expose your current acquired conditioning. Furthermore, during that process you also embarked on loosening the hold and control that your conditioning has had on you. You can now build on this to consider proactive interventions that will make further shifts in your mindset in overcoming your conditioning and which are designed to return you to more resourceful ways of being. These are the domain of the authentic self.

If you look back at the situation we described at the beginning of Chapter 14, of the little boy being bullied at school, you can see how proactive responses to a negative situation can allow us to access and build on the resourcefulness of the authentic self.

Reactive responses to external reality

However, in contrast to the story of the boy and his proactive response mentioned above, if that happened to you, you may have selected more reactive choices to deal with the same situation. These choices may be based on negative and limiting thoughts about that bullying experience. It might be that threatening and fearful thoughts and feelings emerge in your mind. This is because you are attending to different forms of internal representations (we covered this in Chapter 11) that are brought into your mind as associations because of your thought patterns. These in turn inevitably lead to you co-creating different realities. Continually reacting to reality in such ways eventually stabilises into neural pathways that set up the above sorts of predictable headings in life.

For example, intense negative feelings of being unworthy, powerlessness, fear, guilt or denial can be easily imagined (maybe even catastrophised) and our beliefs then form strongly around such forceful and negative concepts of reality, and associated internal representations are brought to mind to embody this as a mind–body state.

Moving away from defaults

As we have already described, neurological research is beginning to understand that negative and limiting choices use very different (default) neurological mechanisms, and form strategies that soon develop into dealing with such issues by focusing and narrowing conscious attention. It turns out that such reactive choices use the same type of circuitry based in basal brain mechanisms in the downstairs part of our brains, which are principally used for automative flight and flight protection responses. This specialised area of the brain is known as the amygdala and it works alongside other basal or limbic brain structures.

The amygdala is a part of the instinctive downstairs brain that acts as a fast response mechanism designed principally to avoid and protect us from many types of negative situations, such as threats and fears. Once triggered, by default the amygdala automatically signals associated pre-wired primary dispositional representations that evoke primary emotions to fire up to recall a predictable and fast response as an automatic solution. However, as above, it turns out that these primal mechanisms can be also taken over by secondary emotions, and secondary dispositional internal representations contained within the inner workings of limiting beliefs. These limiting beliefs via their dispositional representations form the keys to reproducing, reforming and recreating millions of other associated internal representations into a whole mind–brain–body response, reacting spontaneously to the perceived external event in physical reality. These types of strategies become laid down as default pathways. At the risk of repetition, this mechanism evolved intentionally as a hardwired fight or flight response reaction. Its original purpose was an instinctive jump or startle reaction to danger and threat triggered by our primary emotions to aid protection and survival.

My theory is that because of the *perceived* threat of danger from what might be occurring in external physical reality, our consciousness often selects this hardwired survival strategy as a mechanical response to situations triggered by our secondary emotions. In other words our conscious mind always finds the most efficient and straightforward way to deal with external reality, usually by means of a reactive response. I argue that it is not always the best or most appropriate approach though, as we have already covered, as it tends to develop acquired self and limiting conditioning strategies. These then move you away from the more proactive learning strategies employed by the authentic self.

Also as described earlier, secondary emotions are subtler forms of primary emotions and evolved to give humans finer responses to situations, circumstances and events occurring in everyday external reality that are not necessarily innately life-threatening (these, as mentioned above, deal with primary emotions that trigger the hardwired stress response or fight/flight mechanism).

As our mind–brain is highly associative, any similar events that may occur again in the future can therefore be diverted to hijack the stress response mechanism, and so we react, using the hardwired stress response as a one-stop solution. My hypothesis is that this mechanism is selected as the default only because our mind–brain has 'perceived' or convinced itself to act as if it is a fight or flight danger or threat. Also, as said above, it is simply the most economical and expedient solution that was contrived by the conscious mind at that time the limiting dispositional representations were formed from experience, as a marker to hijack and so trigger the stress response mechanism. In addition, it requires no extra (inefficient) cognitive thought, analysis or choice. So no learning or alternative better responses are ever renegotiated or tried and tested. The ruthless conscious mind has no time for such things as improvement if it means compromising on efficiency.

The triggering of the in-built stress response automatically triggers adverse body states and excessive hormonal secretions appropriate to high states of fight, flight or freeze alert. So if the stress response is being activated by the actions of a limiting belief then the subsequent fight or flight reactions often end up producing disproportionate responses to the event being responded to in external reality. As a result, this mechanism leaves us with unnecessary overreactions being stimulated that in the longer term may set up more complicated problems that become harmful to us. The body is not designed to sustain habitualised fight or flight responses.

I believe these strategies end up being responsible for creating the human condition that we have been describing in this book so far. For the many people who I talk to about these types of reactive responses, they have come to believe that these responses cannot be changed, while at the same time desperately desiring relief and freedom from these states of mind. My experience is that it is more than possible to adjust and alter these defaults and use more resourceful strategies instead. So the belief that these cannot be altered or changed is far from the reality. We can choose more proactive responses as long as we are prepared to apply ourselves to the effort of doing so, and through deliberate conscious thought. Another thing that I have discovered is that if we do not take the time to revisit and readdress these limited belief strategies at some point, then we will continue with the same reactions and their adverse effects, ultimately affecting our health and well-being.

The concept of changing established mind–brain maps is now being supported more and more by emergent neurological research, which suggests that this is entirely possible because of the plasticity of our brains positively responding to our willpower. That ultimately we can choose for ourselves to select more resourceful responses that do in fact unfold as new pathways to different structures.

Cognitive behaviour therapy and responsive behavioural repatterning are often quoted as possible interventions by the scientific community that have statistically been proven to be effective. In my own work, I have satisfactorily proved that other similar interventions, such as techniques based on hypnosis and NLP and other related approaches, work as successfully too.

- Chapter 23 -

Applications to break free from your past

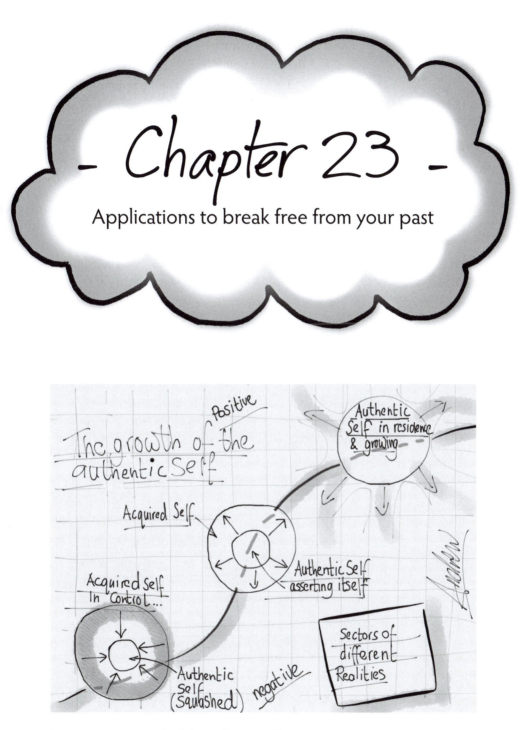

Figure 14: The growth of the authentic self

Interrupting your past patterns – practical application 1

This is the first of three applications. It is a powerful and easy exercise to do on your own, or guided. Best done, if you have some space, in a quiet place. You can do this on your own or with somebody that can guide you through this, such as a friend or a professional coach for example.

However you choose to do this, it is a practical exercise and enables you to access a series of related instances of associated past memories that you feel have contributed to your current issues and problems or conditioning. Its intention is to help you to break the hold of your past experiences, memories, conditioning and responses.

Get a few blank pieces of paper and using a pen or pencil divide each page equally into a series of boxes, so that you end up with around 9 or 12 empty boxes per page. Each box will be used as a space into which you can write separate past memories.

After you have done this, find yourself a comfortable position in which you can reflect and write. It is best to do this exercise by imagining you are able to look at yourself in current, recent and past parts of your life from an objective dissociated position. To do this you simply imagine that a part of you can look at and see yourself as if you are a neutral but interested bystander and observer of yourself looking knowingly at your life.

This is entirely possible: recent neurological research is now working on the hypothesis that our mind–brain really does create a set of dissociated representations of ourselves in exactly this way. This perspective seems to contribute to forming notions of our self and our identity. The important thing for you is that this other you, the observer self, is not to be attached (associated) to the real you, that is, yourself. In doing this, you pretend that you are merely an impartial observer of yourself and your past situations, passing by and observing you from a neutral perspective, like watching a film about you. Your observer self is then able to look at your life situation more dispassionately and objectively.

Your simple pre-made template is merely a series of 9–12 empty boxes – an empty matrix or table. You allow your imagination the necessary time for your mind to fill each box with a certain memory, one after the other. A bit like a cartoon strip if you like. Add a single word or phrase to describe each separate representation in each box if you find that that helps you. You need a starting place, so I suggest starting in the top left box and using that as the now position and slowly go back chronologically in time, moving from left to right, as if you were writing a book.

You will need at least an hour to do this. During this time, allow your mind to relax and then give yourself permission to think about, for each past event, your issue or problem or past conditioning, in turn. In this calm and relaxed state of mind, start with the most recent image representations, and bring them into your consciousness. Either represent them as a picture or as a statement – whatever works best for you. Going from left to right, recall a series of related and relevant past images going back in time in chronological order. If you can't remember them in the exact time sequence, then don't worry, it doesn't really matter, the sequence is not at all important. Its intention is to help you to bring back to mind your past experiences, memories, conditioning and responses. In this way you can later begin to make sense of them in new and different ways. A key to this exercise is to keep in mind that while the events of the past don't change, our attitudes and perceptions to them can change in infinite ways and it is this aspect that is important.

Remember, too, to see it as if you are an observer of yourself, so that you remember yourself, your feelings or your actions in the content (as I said this can be pictures or a statement – whatever helps you to evoke, describe and remember each event) you put in each separate box. Every box will contain a brief and small reminder or description that your mind–brain has associated with these kinds of thoughts. The only difference is that you are pretending to be a passerby, a neutral bystander. If possible, you can add a rough time and place marker in each box, or how old you were or roughly what year or date each memory was for you. Alternatively just number each one later on once you've finished. Again accuracy is not necessary here, unless it is important to you.

Continue to move left to right and top to bottom in your template, going backwards through time, and note each scenario in sequence as you do this. Use as many sheets of paper as you wish.

If you prefer, you may start at the bottom and move right to left going forwards or backwards in time. Again, don't worry if you get some out of time sequence. If you do, then just allow it to be, or number them differently if you wish, it is not that important. It's not about getting things right in time or moving in a certain predefined way through the template. Instead it is about allowing you to see your past in a series of images that have been negatively associated with one another.

Allow your mind as much time as it needs to fill in each blank box, however and with whatever it feels is relevant to your current conditioning, situation or predicament, and in any way that makes up the reasons for your current situation. Don't over-think these; allow the process to flow and trust that your mind will deliver what is necessary. This exercise is not complex and there is no right or wrong. The boxes are merely a form to allow you to express a part of your life so you can learn from it and its patterns and repeating nature.

The first boxes represent recent events and situations. Successive boxes represent your past significant and relevant situations that all are linked to or contribute in some way to your life as it is today. Each box simply represents a significant aspect or notion of your life at a particular time. The whole collection of these, once complete will represent a series of associated and significant, relevant and contributing aspects of your life leading up to the present moment.

The purpose of this practical, experiential exercise is to map out a self-inventory of how you would describe your current situation and how this has evolved directly from your past conditioning. And how it is linked, where it came from and other things that you will discover will be all useful learnings. This in effect becomes the story, or storyboard, of the significant aspects of your life in the context of a particular issue or part of you. All these aspects have contributed to making up the life that you are currently leading and are formative or key events along the way.

The important thing to remember is that you can't go wrong with this exercise as it is fluid and flexible with no specific way of doing it.

Here are some guidelines for you to consider as to what aspects this exercise might represent for you. You might also do the exercise several times for different aspects that you wish to explore:

- Review what the main sticking points are in your current life and where these emerged from.
- What you feel is stuck in your life recently and review how your past contributed to this.
- How do you currently feel about yourself and where did this originate and evolve?
- How do you view what others might perceive you as being now and in the past?

- What are the reoccurring themes that you think a lot about (e.g. anxiety, worry, panic, anger, fear, procrastination, avoidance, conflict, feeling uneasy, unsure, insecure)?
- What are typical examples of the way you talk to yourself and repeating patterns of inner mind chatter language?
- Deep down, what beliefs do you hold about yourself and how or where did these form?
- What current behavioural limitations, controls, habits or 'OCD' type tendencies have you noticed developing and how have they changed or adapted over time?
- What current physical conditions or symptoms do you experience that are not inherently part of you (e.g. skin rashes, hand wringing, shortness of breath, asthma, itchiness, sore patches)?

The boxes as a whole represent a simple timeline of recent and past events or situations that are relevant and provide supporting evidence, linkages and patterns of what has formed your behaviours, thoughts and feelings of your conditioning to date. Each box therefore represents a useful snapshot in time that has contributed to the you today. Use your self-inventory journal to capture your reflections, changes and learnings and what might feel different to you…

When you have finished give yourself a chance to think and reflect on it. This exercise is initially about information gathering. It also helps you to build a comprehensive picture of yourself in relation to this aspect of you and your life. Once complete it is important to invest time in standing back and reflecting. This is a very important part of the change process, as it helps you to develop your own self-awareness.

Another aspect of learning, particularly from the recent and past situational snapshots, is to consider where these aspects of your conditioning arose from, from whom, when, why etc.

When you are good and ready, cut each box out so each can standalone and place them on the floor or on a blank wall or table. Either put them in a long chronological timeline or bunch them into clusters or groups using rows and columns that seem logical to you. Add any further memories using other blank boxes as you see fit. Sort and sift them in any way that feels right to you. Notice what you observe and learn from this perspective.

These sorts of reflections will help you piece together and to understand possible underlying reasons, or perhaps just patterns, as to why things are the way they have turned out.

What next…?

Now, reorder each box in the timeline, seeing them in reverse chronological order, from the earliest to the latest. Become aware of any changes that you might now see from this perspective. As an additional option, you could place them on the floor, so you can physically walk next to them. In this way you apply your whole body to the learning. This is a very powerful approach. However, if you prefer just to look at them quietly and reflect then that is okay too. Pay attention to what you notice and reflect on whatever messages this provides you with. Use your journal to capture any relevant aspects.

After you have spent sufficient time in reflection, the next stage is to mix all of the image boxes up, so that they are in no particular chronological order. Now lay out each of the boxes in a long line. The scrambling of the time sequence is intentional and important for this next part of the exercise. Now quietly spend time reviewing each one of these items out of time sequence and move on from one to the next, repeating this one or two more times.

This process starts to unconsciously disrupt and break the hold and association to time and sequence about such associated events and how they affect you. This disruption has a powerful releasing effect and begins to break down previous holding patterns that each had on the other.

After a short while of reviewing this, I want you to look at each of the images and start to move them into different clusters that represent new and different ways of observing and perceiving them that up until now you haven't previously thought about.

After you have spent a little time reflecting on what has altered and what new ideas have sprung to mind, I now want you to slowly bring all these images together and, closing your eyes and taking as much time as you need, use your imagination to consolidate these into a new single representation that converts this learning into something completely different and more resourceful and that enables you to feel good about yourself and to learn from this knowledge, move forward and to apply this in a new way in the future.

Practical applications…

Once you have stabilised this, use your self-inventory journal to record how you have now represented this new awareness. Over the next two or so weeks it is important to be deliberately conscious of and aware of new changes that start to occur as a result of doing this. Use your journal regularly to record these changes, and celebrate them too. And there will be changes.

As a suggestion, see Chapter 27, 'A practical anchoring application to feel good about yourself', and use it to deliberately, physically 'anchor' this new resourceful change into your conscious awareness.

Changing your past perceptions and seeing with new eyes

> The real voyage of discovery consists not in seeking new landscapes, but in having new eyes.
>
> (Marcel Proust, http://www.brainyquote.com/quotes/quotes/m/ marcelprou107111.html)

Time and time again, I am struck by how true this remark is. I have found that this statement is fundamental to making personal change from the grip of remembered past events and circumstances. As described in Part 2, it is the associational power of your acquired limiting beliefs and their dispositional representations' hold your past has on you that continues to shape your current experiences and hence your reality. As we have also learned in this section, without change these patterns will continue into your future, as ongoing predictable responses.

So one of the fundamental principles in making personal change is to be able to perceive those past events, situations and circumstances that caused you pain or difficulty with a new attitude. With new eyes. The application of the second approach in this chapter is to revisit and replay a significant past event to re-pattern the experience of it by perceiving it anew.

This approach is about revisiting those circumstances and replaying them again in your mind's eye from a new perspective. This time, however, the intention is to learn something different from your past situation. You do this by reviewing that past situation or event differently by using the power you have in this present moment now to review your past issue. This often produces powerful change. This is because you will be appraising and assessing that past event more objectively as a more mature grown-up you in a (now) different time. In this present moment you are a different you from the you you were when you first experienced the event, situation or circumstance as it actually happened. Time has passed, and time is often a great healer.

In this practical exercise you have the opportunity to evaluate it and see it again, but as it would be today, now, in hindsight with new eyes.

As we have discussed, your own such past issues and experiences have tendencies that end up shaping your conditioning and limiting beliefs. Such acquired beliefs are formed in our past, often when we are much younger. So in these new, different and current circumstances you have an opportunity to revisit the events that formed your past experiences, and see them differently as an adult with new eyes and new perspectives.

The following practical application requires you to use the power of your imagination to relive and change your perspective of a past issue that helped shape your limiting belief patterns by seeing it with new eyes.

Revisiting the you of the past – practical application 2

To orchestrate this properly, it is important that you find yourself in a quiet place on your own (you can do this as a guided exercise, too, if you prefer). You will need about an hour or so's time to complete this exercise.

Make yourself comfortable and close, or soften, your eyes. But don't fall asleep though. Take time to relax yourself and breathe steadily for a while, to get into a nice, easy, centred and mellow, calm state of mind. When you are ready, imagine you are able to go back in time to your past as the you of today and revisit a particular situation or set of related situations that have caused you difficulty. Choose an event from the previous self-inventory practical applications that you have traced back as being the formation point of an acquired limiting belief that has been conditioning you ever since.

This practical application exercise can be done by using a meditative state of mind. Later in this book you will find a chapter on meditation and self-hypnosis. That will help you to do this in deeper ways.

Any past event can be recalled and replayed by remembering it. Often the circumstances that cause pain and threat or difficulty, for example, can be easily recalled due to their dispositional nature and associated emotional effect.

However, this practical application requires you to recall the experience(s) that led to your conditioning that has a hold on you, but in a subtly different way. Many people can readily recall difficult things that happen to them, as if they are happening all over again to them, here and now. In this exercise you need to pretend again that you are the 'you' you are now having the power to go back in time and visit the person you were at the time of the issue you want to revisit. We are using the same dissociated technique used in the last exercise. In this way you can literally revivify your own experience(s) and see it again but this time through new eyes, the eyes of the you today acting as the neutral observer, not the old you back then. This is an important distinction, as the dissociation subtly allows you to relive an event without having the associated emotions of the you then that experienced it back in the past.

Spending time on your own, in a comfortable and relaxed state is the best way to re-imagine this and carry out the process.

You then use the power of your imagination to replay it again, but this time, as suggested, as if you are a neutral observer, watching the poignant moments of that issue being recalled. You see the you that was there at the time, re-experiencing it all over again, as it actually happened. As explained, this technique is called dissociation. You imagine that you can see the past you are watching as the you today. The you today is an interested but neutral observer that perceives it objectively. The dissociated (most recent) you is not overly involved in it, but looks on at it from this new perspective.

In this way you spend as much time as you need, revisiting all the details of the particular associated past memories that created your conditioning and limited beliefs that have formed your acquired self. In this exercise you recall your 'then' self experiencing the event in as much detail as you can remember, exactly as it actually was. Being the neutral observer, the you today, gives you new and different, updated perspectives, thoughts, feelings and insights to your past issue. This new viewpoint allows you to make different choices and changes, to see things that, at the time, you were unable to see. This is because in this dissociated perspective you are not emotionally attached, as the past you that first experienced the real event was. In addition, by imagining this event being replayed again, you are going back in time, as the you that you are today. This makes you see what was and what occurred in a new light.

That doesn't mean you can change the actual past event, of course. That stays the same. You can't alter past events. But the important and powerful thing you do have is the ability and authority to choose to change the way you look at it, think and feel about it. This in itself possesses remarkable releasing power.

Here's a personal example for you…

When I was a young boy growing up, we moved to a different part of the country. That meant I had to move schools. During this unsettling period, I happened to have crossed swords with an older boy who ended up making life difficult and particularly unpleasant for me. This boy had a knack for turning my peers against me. This issue, the specific details of which are unimportant, didn't really sort itself out and seemed to linger interminably. Eventually we all grew up and went to different senior schools and in time the trouble eventually petered out, but not before culminating in a dramatic confrontation, which at the time I found very painful and upsetting. From then on, I believed that this entire spate of events had permanently altered me. From that time on, all the way into adulthood and into early middle age, I ended up with the acquired limiting belief that people did not like me. My conditioning deeply affected me. This was solely due to this issue.
I believed that I was somehow always at fault;
I was never good enough, or liked by others, that others always talked about me;
I made mistakes that affected others;
I was a flawed person;
that others laughed at me;
who, during difficult interactions, became moody, sullen and took myself too seriously.

I did this very exercise that I had invented for myself, and spent time reliving the most difficult part of this past issue from my younger life – where things had come to a head between me and this older boy – which had become etched in my mind. During the process of revisiting this culminating past event and re-imagining it through adult eyes, I played the part of the neutral observer. As I did this I began to realise that, by looking at the me then and that older boy again, a new perspective began to dawn on me. I found in this relaxed state that I was able to interact and even talk to the me then and the other boy too. As I watched the whole scene unfold again, with the adult me watching on and momentarily interacting with each boy, in turn I found myself asking them questions with the instruction for them not to answer me, but each other instead. I suppose I acted as a pretend mediator. On reflection, however, the real moment of new perspective came from simply reliving it again and replaying it in front of me as an adult observer: that was the change that made the real difference for me.

At that moment, what I had thought of as 'bullying' was not actually that at all. I came to see that here were two boys, just two exuberant boys who were just growing up, finding their way in life, and learning how to cope with being different from each other and learning how to cope with dislike and disagreement. He was learning and so was I. It was an experience for us both, but just different for him and me.

So during this process I learned that I was actually never bullied, we were just incompatible and that I was actually a well-liked boy who made friends easily; he simply didn't know how to cope with me nor I with him. He and I acted with the resources we had and knew at the time. It didn't mean that what happened then had to shape my future at all. This was a huge realisation for me.

Reliving the past event using this exercise instantly released me from the hold of that limiting belief that had formed there and then all those years ago. What I hadn't anticipated was the dramatic effect that changing this one past event would have on all other similar past events that had happened to have been coloured by that limiting belief formed through this one past episode for me. I remember experiencing a physical shudder and, right there and then, I mentally experienced a shift in all the subsequent times from that beginning event onwards, right up to the day that I did the exercise, my perceptions of which also changed right in front of me. I found the effect physically made me 'reel' for a moment too. And I remember having to steady myself. Mentally I realised something big had happened.

When I made my realisation of perspective change, this became an instant ah ha! light bulb type moment for me. As soon as I had made this mental shift, then my whole mind–brain–body seemed to realign itself. This all happened extremely rapidly, and felt like a physical release, a freeing of the hold that this acquired belief had had on me for so many years. I was now able to regard all the related past memories from that point on completely differently. It actually felt quite spiritual, like a conversion experience.

From that one shift in perspective, I had gained a completely new way of thinking, feeling and being without any redress to the previous emotional body states and sensations – no panic, or fear, sense of threat or wanting to run away. No guilt or unworthiness. The change had suddenly, dramatically, cascaded through my entire experience. It felt a bit like rapidly flicking through a whole roller-deck of cards. Each card represented a similar past experience that had been released from the powerful hold of my former acquired limiting belief. This was now gone.

The realisation was that, actually, all along, people have liked me, that I am good enough as I am. I may be different, but that's all. I realised I felt differently about the boy that had given me all the hassle back then over so many years. I was able to realise his true self and to let him go and so I saw him with completely new eyes.

I hope that you find this application as powerful as I did. I adopted the process of reflection specifically in response to this very example. It works like magic; however, what's really underneath it are a few practical principles.

Firstly it is about shifting time and using this as change mechanism: you are using the you today and going back in time to revisit the past you at a particular poignant moment. The you today has changed from the past you that has been stuck in a holding pattern. You are therefore using the more mature and grown up you that has new perspectives and experience to revisit the then you that was not so mature. Your unconscious mind will get this and make the necessary adjustments and changes based on what you learn from the reliving process. This is because the you today revisits that past you reliving that event as an observer, a neutral watcher. Your unconscious knows that the event happened and can't be changed. But the speciality of the unconscious mind is to see things in new ways that provide different realisations. It is able to experience the same things in an altered way, to gain new knowledge and understanding from this altered perspective.

Once new realisations about the past event are discovered, the mind immediately realises this. It is like when you have an argument with somebody and assume they are to blame for it because of their actions, and go off in a huff. Only later you find out a different take on the same event, and you immediately say, 'Oh, I see now', and let go of your anger and your relationship is restored with no animosity, as if the altercation never happened. Or a mystery has occurred, something has gone missing and you can't get it out of your mind. The unresolved issue continues to act like a splinter in your mind. Then sometime later you go back in your mind's eye or physically you retrace your steps, examining the events surrounding the disappearance, and you find it again. At that point you are joyous and celebrate and everything falls into place and you laugh, and call all your friends to tell them about it.

The same kind of thing is happening here too. The new realisation creates a large shift in the previously held psychic energy that kept the acquired belief in play. Importantly, the new realisation brings new perspectives. These are made up of entirely different internal representations, which have no such dispositional hold over you as the previous ones had.

These new representations use the released energy to form newly activated neural pathways that use different parts of mind–brain structure. They do not use the same flight or fight triggered response and mechanisms the downstairs elements of your brain used previously.

You have literally re-patterned your brain to use completely different internal representations of the same event to create different pathways from what it was using only a moment ago. That is the power of your imagination and the instant power of realisation and new perspective.

Now, in the next application you will discover how your present point of power can influence and change the past. But interestingly, it also profoundly affects and alters the future too.

The next practical application purposefully helps you to choose a new future for yourself. This, as you will see, interrupts the pre-organised and conditioned predictable future. This application has done something similar too. Neurologically, the way you now perceive the past event has, in that process, set up completely different internal representations that now associate and represent it. So, by your willpower your neurology is now selecting more resourceful representations, you have changed course from a predictable future and set a new course on a different heading. Therefore, by changing the patterns of the past in this way, you change your responses now and set sail into your new future.

As you have changed your internal reality, this will, in turn, enable you to experience a new and different, more resourceful external reality. This new reality will in turn reinforce your internal reality with new internal representations that will permanently change your responses and the future direction of your life.

Setting a new heading – practical application 3

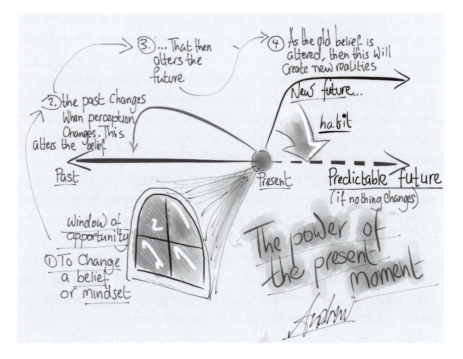

Figure 15: The power of the present moment

This application builds on either or both of the previous practical exercises. A further exercise follows shortly.

If you have been used to reactive responses, then an element of your internal psychic energy and consciousness has most likely been deliberately diverted to form coping strategies that trigger and sustain these. However, as Part 1 of this book described, consciousness is ultimately the most creative force in the universe. In itself it has no limits and has the power to access infinite choices, experiences and resources. It is therefore only your thoughts about yourself and the default approaches that you have adopted that restrict and narrow your consciousness, your reality and responses. In other words, through your thoughts and actions you have conditioned yourself to believe that the responses you have acquired are fixed and unchangeable.

However, available to you at any time is an infinite sea of other more resourceful choices, an ocean of potential, myriad other choices and vastly different approaches that will produce many preferable outcomes instead.

It is merely the way you specifically think, and react and respond, or programme and encode your experience that sets up your limitations. It is not outside circumstance, but internal thought that creates the reality you experience. I call these ways of thinking, or mindset attitude, 'presuppositions'. What you presuppose is what you end up manifesting into external reality. Yes you are much more than you think.

Presuppositions are linguistic structures, internal statements that often make up part of your inner mind chatter. They are the belief systems you hold about the world around you. They are your attitude and mindset to life and what you experience.

We will be exploring these in more detail in the next sections. These internal statements set up (presuppose) your thought reactions and mindset responses and they really govern the way you respond to things and create your experience. If you presuppose for example that nothing ever works out for you, or that things always seem to go wrong, that you never think about this or that working out… this is because this kind of thinking will make it not do so. The interesting thing is that whatever you habitually presuppose inside you will end up eventually working themselves out through you, into the reality you end up experiencing. Likewise if you can change the assumptions of what you presuppose then this will correspondingly work through into reality.

In this way any possibilities, resourceful or otherwise, can be presupposed and consequentially experienced. This means that any reality can be literally created and experienced by changing the patterns of the way we think, what we presuppose (reactive, proactive; negative or positive). Different thought patterns and mindsets use different pathways within the structure of our brains. The plasticity of your amazing mind–brain connections and emotional body responses subsequently create corresponding shifts internally, which in turn manifest externally. You create your reality.

As we have demonstrated through the pages of this book, responses born through fear and threat, however, always create less constructive consequences. Eventually belief systems that use these create artificial constructs, called limiting beliefs. As we now know these structures always operate using principles of avoidance, postponement or other diversionary tactics to find ways around the issues you are experiencing.

These in turn fast-track into carving out habitual grooves that quickly create certain repeated reactions and behaviours that are so ingrained we act on them without thinking. Limiting beliefs, then, are deeply embedded default approaches or bearings that we habitually take to avoid experiencing threatening situations. However, despite intentions designed to protect from future harm, threat or danger, their very existence in your internal reality means that they continually attract corresponding and similar events happening in external reality. These acquired ways are self-created programmes that control you.

Predictable futures

As we have seen, our past conditioning, which includes your thoughts, mind chatter and mindset, creates certain responses that produce predictable outcomes corresponding to these patterns. You may have noticed that these outcomes seem in themselves to lead to repeating similar patterns of experiences that happen to reiterate time and again over and over in your life. These negative and powerful forces create a predictable approach that bears you towards a corresponding reality.

Depending on the pattern of your mindset and the beliefs you choose to live by, you create corresponding predictable approaches in life. These can have good, bad or indifferent consequences for you. Whatever your beliefs and the subsequent choices you make through them, these become the coordinates that chart your course through your life; in effect, if you never change them, then you keep yourself on that bearing and manifest a corresponding sector of reality matching these coordinates. Such is the hypnotic power of acquired conditioning.

What you are learning here is a subtle take on external reality forming your internal reality. The concept I am now introducing is that internal reality also shapes external physical reality using the same mechanisms as the former, but in the reverse way. One begets the other.

I can't emphasise this point strongly enough. These patterns have a two-way effect. External experience of reality is correspondingly re-presented internally, and internally represented reality works its way through to physical external reality. It is all driven by the way we are using our mind–brain and how we react habitually to external circumstances. This means past conditioning has an incredible power and hold over you, because it takes you to a certain predictable approach in external reality. The more you use the same pattern, the quicker reality corresponds to it. At risk of repeating myself, what is recalled and re-presented on the inside of us also manifests what happens outside of us. That predictable approach maintains a particular pattern of events occurring in similar ways in our experienced reality in the physical world around us. The programme becomes set.

Author Vadim Zeland, in his book series *Reality Transurfing*, expresses reality as existing in infinite sectors like coordinates on a map. Extending his analogy of attracting reality in the same way that a sailing boat catches the wind, imagine your mindset as a sailing boat, sailing on the sea of infinite potential. Our internal thoughts, beliefs and mindset are the charts captained by you (your conscious mind) and are the instructions given to the helm (unconscious mind) as a bearing. The helm then dutifully turns you, the boat, to correspondingly head for the set course. As the boat bears to the course, the sails fill full of the winds of that particular potentiality, and the boat then heads along the set course towards that sector of reality, which matches the captain's intentions and wishes. Taking this heading regularly will enable the captain to become familiar with its waters and its tendencies and conditions. To the captain, this sector (of the sea) of reality becomes known and predictable, and the winds blow in a prevailing direction. I call this particular type of bearing a 'predictable future heading'. This is because this is exactly what happens to you, all the time and will continue to happen to you. If you continue to be at the mercy of your internal thoughts that programme your internal conditioning, then the same sort of patterns of events will keep happening to you. This is the programme on the chart. Thus you create a predictable future that is based on past conditioning patterns.

> Based on what you have been noting in your self-inventory journal, it is now time to consider noting how your own conditioned responses produce various kinds of predictability and repeating outcomes that have continued to manifest in your external reality and to start to identify them.

In this way you can make the choice to take a new heading that manifests a new external reality.

Many people get stuck and addicted to all sorts of predictable patterns. We can get so conditioned to these patterns that it becomes a way of being. This acquired conditioning creates 'safe' and predictable headings through life. Often these types of experienced reality are dominated by limitations and fears and our heading sails us far away from the real world of true authentic living. It is a world that is created entirely through acquired and conditioned choices. It is a self-fulfilling prophecy that has pulled the wool over our own eyes. It has created a self-imposed prison that holds people to certain predictable futures.

From time to time the unconscious mind will produce glimmers of this 'stuck in a rut, or the doldrums' predicament. But panic then quickly sets in and any chance of change seems too hard or pointless. So it is easy to simply give in, and slide back into a comfortably numb feeling. Such is the power of acquired conditioning. Resulting reality denies hope.

Deep, deep down though, an uncomfortable inner truth remains: that this conditioning has been created through choice.

Many people stuck in their own conditioning and resultant reality may continue to ignore, fear and so deny that they have the power to liberate themselves from this self-imposed limited control. Others can't accept (or believe) that they can choose to change. For many people they have never considered the possibility that different choices can be intended instead. Such patterns of predictability only remain predictable if you continue to accept the circumstances of your conditioning as being part of you. Perhaps you may believe that you cannot change at all.

So if you are dissatisfied by the sector of reality you have been sail-ing in and continue to experience, then it is time to be proactive and get down to desiring to change the coordinates of your internal beliefs. Sure, this may be hard for a while, as it will take some effort; however, with the right motivation we can challenge any set programme. Neurologically, the reason change is initially difficult is that any new approach has to fight for the cortex real estate in your brain. But what fires together will start to wire together and what you don't use, you lose. A gritty determination is what is required to ensure that the law of neurological plasticity makes these new circuits on your behalf, and your brain will dynamically reorder associated brain patterns and diminish those that are no longer firing. If severe stroke victims with the right motivation can relearn to completely regain what was destroyed in one part of the brain, by using another brain map elsewhere, then you can certainly do the same to rewire new ways of being. You are more than you think.

Using your self-inventory journal write down what it is that you want to experience now. How do you want to feel instead? What new course would you like to head to?

This will start to alter the patterns and holds of your past conditioning. By doing this you are in effect setting your sails on a different heading and trajectory. This will eventually take you to a correspondingly different sector of reality.

So once again, the internal thoughts, beliefs and mindset (conditioning) you hold about yourself is the key to changing your heading. By being aware of this as a principle law of reality, we can then utilise this same principle to intentionally set a new heading to sail to another sector of reality to desire and get what we want now.

Whatever your current conditioning is predicated on, be it fear, judgement, control, excuses, avoidance or worry, anxiety and so on, you will recognise its patterns, which continue to unfold and play out in front of you. As you become aware of them, the more you expose yourself to the right analysis, bit by bit and layer by layer you begin to awaken from the hold of the acquired self. Once you start to waken from this, then it is readily possible for you or anyone to choose to chart a new course, and journey along a different heading or bearing from the one you have chosen so far.

So how do you change from one sector of reality and chart to a different one? What resources and tools do you need to transition from the predictable outcomes of one sector to the freedom of better, more authentic future choices of another?

Well, firstly we have to become aware there is a possible choice. In his book, *The Seven Cs of Coaching*, Mick Cope describes this as the choice point.

I call this choice point the present point of power, and it is always here in this very moment. It is here in all moments now and in future nows. All moments are potential present points of power. In Chapter 6, we saw how the present point of power, when acted on, affects the past, the present and the future. Its significant power represents the power of the present moment, the power of the choice to act now. It is the power to decide to choose and act and take action. This is *the* true power that can be invoked by any human being at any time. The present moment has power – the power to decide, to choose, to act and to do something different.

To use it you have to be fully alert in your consciousness. The present point of power cannot be used to advantage if you are unwilling to overcome your conditioning of the acquired self.

So the point of choosing to change firstly represents your desire and motivation to want to change trajectory. Secondly, it represents the will-power to break free from the hold over your acquired self. The present point of power provides the capacity, capability and energetic impetus to overcome the patterns of your limiting acquired conditioning and replace them with more resourceful ones.

It is your past limiting beliefs and their rules that hold you in a self-made prison. A prison for your mind. And it is these very patterns that set up a predictable future based on these conditioned rules that then imprison us.

The present point of power merely represents the liberating moment you consciously awaken and open your mind to realise something has to change for the better in your life. You declare that change and decide to start right now. I cannot overstate the power of this choice. In that moment you reject the hold that your past beliefs have conditioned you to. Instead you choose to open your mind to something different. You make a statement to yourself and the point of power becomes the juncture of conversion where energy held in the controlling grip of the sector of what you once believed transfers to another that you become open to accept. At this point you won't have the answers as to how it will come about or even have an exact plan, you merely make the decision in faith to do it, trusting that you will determine how to go about it later. That vow, or oath if you like, is the difference that makes the difference. It represents the will to live a life free of your conditioning and past patterns from now on. To do this you simply have to open your mind to its possibility and potential and commit to change. It's perhaps rather like a spiritual conversion. Taking the present point of power is the commitment you make to yourself to change. Your boat of your consciousness will then tack to the new heading, your sails will fill with new intention and you will start to head towards that bearing. Your unconscious mind and authentic self will take you there. Trust in these is all that is needed.

This, in effect, is like your personal Damascus Road experience. It is not yet full enlightenment, but the commitment to journey along its path is now made.

The moment of making this choice is a critical, and a poignant moment in time, and creates a burst of energy to awaken you sufficiently to push and break through the old patterns that held you so tightly just a moment ago. That energy is created through your intentions. This moment in time represents the passing and letting go of control by the acquired self, and intentionally turning to the freedom of the true authentic self. It is a rapid transformation of psychic consciousness from old to new. In spiritual terms it is sometimes referred as rebirth or being born again. For some people it may feel just like this.

From the old self to a new self

It is the moment of bursting through the chrysalis and emerging as something new. This moment in time is the coming together of many aspects of consciousness that enable this moment of freedom. This intentional energy will sufficiently fill your sails to head you towards the appropriate sector of reality that enables your authentic self to fully operate.

It is often experienced by many people as an ah ha! moment of significance. The point of present power is always a place where mind–brain–body meet and the authentic self is given authority to awaken and be fulfilled. It is the point where your conscious will is sufficiently focused in that moment to concentrate the huge amount of psychic energy necessary to burst through the old self to the new self. To do this, your consciousness has full use of the power of your imagination in that very moment and it is like a crown being handed over to its true owner, and worn by the authentic self. Your imagination is an inexhaustibly powerful supply of available human energy. In the choice point moment, this energy is rapidly built up into a stream of highly focused energy that has the power to break the hold of your previous beliefs and conditioning in a single moment.

For many people this moment of breakthrough is remembered. It is like a release, the lifting of a weight. The passing away of control. Some people describe it like prison chains falling away. It is a moment when physical and mental energies work together to shake off a past life, an old skin, and what emerges is very new, very awake and very alive.

Neurologically this transformation is created through a momentary change in consciousness control, or rerouting to new intended pathways. As described in the opening chapter, the conscious mind has a propensity to dominate and for over-control. It was never intended to be the master of your life but a faithful emissary instead. When it operates in this way, your conscious mind is at its very best. Left to its own devices, and without balance from unconscious ways of being, it can become a petty tyrant, an impostor, a false king. However, during the choice point moment, the neurological patterns of these former automatic mechanistic controls are rerouted to more resourceful pathways and balance is quickly restored. On this new heading you will be free to explore more of your true, authentic self. And this will be the same for your journey through this book. However, for now, all human beings on the planet are able to live a life that honours the authentic self, and to break the patterns and hold of the acquired self. This is a rite of passage for all of us. But the tragedy is that few take it. It is easier to ignore it or deny it. But deep down we are all aware that this present point of power can be made. The choice point is simply the moment that this choice is made. Once you commit to a new way of being, you will then have to deserve the right to have it. There will be struggles ahead. I didn't say it would be easy, but we do have to find the courage to get to the reality we desire.

How do you recognise the present point of power and act upon it?

So you now understand the point of choosing in the present moment and its power to transform, what it is and why it is so important. Let's look at what you do to practically implement it.

While the present point of power is a concept, it is one that needs to be practically applied in real life.

Earlier I told the story of my own personal points of power and of seeking change and betterment for myself. When I reflected on my journey, I could see my predictable future unfolding ahead of me. I didn't want this and it was this realisation that inspired me to make changes for the better in my life. So I know that change is possible, and through my own story and journey, I have come to believe that if I can do this, then so can anybody else. Most importantly, so can you. There isn't a man or woman or child on this very planet that hasn't had something they needed to overcome and struggle with. We all know it.

My own story, I hope, demonstrates that this is possible, and through better choices you can get what you really want, what you desire and reach for those things that you dare only to dream of. They are a possible reality. You only have to make the choice, plan your course and set sail to these coordinates. Along the way there will be help. There always is.

Changing course also means that you will have to prove (to yourself) that you deserve the rite of passage to take this new course. My own experience is that it doesn't come easily all the time, but neither will it be beyond you. You see, it has to be deserved. The power and hold of your past conditioning will create resistance. As we have learned, the acquired self is very resistant and 'sticky' to any change. Author Mick Cope describes this as an 'elastic band effect'. And it feels a bit as if our past conditioning acts like an elastic band that tries to pull us back to resist change at all costs. My experience is that you will therefore need to be aware that you will require energy and willpower to overcome your own internal resistances. We know this to be neurologically true from Chapter 15.

So in such ways you will be tested as you pass through stormy seas and uncharted waters. This is the inevitable tussle when two opposing winds meet at a certain point. Choppy seas and stormy waters may be ahead and need to be crossed. This is a time of testing for your authentic self. However, there will be help along the way. When we make the decision to change, to return to our authentic self, then serendipity and the laws of synchronicity benevolently begin to operate to our advantage and meet us along our journey. A bit of beginners luck is always useful. If you stay committed to your new heading then, bit by bit, you will begin to deserve this rite of passage, and at that point the wind will change for you favourably, and the new winds of new potentiality of your authentic self will certainly help you along the way too. This test of courage will re-hone you and allow you to face the 'monsters of the deep' and those dragons that require slaying, which may be stirred up in the process of changing to a new heading.

My own journey was a process of realisation and change and has been a blueprint for me to help others. It's worth repeating that the intention of this book is to map the way to sail through this infinite sea of potential and possibility. This book will hopefully help you to map your own heading, faster and more directly. It is intended to give you purpose and intention in your sails and to chart your own course and understand more coherently the critical success factors and steps involved,

Practical application...

Using your self-inventory journal and the figure below, fill in the blank boxes with descriptions that fit with your unique circumstances.

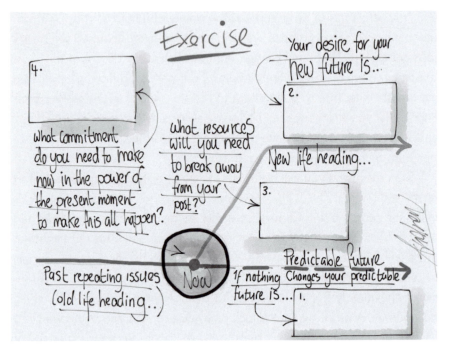

Figure 16: Changing headings working template

This is a powerful exercise, as it will provide you with the overall motivational reasons as to why you want to change. By setting up your future intentions in this way, it will provide you with meaning and purpose. This is a vital initial component to personal change. Setting your intentions is about setting your sails to catch a new wind that changes your direction. Choosing your new heading will enable you to purposefully steer yourself on this new course. This bearing will eventually take you on to discover your new future. This journey will mean charting new waters and along the way you will discover your authentic self.

Start with a statement that encapsulates a description of what your own particular predictable future would be if nothing changes. Refer to Part 3 and use your self-inventory journal notes to help you.

Then spend time to think about what you really dream and desire for yourself and for your life, and how you really want to be. Set yourself some sort of purpose to head for. State this in the box provided for your new future. This will begin to activate your authentic self. The output in your self-inventory journal from the last two practical applications may be useful here.

Then spend some time considering what internal resources and strategies you might need to draw on to motivate yourself. This is the application of the choice point that will head you towards your new desired future. Having made the choice to change, it is critical to evaluate and note what will give you the necessary energy you will require to overcome the hold of your past conditioning, which will attempt to pull you back to your acquired self's predictable future.

Finally you need to make a commitment to yourself to maintain the impetus to make this happen in your life and also to watch external reality begin to shift. You may not notice anything changing in the short term. However, after a few weeks you will notice differences. Also, watch out for any synchronistic moments of serendipity happening to you for each change. Expect them, look out for them and celebrate the feeling that gives you. You will be amazed. Remember to give things a chance and use supporting thoughts. Don't allow your inner mind chatter and thoughts to doubt what you are doing, as doubting feeling will quickly take things away before they've have begun. Remember, too, that it's really important to feel good about yourself. So you need to have hope and faith in yourself.

You may also wish to refer to Chapter 27, 'A practical application to feel good about yourself', to anchor what you imagine your new heading might look like, sound like and feel like.

- Chapter 24 -

Breaking through limitation towards a new future

All limiting beliefs are biases and distortions of the truth that we have built into our mental maps about reality. As you become more aware of your own limiting beliefs and their narrowing effect on your own experience, the question to ask yourself then becomes: 'What is it most useful to believe or to presuppose instead?'

Limiting beliefs tend to come in 'swarms' or 'clusters' – like buses, they seldom come alone.

When working with challenging limiting beliefs, it is very common to sort one belief out only to find that another one pops up that has hitherto been out of conscious awareness. This phenomenon, although it can be frustrating, is highly productive. Think of it like peeling the layers off an onion.

Your limiting beliefs set a ceiling on what you can or can't accomplish. Simply having empowering thoughts alone does not guarantee success in an area, but they are a necessary precondition. Beliefs, empowering or limiting, act like an inner compass determining what is and what is not possible for you.

Whether you believe you can, or you think you can't – you're right.

(Henry Ford, http://www.goodreads.com/quotes/978-whether-you-
think-you-can-or-you-think-you-can-t--you-re)

Beliefs are not fixed and unchangeable – although traditional therapies have often assumed they are. Prove this to yourself by thinking back to something that you used to believe but no longer do (in fact you might even be a bit embarrassed that you used to believe it). Examples could be Father Christmas, the tooth fairy etc.

What follows in this chapter is a series of self-inventory practical exercise templates to help you to break through the hold of your own limiting beliefs. It is best to do them in sequence as each builds on the previous one. Take as much time as you need to do these exercises, either on your own or guided.

Redefining negative expressions or emotions

Now that you have applied the practical examples from the previous chapter, you have learned how to break away from the significant effects of your past conditioning.

You have powerfully shifted your perspective. You have changed major acquired patterns that conditioned you to adopt reactive responses. So by now you have started to considerably open up your mind.

What remains is to sweep up a bit, and shift other residual and habitual patterns at deeper levels. You see, acquired limited beliefs and dispositional conditioning seem to insidiously take hold of us at many levels of our being.

An important area to work through next is the effect that our beliefs have on our emotional and spoken language. Our acquired limiting beliefs, and their associated inner mind chatter, as described in Parts 2 and 3, need to be softened and changed. Otherwise they will continue to have a hold on you through habitual language and the linguistic constructs that you use about yourself and in your inner mind chatter. So our language about ourselves, others and our reality will all need adjustment and alteration. This will ensure that you continue on your journey of discovery and are able to return to your authentic self.

The remaining chapters in this part also provide further important practical applications to do just this, so you can continue to free your mind, to sweep away other effects of the acquired self in its limiting patterns of conditioning.

So you now need to focus on changing the language of your residual limiting beliefs.

To do this, you begin by becoming aware of the way you use feeling language (either expressed, or as inner mind chatter) when your emotions are aroused.

Softening or moderating such emotive language helps you to gain more control over your feelings about the events, situations and circumstances you are responding to as you experience them. This is particularly useful if you tend to find yourself defaulting into an emotive negative forceful state very rapidly, or find it hard to keep control over your negative emotional states. By learning to soften or attenuate your emotive thoughts and feelings in this way, you will be able to dramatically reduce their internal impact on you and you can therefore begin to exercise more self-control and have more resources to choose how you respond. Just as with the previous practical applications, these more subtle changes will in turn proactively project into your future. Taken as a whole, they will allow you to shed the acquired controls of the past, and instead experience a new type of reality that will stimulate and activate your authentic self to become the driving force behind your being.

Have a go at reframing the following practical applications. As a starting point I have included a few reframed words. If you prefer your own word instead insert it to the right of my suggestion.

Table 1 Toning down evocative emotional words

Negative expression or emotion		Transform to…
I'm feeling…	to	I'm feeling…
Afraid	to	Uncomfortable
Angry	to	Disenchanted, slightly miffed
Anxious	to	A little concerned
Anxious	to	
Confused	to	Curious
Depressed	to	Calm before taking action
Depressed	to	Minor set back
Disappointed	to	
Disappointment	to	Underwhelmed
Disgusted	to	Surprised
Dread	to	Challenged

Negative expression or emotion		Transform to...
Embarrassed	to	Aware
Embarrassed	to	
Failure	to	Learning, stumble
Failure	to	
Fearful	to	
Frightened	to	Inquiring
Frustrated	to	
Furious	to	Passionate
Furious	to	
Hate	to	
Humiliated	to	
Hurt	to	
Impatient	to	Anticipating
Insecure	to	Unsure
Insulted	to	
Irritated	to	
Jealous	to	
Lazy	to	
Lonely	to	
Nervous	to	
Oh Sh.., Oh F...!	to	
Overlooked	to	
Overwhelmed	to	
Painful	to	
Petrified	to	
Pissed off	to	
Rejected	to	
Sad	to	
Scared	to	
Stressed	to	Slightly distracted
Stupid	to	
Terrible	to	

Adapted by Roger Terry (original source, *Awaken The Giant Within*, Anthony Robbins. Pocket Books, 2001)

Table 2 Your attitude to your experience of external reality

Limiting attitude	If you believed this, how would you get to feel?	Empowering attitude	If you believed this, how would you get to feel?
Life's a bitch and then you die		Life's a bowl of cherries	
People are out to get you		People go out of their way to help me	
Change is slow, painful and never really long term		Change is a natural inevitable process – which can be enjoyed and learned from	
Life is tough		Life is what you make it	
Add your own examples		Add your own examples	

Source: Roger Terry

Using the power of language to change habitual patterns

The statements you habitually choose and use about yourself form your attitudes and are driven by underlying beliefs. By becoming aware of your default statements, you can decide to choose to break their habitual persistence, simply by adopting different language for yourself. Using the template below reframe your own typical negative statements that you make often unconsciously into ones that feel positive and empowering instead.

Check how you would feel about the statements by contrasting the reframed empowering statement with the negative statement.

Table 3 Using the power of language to change habitual patterns

	Habitual negative statements	Reframed – empowering statements
1.		
2.		
3.		
4.		
5.		

Source: Roger Terry

Trapping and reframing your own limiting beliefs

Think of five bad or negative experiences (events, situations, circumstances) that regularly repeat themselves in your life and list them in the left-hand column. What is the underlying belief that you must have assumed to get the meaning or feeling that you got? Put this is the right-hand column.

Table 4 Trapping your own limiting beliefs

Experience	Belief

Source: Roger Terry (idea from *Unlimited Power*, Anthony Robbins. Free Press, 2003)

Think of five different aspects of your life that are positive or empowering experiences (events, states, peak moments). List them in the left-hand column. What would be the underlying belief to get this meaning or feeling? Put this in the right-hand column. What might happen if you began to believe in these statements instead of the ones in the table above?

Table 5 Reframing your own limiting beliefs

Experience	Belief

Source: Roger Terry (idea from *Unlimited Power*, Anthony Robbins. Free Press, 2003)

Turning around and re-patterning past beliefs to work for you, not against you

The last few exercises were specifically designed to help you to become more aware of your own underlying beliefs and their associated language patterns that create limitations of some sort or another. As you have now seen, your own inner mind chatter provides insight into your particular limiting belief systems. These patterns have a hold on your emotional language, and your attitudes. They also form the habitual statements you use to describe your own map of the world around you, and so they colour how you experience your own internal and external reality. In the above exercises you also got used to how to reframe your language. The idea behind this is to help you to become aware of and to understand the limiting and negative effect your spoken self-talk and inner chatter has on you and the way you perceive the world around you. How you talk to yourself and to others has a dramatic effect on your reality both internally and externally. The majority of inner self-talk seems on the surface harmless enough. It is often expressed as spontaneous phrases that slip off the tongue. They are everyday, simple, short statements and usually only four or five words long. Yet, when you become more aware of them, you might begin to realise that their habitual frequency and repeating nature have some kind of hypnotising power over you. Such statements come loaded with intonation and emotionality. They are not innocuous as you might have previously thought.

Negative or limiting inner mind chatter always works against you, not for you. Your associated thoughts narrow down your options. This is because, neurologically, the underlying language used in your consciousness continues to automatically produce internal representations that match the words you use due to your mind–brain–body connection. Using words like 'pretty' versus 'ugly' or 'intelligent' versus 'stupid' for example, will produce completely different internal representations and different pathways, mechanisms and responses. These representations correspondingly have unique patterns of neurological and emotional mind–brain–body responses.

Such inner language therefore truly is your window into the way you respond and react to the world around you. It is a map of your internal world, which leaks out as being orally expressed thought representations of your underlying belief systems.

Many people think that their inner language is harmless enough – after all don't we all do it? It's just a thought, isn't it? It is not: thoughts have power and they ultimately influence the external reality that you perceive and therefore experience. What you think actually does shape your experiences and your reality in your life.

Now that you have an appreciation of the inner self-talk that chatters away in your mind, and its power and influence over you and how you emotionally feel, I will show you how to change it. By updating your inner habitual limiting statements and the language that you use you can break the operation of the underlying limiting belief system, as the neurological pathways re-establish in different ways.

This is a very subtle but powerful process as it allows your inner language to work for you, rather than against you. Also, even more subtly, the more you spend time on changing your inner self-talk and language patterns the more it gradually allows you to open an inner door that gains you more access to your true authentic self.

Practical application – changing a limiting belief into an affirmation

Table 6 Practical application – changing a limiting belief into an affirmation

Limiting belief statements: 1. 2. 3. Choose one to reframe **Reframed statements…** Workings….   Final statement…   **Two reinforcing actions…** 1.   2.

From the previous exercises, and using the box above or your self-inventory journal, note down one, two or three limiting beliefs that are holding you back. The premise is that if you change these they would make a significant difference to your life. As you have completed the previous exercises these should now come more easily to mind as your thinking will have become used to the context. For some examples of typical real limiting beliefs, refer back to the limiting beliefs chapter (Chapter 14) and the inner mind chatter chapter (Chapter 19).

Typical elements of limiting beliefs

Global beliefs:

- I am
- People are
- Life is
- I can't
- People should
- People shouldn't
- The world is
- Men are
- Women are
- Americans are
- Old people are
- Teenagers are
- Organisations are
- Change is
- The future

If, then rules:

- If you trust people, then they take advantage of you.
- If I even look at a biscuit, then I put on weight.
- If you want to make it in this company, then you have to be tough.
- If I can't get my own way, then I must get angry.
- If you loved me, then you'd understand what I need without me having to tell you.

Work on your own, or guided if you prefer, choosing one of the limiting beliefs you have listed in Table 6.

A working example for you as a guideline

> People never like me and don't want to be around me because they find me awkward, prickly and difficult.
> Or
> All people can't be trusted and are dangerous.

Change this to a positive statement

As a first step, take that belief and, purely as a grammatical or linguistic exercise, take out all the negative words, such as can't, won't, need to, have to, must do, ought to, etc. or, if necessary, simply replace these with a positive modal operator instead.

So changing the grammar from negative to positive becomes…

> People like me and want to be around me because…
> Or
> All people can be trusted and are…

If any of the descriptive words in your modified statement have negative connotations, then replace these as well with positive ones. For example awkward, prickly and difficult might be replaced with words like 'easy' or 'relaxed' instead. Also reword the statement so it still makes overall sense as a sentence.

In my working example, this becomes…

> People like me and want to be around me… because they find me easy to be with.
> Or
> All people can be trusted… and are safe.

Make final adjustments

Adjust it so that it feels right to you: shorten or simply change the sentence so you feel it is easier to say and is more powerful (less is often more). Usually the shorter it is the easier it becomes to believe for many people. For example, the above could be shortened to become simply…

People like me and want to be around me.
Or
People can be trusted.

Compare limiting statement to reframed statement

Now, in your mind compare your own new empowering statement to the original limiting belief statement in Table 6 and repeat the new empowering statement to yourself…

People never like me and don't want to be around me because they find me awkward, prickly and difficult.
Compared to…
People like me and want to be around me.
Or
All people can't be trusted and are dangerous.
Compared to…
People can be trusted.

Without making a judgement just yet about the new empowering statement, as to whether you believe it or not, simply compare the effect each statement has on you neurologically and emotionally. Spend a few moments to reflect and imagine what pictures, sounds, feelings and sensations each of these produce. As you play these statements through your mind one at a time, you should start to notice that, representationally, they produce completely different images, sounds and feelings inside you. This is the representational power of words. Different words have very different emotive effects on us. This means that neurologically they are very different.

Add bridging language to overcome resistance and create acceptance

The next step is to play this new empowering statement in your mind and weigh it up.

Is this new empowering statement believable and acceptable to you, or does your unconscious disbelieve it, or reject it in some way? If it is satisfactory then skip the next element.

Sometimes when I help people do this for themselves, they report that the new empowering belief is what they certainly would want and desire. However, occasionally they may report it seems a step too far for them to get to. That it sometimes feels too big a jump from the original limiting belief to the new empowering statement. So, to bridge the belief gap, I have found it useful and sometimes important to provide some starting point, as well as some intermediate language, to bridge the gap and make the jump from the original limiting belief to the new empowering statement.

Here's an example of what I mean by this bridging language…

People like me and want to be around me.
Could be prefixed with…
I am learning that… people like me and want to be around me.
Or
Every day in every way I get better and better at accepting that… people like me and want to be around me.
Or
All people can't be trusted and are dangerous.
This became…
People can be trusted.
It could be prefixed and additionally bridged with…
Even though I believe that… all people can't be trusted and are dangerous… I am (getting better at) learning that… people can be trusted.
(A further option was placed in brackets.)

I have found from experience that this step is the difference that makes all the difference. It provides the impetus for success and often makes the new empowering statement stick.

These softening prefixes and bridging additions seem to immediately take away any resistance to the new empowering statement. Instead it makes it possible for people to believe themselves more when the new empowering statement is softened in such ways.

The reason why this seems to work so well, in my experience, is that the new empowering internal language must first be accepted by the conscious and unconscious minds. Once the statement is acceptable, there will be little or no conscious or unconscious resistance to the change, then you have to buy in to it. So the new empowering statement becomes easily accepted. My reckoning is that this is because to accept and believe a new statement instead of the original limiting belief requires the power of your imagination. Your imagination also provides the necessary psychic energy that is required for it to be accepted, to replace and supersede the original limiting belief.

Repeat out loud to yourself until you sense something shifting

The penultimate step is to simply repeat this new empowering statement out loud around a dozen times or so. This is for several reasons.

This will be the very first time you have ever said this new empowering statement.

So hearing yourself saying this to yourself reinforces its existence in your mind–brain–body and begins to take a neurological effect. During the repetition, it starts as an awkward feeling, and the more you say it the easier the statement begins to sit within you. Eventually, after some further fine-tuning it will feel comfortable and right with you and you can accept it. This creates a breakthrough.

This final new reframed statement in its empowering form could then be used in the earlier practical exercise – setting a new heading, based on the choice point at the end of Chapter 23.

The other thing that you will notice is more subtle, and this is that your own demeanour shifts, that is to say, your emotional body state shifts and associated sensations change in your body as well. For example, taking note of any change in emotion will affect the way you feel about yourself and will also reflect in your thoughts. Other shifts are more delicate, such as becoming aware of a sudden rush or a flush, or temperature shift, a different feeling in your body, a sudden flutter, or judder, a leaning back, breathing changes, a feeling of being lighter, happier, joyful or energetic perhaps (see Chapter 8). These are all indications that you are returning to your true authentic self.

Before this practical exercise, this statement was a real limiting belief, which had a right to exist in you, because you acquired it. Until now it has never been changed. It has operated in you since you acquired it.

Your mind–brain was able to acquire the limiting belief in the first place, often through repetition, and using the brain's plasticity. So, in the same way, by using repetition, you are now able to learn to accept the new empowering statement instead of the old limiting pattern, again through the same brain mechanism that created the limiting belief. Although this time you are accelerating the process by instilling it consciously.

The original limiting belief was beginning to create resistance within you, otherwise you wouldn't be wanting to change its effect on you. In accepting the new empowering statement instead, over the original limiting belief, you have simply turned the language of the limiting belief around. It now works for you, rather than against you. This is important and subtle. What

I mean is that psychologically you haven't 'rejected' the limiting belief and said that it is all wrong. Remember that even your acquired limiting beliefs had a right to exist. Instead, what you have done is taken the limiting belief and 'updated' it by rewording its context. You have turned it around, that is all. It is still, in its basic context, the same statement. It now simply works for you and not against you. As I said, this is subtle and critically important.

Add two actions to reinforce it as a habit

The final step is to consider and write down in your journal or in the above template two practical actions that will help you to continue to reinforce this empowering statement as a new behaviour and habit into your neurology over the next two weeks or so.

Some common examples are to write down the empowering statement, put it on the mirror and repeat it every morning and evening.

Visualise the outcome.
Put it on your vision board. (See Chapter 33.)
Draw the outcome as something you desire.
Inform your best friend so that you can commit to them, and they commit to keeping you on track.
Screen savers, poems and verses are other examples.

Practical application...

See Chapter 27, 'A practical anchoring application to feel good about yourself', to anchor this new resourceful empowering statement about yourself.

A short real example...

I have had considerable success teaching this technique when I present on this topic to larger groups of around 100 or so people. It works really well doing this exercise in that type of group atmosphere. The technique is executed initially as each individual working on their own to reframe the belief, in exactly the same way you have done using the above. The only difference I add to this with a group is to do the repetition of the empowering statement and action/commitment part by working in pairs in a guided way.

I ask the whole group, as pairs, to stand up and do this all together inter-actively. Firstly they quickly introduce themselves to each other and use each other's name. Within their pairs they work very quickly together: one acting as the guide, and the other working on their reframed empowering statement. They swap roles after a couple of minutes and repeat the same exercise.

I also ask the guide to smile and nod as their partner simply says the empowering statement out loud back to the guide. The guide then says, 'Thank you, can you repeat that please?', and their partner repeats the same empowering statement again. They continue to repeat this process, over and over, getting faster and faster until the guide believes them. The process ends by the guide spotting some sort of a shift in the other's demeanour.

The whole exercise, done rapidly this way as a group and simultaneously by each individual pair, creates a huge amount of energy that contributes to its success. Furthermore, doing the process in pairs also means that rapport and commitment is symbiotically created between them. The guide smiling and nodding also reinforces to the other the belief that they are okay and on the right track, which encourages acceptance for them. So this process works, whether done as an individual or with a guide. Group work is not a prerequisite for its success at all. I merely mention it to hopefully convince you that the process works. If you can get results by doing it in a group and people get breakthroughs this way, which is hard, then you can also more easily succeed doing the same thing either individually or guided.

Many people also tell me that what made the difference for them was the bridging statements that made the empowering statement believable, so that they were then able to accept it readily after the repetition process.

The energy created in this way often produces quick breakthroughs and some people experience this for themselves in dramatic ways.

One of the other factors that helps to create success doing this in pairs or in a group situation is that the guide is asked to spot some sort of shift and change in the other's demeanour. This, too, is an important part of the change and easily applied in guided pairs. If you work on your own here instead, you need to become aware for yourself of the internal state shift and associated sensations that change. Again I add this to help convince you of the success of this practical exercise.

Guides helping people to shift limiting beliefs in this way, and doing this exercise notice many changes of demeanour…

Eyes change, crying, eyes glisten or sparkle, pupils dilate…
Eyebrows raise, skin tone changes, facial features soften…
Hand and arm movements become fluid.
Statements become more fluid and easy.
Leaning back, or sudden head movement.
Shoulders rolling or going backwards.
People raising themselves to the balls of their feet and rocking back and forth.
Smiling or breaking out in laughter.
Stance becomes confident and more centred.

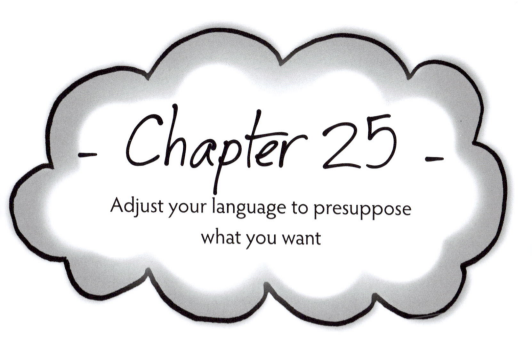

- Chapter 25 -

Adjust your language to presuppose what you want

In the last chapter we looked at how to change the language of acquired limiting beliefs and modify associated inner mind chatter. You now understand the hold that negative and limiting language structures, caused by underlying belief systems, have on you. That these structures have a huge influence over your mind–brain–body via neurological and emotional body states. They also affect your thoughts and feelings about yourself. You now also understand how these constructs shape your inner and outer reality and ultimately your life experience.

In this chapter I would like to turn your attention to the way you use everyday language. As we have already seen, inner mind chatter language has considerable power. This is not only true of the language of any belief system but also true for your everyday language as well. The language we choose, whether in thought or in oral expression, focuses our attention, and therefore sets up our patterns of reality. What I mean by this is that all our thoughts are powerful means by which we constantly form, organise and co-create our reality every moment of our lives.

Forms of acquired self always use ineffective language patterns. They are based on getting away from what you don't want. *Therefore it is far more effective that the language you choose to use always states what you want, rather than what you don't want.*

The interesting thing about our mind–brain connection is that the brain cannot distinguish between what you want and what you don't want. To it, it is the same thing. If you focus on what you don't want, then your attention is focused on exactly that: what you don't want. As you are therefore attending to that type of thought pattern your brain is effectively understanding this as a direct command and sets up corresponding patterns that look for evidence of this, and the next moment's predictions are selected on this basis.

As we have already seen, the underlying mechanics of consciousness behind this is the mind–brain–body's miraculous ability to produce millions of internal representations of every moment. As we have already stated, this is exactly the same for the language we choose. These visual, auditory and kinaesthetic pieces of sensory information are used by your consciousness via your mind–brain–body to build up a coherent internal reality that represents external reality in a sensory way. Your body then amplifies these as emotional body sensations to inform our higher level consciousness via your thought structures. So focusing your attention on what you want or what you don't want results in you getting exactly that. The phrase, 'Be careful what you wish for' holds true for what your thought patterns are. The way you use your thoughts bends the reality you end up experiencing to give you what your thoughts have been tuned to. I use the term 'presupposition' to describe deliberately choosing language that works for us, or not. In other words, what is presupposed is what we end up getting.

So for example…

Table 7 Effective versus ineffective presuppositions

Ineffective presuppositions	Effective presuppositions
I don't get on with her	She's different to me
He makes me angry every time I see him	His values are different to mine
I make every effort to try to avoid this or that happening	I want to learn how to overcome this

Ineffective presuppositions	Effective presuppositions
I need to be careful that I don't fail here	What will I need to do to succeed here
I am so nervous, or am really worried about this or that	I want to be calm and relaxed and trust that it will work out okay
You have to take life seriously and always be responsible	Enjoy life as it comes; I will know what to do when I need to
I don't want this to fail	I want to learn how to do this well and succeed
Don't get this wrong again	I wonder what I will learn
This is hard and difficult	The more I do this the easier this will become and the better I'll be at it
It's not my fault	Be open to learn
I'm not sure. I won't be able to do this	I want to get the hang of this
You need to take control otherwise it'll fail	I want to hold this loosely enough to allow it to work

All these language patterns are examples of presupposed linguistic choices that will end up with you getting a result one way or another: more of what you don't want, or alternatively what you do want instead, every time. So how do we tune our thoughts to be deliberate so we get what we want and not what we don't want?

What you presuppose in your thoughts and what you verbalise has power. What you presuppose is a precondition of possibility. Whatever you presuppose sets up your assumptions as to how to use your attention, which in turn drives your thoughts. Your thoughts direct your conscious mind and ego to look out for this in the external world. What you presuppose implies you are conditionally seeking out responses in external reality that match, cohere with or make necessary that particular internally preconditioned thought. Presuppositions are therefore the assumptions that lie behind any language we are choosing. They are, however, subtle and not always apparent. They not only affect you, but also affect any receiver or listener too, even if that was not intended by you the communicator. This is because our unconscious minds are highly tuned to the effect of language and nuance on our whole being. Our unconscious picks up all information, even if you are consciously unaware of it.

Practical examples

Some words to watch out for are – 'if', 'try', and 'but' and their alternatives.

Table 8 If, try, but results

Word	Statement	Probable result
If	The use of 'if' presupposes that you have a choice (if–then). So you should only use it when you mean to be offering someone a choice	
	'If you can arrange a meeting for 10:00 am…'	The meeting doesn't take place – 'I couldn't arrange it.'
Try	The use of 'try' presupposes failure. So only use it where you want to increase the chances of someone not being able to do something	
	'Try to get it done by Friday.'	'Yes, I gave it a try, but I didn't finish it on time.'
But	The effect of 'but' is to negate the previous statement. So be careful to use it correctly, because when you use it incorrectly the effect is to build resistance up in the listener	
	'Yes, we have considered your idea, but we are going to …'	'They ignored my idea.'

Source: Roger Terry.

Setting up your mindset and attitude

In the 1970s Richard Bandler and John Grinder invented a holistic approach to personal development, betterment and human success they called neuro-linguistic programming (NLP). At the time it formed a ground-breaking new way of being, based on their studies of human excellence, and these philosophies continue to be taught and applied today. Grinder, a linguist, understood the power of what we presuppose in language and Bandler was interested in how we affect reality. So together Grinder and Bandler developed these language constructs further and founded a whole new approach to presuppositions. As a consequence, underpinning NLP is a series of ready-made predefined presuppositions (a sort of set of resourceful beliefs). These sets of presuppositions were strategies used by successful people and are principles they adopted to have the right mindset and attitude to succeed.

Grinder and Bandler purposefully used them as everyday tools that anyone could adopt and use as a basis to influence and improve peoples' reality. Their presupposition about these predefined presuppositions is that by following the sentiment behind these will allow you to take a more resourceful attitude to the world, towards others and to personal development. They are called 'presuppositions' because by adopting one or more of these statements you presuppose them to work out for you. There is no claim that any of these NLP presuppositions are true, that's not necessary. What is important, however, is to simply try them out, and act as if you believe or pretend (or literally presuppose) that they are true. They do not have to be believed, but simply applied as a principle as a starting point. In this way you influence appropriate sectors or reality for yourself and those around you. By practising doing so, you allow the corresponding reality the statements presuppose to unfold into existence, simply because you have presupposed it to be so.

Moving away from the strategies of the acquired self and returning to your authentic self is not about using fixed ways of doing things. It is about seeing things with new eyes, and new perspectives, being flexible and willing to experiment and be open to different and novel choices of 'trying on' other ways of thinking and behaving. In this way you learn to develop greater freedom, more choices and opportunities for yourself.

As an experiment for yourself, commit to applying two or three of the following predefined presuppositions in your interactions with others and notice what happens as you use them more and more.

Their practical application works very well. Test them out, as attitudes or principles for your life as a starting point. Try them on like a piece of new clothing for a while, and see how they change your reactions to the world around you. Again you don't have to believe them, merely act as if they are true and notice the difference they start to practically make in your life and how they shift your reality.

There are many of these predefined presuppositions found in NLP; however, here are some of the most common ones and some others that I have found to be most useful.

1. The person with the most flexible behaviour will control the outcome of an interaction or situation.
2. Respect other people's model of the world.

3. Different people have different maps of the world. Some maps are, however, better than others.
4. Every behaviour has a positive intention.
5. There is no failure, only feedback.
6. You are in charge of your mind and therefore of your results.
7. It is better to increase your number of choices.
8. If what you are doing isn't working, *do something different*.
9. Resistance in a client is a sign of lack of rapport.
10. There are no unresourceful people only unresourceful states (and we can always change states).
11. People have all the internal resources they need in whatever context.
12. A person's behaviour is not who they are (it is contextual and is not about their self or identity).
13. People make the best choice they can at the time.
14. People work perfectly.
15. The meaning of the communication is not simply what you intend, but also the response you get.
16. You already have all the resources you need to achieve what you want.

For me, I have tried and subsequently adopted many of these presuppositions and tested them over a number of years. I have used them as working strategies and attitudes in my own life, and when interacting with others. These presuppositions certainly created shifts that made all the difference for me. When I work with these sorts of predefined presuppositions with other people, they too have found them useful to break old judgements and ways of being. Having trained in NLP techniques and taught them to hundreds of people over many years now, many people I have personally taught experience profound personal break-throughs from them, and are able to use them in highly effective ways to enable them to return to their authentic selves.

Getting what you want begins with what you presuppose

These predefined presuppositions are certainly a useful starting point to re-pattern your attitudes. However, the real practical application of using the power of presuppositions ultimately comes when you start to presuppose your own constructs that help you to achieve your own specific outcomes.

Whatever internal language you use about yourself and your attitudes to life presupposes your outcomes and sets up your successes, or not. It also requires a disciplined approach to resetting your mindset and attitude. In the section on mindset above, and the ineffective and effective presupposition comparative examples…

Whatever we presuppose will get you either what you want, or don't want.

Using the right internal language to presuppose the right things in your mind begins the process that drives you towards your own successful results.

Start to become aware of and monitor your own use of the language you use about yourself and the everyday circumstances and situations you find yourself in. This is important because it will help you to understand your assumptions about who you are, what you are about, and ultimately what you want, and also what happens to you. All these things begin to be set up by what you are assuming about yourself: what you believe is possible or impossible, what you fear and avoid or what you learn about courage from making mistakes.

This is how your real reality creates itself. You see, what you presuppose and assume either continues to support the strategies of your acquired self or has the power to begin to return you to your true authentic self. At the highest level, this is the ultimate principle of choice.

In the next chapter we take the presupposition principle further.

- Chapter 26 -

Letting go of control, critical judgement and anxiety

Letting go of control; holding things loosely

In the last chapter or two we have explored how to break the patterns of the acquired self using practical applications. This chapter will explain how to break limiting beliefs and patterns of the past and to move towards a new future. In the last chapter we discussed how to reframe language patterns and the principles of using presuppositions to get more of what you want instead of what you don't want. The next two chapters conclude Part 4 by breaking the attitudinal patterns of the acquired self; that completes a set of personal change strategies. If you use these in succession, they will progressively and successfully break you free from the grip of your conditioning and your acquired self. Part 5, the final part of this book, later examines practical applications that return you to your true authentic self.

The acquired self builds up its survival and protection strategies through principles of control and judgement. These are coping strategies that gradually built up layer by layer, one acquired strategy on top of another to form our conditioning. Many of these 'presuppose' you being in control and 'presuppose' judgements of one kind or another. Underlying these can often be states of anxiety.

From my experience, being 'in control' becomes an insidious habit. People happily confess that they are 'control freaks'. For some it is viewed as a sort of pinnacle of excellence. From my experience I believe that this is a distorted and false view. I believe that to return to your true authentic self you first have to master the right to let go of control and judgement. Over-control and hyper states of worry or anxiety are the hallmarks of the acquired self. As we have seen, they take advantage of and distort conscious mind and egotistical principles and their 'sticky' adherence to familiarity, what is known, and to prior experience.

Control, judgement and underlying states of worry or anxiety stem from the acquired self. They are derived from having to rely on what is already known and experienced by you. They require the exclusive use of familiar and highly honed strategies constructed from your (re-presented) internal representations that have a predefined reality. Ultimately, control and judgement are based on ways of mastering states of anxiety and worry. These, as we have already pointed out, are underpinned by the primary emotions of fear, threat, avoidance and protection. They are intended to allow you to get what you want, because they are really based on not getting what you don't want. To ensure that you get results, these strategies require you to hold tightly and control by force everything you want to achieve, and through sheer willpower you end up having to force and 'wrench' the things you want into existence to attain the goals and objectives you have set yourself. You do this because you know them to be hard and difficult to achieve. So to get what you want, using this approach, you know you will have to lever a huge amount of your energy to make it happen.

Neurologically, as we now know, these states of control are acquired attitudes we adopt, and in themselves are representationally and dispositionally based. They make up our limiting beliefs. So this means, like all states of mind, they produce particular emotional body states. These mindsets are inclined to tighten and stiffen body posture and create a physical and mental rigidity. Fist clenches and nervous or fidgety hand movements are common outward physiological signs, as is facial strain, such as 'hard' eyes that have been conditioned to look out for justifying and controlling aspects of experience. A clenched jaw and grinding teeth are also common outward signs. The body becomes conditioned to such physiological ways and eventually resets as an acquired baseline state. Extreme states of prolonged anxiety and worry turn into hyper-alert sensitivities, where physiological responses are quickly and easily triggered.

You are also aware of the laws of importance and reverse effect (discussed earlier in Part 1) – that is, the more you try and the more you want it, then the more control you have to apply to win over the opposing forces in order to make it happen your way. To achieve success in this way, you know it requires conscious willpower and huge mental effort to have it your way. However, as we saw in Part 3 (with the cycle of grief), success in this way comes at a cost and is extremely fragile and temporary.

The principle of control and judgement requires you to:

Fight for the right to deserve your place under the sun.

When you are young this strategy might work for you, but only for a while. The consequence is that this achievement came only through control and effort.

Instead, along the way you might have learned different things; you may have learned to achieve things by letting go and holding things loosely. However, later, as you mature, your available energy is naturally meant to be diverted to other parts of you. The authentic self relies on you going beyond these acquired strategies. You need to learn to develop the discipline to opening your mind to presupposing different choices.

Your authentic self trusts and depends more on unconscious mind principles to determine its responses to what occurs in reality. It relies less on what is familiar, already known and re-represented. Instead it learns to use what is possible, what is emerging and unfolding. What potential there might be and what other options or different approaches might be available. For example, letting go, holding things loosely and becoming accepting of your situation are more an unconscious mind style and strategy for success. When things don't turn out your way, the key principle of the authentic self is to have the discipline to evaluate this from an accepting perspective and by remaining curious and flexible.

In contrast to the acquired self above, the principle of the authentic self of letting go merely assumes that:

The world takes care of me, and things come to me because of this.

Practical application...

Below are a few presuppositional principles that I have developed to help you to understand how to let go of your own acquired control and hold things more loosely. They are very effective.

Remember, this requires a whole different way of being. Living by these principles requires discipline, but it is rewarding and liberating.

With new eyes, based on your new understanding of what you have learned from this book so far, start to practically apply these either directly as they are, or alternatively develop different ones that are based on these, but work for you.

They require you to use them regularly and deliberately whenever you are planning and setting up your day, or embarking on anything new, and when you are waiting for events to come your way. They are useful when you apply them to work situations as well as in general life.

In your self-inventory journal, notice what changes and what is different in your life when you experience letting go, holding things loosely and accepting rather than judging.

1. Always begin new endeavours with presupposing the outcomes you want.
2. Never worry about what you don't want, instead always presuppose the outcome you do want and focus your thought energies on it.
3. Allow reality to shape itself based on what you presuppose as a starting point. And watch as it manifests.
4. Presuppose a positive outcome and success, and see where this goes. Likewise never focus on what could go wrong, because it then will.
5. If things go wrong, then accept this. Focus your attention on the patterns and potential learnings for the next time.
6. If something doesn't work out, or you make a mistake, then this is okay; learn to accept it and let go of it.
7. If things work out differently to what you presupposed, then wonder: what did I learn and was it meant to be; what do I need to presuppose instead?
8. Let go of your need to control. Let things shape up the way they are meant to and watch them unfold in front of you as they do, then act. By all means, though, guide them gently.

9. Look out for synchronicity and serendipity by wondering what might happen next.
10. Always expect new things, you don't yet know about, to come your way and feel excited about this. Watch for these to manifest.
11. Always expect things to work out the way they are meant to be.
12. Never act out of fear or anxiety. Don't avoid and try to protect. Use courage and be brave and be curious instead.
13. If you are criticised or judged then be open to learning. Never be defensive, but be open-minded. That doesn't mean you have to agree, just be open to listening.
14. Letting go of love gently (not holding it tightly in other words) allows love to remain and to constantly return to you. And it will.
15. In the stillness we can participate. In the silence we can hear and in the dark night, see. Empty yourself to be filled.
16. When you do not know what to do, then allow time for the right solution to find you, to come to you, and look out for it and expect it to arrive.
17. Choose to accept and not to judge, forgive not hold a grudge.
18. Never attack, justify or defend unless you have to. There is power in allowing the moment to be.
19. Never judge or hold grudges about others; learn to accept what happens to you in spite of the actions of others; their actions do not have to affect you.
20. Be graceful not spiteful.
21. Money and riches are not desires in themselves, rather they come to you because of the help and benefit you give to others and for this you are rewarded.

Accept, don't be critical and judge

States of inner anxiety and worry can often affect the way we think about and judge ourselves, often extremely critically. We therefore habitually impose self-limitations by berating ourselves. However, these in turn adversely affect our interpersonal relationships and interactions with others, as well as our view of ourselves. So we end up criticising and judging ourselves and judging others around us by our own standards.

For example…

She always gets angry with me.
Typical – he has messed this or that up, as always.
Gosh he looks really… ugly, weak, pathetic, a rough sort, idiotic.
She never stops talking about herself.
That family is all bad sorts, never mix with them.
They are common and crass, don't associate with them.
She's not very clever or pretty, don't be seen with her.
He's really fat and smells, don't sit next to him.
Nobody likes him/her, therefore don't associate with them.
She looks mental, whatever you do don't give her any eye contact.
This person smiled at me, so they must want something.
Don't look at others, otherwise they might want to engage with you.
I'm… too stupid, too ugly… too common to talk to them.
They're better than me, so I don't like them.
I'm better than you.
Other people make me angry if they are not like me.

All these acquired critical judging thought patterns lead to limiting yourself and your reality. Making mindset judgements allows them to neurologically re-present themselves as adverse, emotional mind–body states that then also affect you physiologically. Like states of control, longer term they re-pattern your baseline state and end up working against you. Furthermore, you become what you think, and others can then pick this up from your demeanour.

For example, have you ever come across a person that just simply appears to be an angry person on a bus or train or in a queue? You might never have talked to them to confirm this or witnessed any angry actions from them; however, you can just tell. So it may be that this is what that person is giving off, and/or it might be your own judgement of that person. So when that person looks at you they detect your disapproving nature. And then begin to wonder about you too. So be careful how you judge. It is interesting to wonder how that person's demeanour may change towards you if you were to hold a different and more benevolent impression and assumption of them. So these conscious and unconscious effects are all driven by what we consciously presuppose.

When you criticise and judge others, then they too will start to become consciously or unconsciously aware that you are adversely judging them and will either avoid you or behave in corresponding ways to you. As such interactions become more unsatisfactory, so the noose of judgement tightens around you even more.

To break these presuppositional judgement and control patterns is extremely beneficial. You simply have to consciously learn to change the maps in your mind by using your present point of power, which we discussed earlier, and choose to become more accepting, rather than judging. By doing this you generate more resourceful maps by which to direct your mind. As part of this change, you also need to become conscious of your inner mind chatter and begin to direct your mind–brain to learn different, more accepting language about yourself and about others. You need to build into your new maps presupposing accepting patterns, such as you are okay and so are others.

Practical application – simple acts of kindness when engaging with others

Some easy practical applications are simply to regularly practise engaging with other people in more accepting ways. Being purposefully and consciously graceful and kind in your thoughts about others changes your internal paradigms.

As you smile at others, so others will smile back at you.

Practise regularly talking and engaging with others whenever you find yourself with a little time, such as in the supermarket queue, waiting for a train, while you are on a train or plane, etc. Learn to be curious about others and strike up conversations with whomever you come across. If you presuppose genuine interest and curiosity and an overall friendly nature then you'll be amazed at how good it makes you feel and makes others feel, too, during your interactions. In this way you learn to create internal maps that automatically generate resourceful internal representations that work for you. The more you intend these and presuppose these, then neurologically the more they will wire up for you and become part of your neural real estate.

Remember the tale of A Christmas Carol and the turnaround of Scrooge from being a grumpy old miser, to a generous man full of joy and merriment. This is a fantastic tale of overcoming the inevitable consequences of the acquired self and embracing the positive reality created by the authentic self. Both sectors of reality existed as optional possibilities and each would lead to very different future realities. Scrooge had to choose, and ghosts of the past, present and future helped him to make that choice point.

If you presuppose you like people and are interested in them, then they will correspondingly like you and be interested in you.

Compliment others, and they too will compliment you. Also perform random acts of simple kindness like opening the door for someone, buying a stranger in the queue behind you a coffee or preparing a small creative gift for a guest. You will be amazed at how good feelings are hugely contagious.

Treat others with acceptance and grace, and kindness and they will do the same for you.

The more real you are with others the more real they will notice you to be and in return be real with you.

Accepting yourself and others has an amazing ability to make you feel really good about yourself and others good about themselves too.

Neurologically, feeling good about yourself generates very resourceful maps that create corresponding emotional mind–body states. Regular practice of the above practical examples will help your brain to learn to generate new maps and patterns that will allow you to habitually change your mind to become more accepting and less judging. Your physiology and mindset will also let go and loosen up.

The state of grace in human beings has power and strength that goes far beyond controlling and judging attitudes and is beautiful to behold.

Develop your sense of gratitude – a practical exercise

This is a simple and powerful approach to changing your thought paradigms and the way you think about yourself and others.

Simply enjoy spending a little private time to relax and take these moments to reflect on what has happened in your life up until now that you can be grateful for.

Even in the less good times, you can still take time and learn something from every situation that makes you grateful. Even if it was simply learning about something that you don't want to repeat. You can be grateful that time has passed, and how it has changed you for the better.

For situations that you really regret or are embarrassed about, or have feared, even these have something you can see from the perspective of gratitude.

It is amazing how this simple reflective approach can change your mindset, mood and attitude to life.

As you get better at this, you can become grateful for the situations, people and things that you have experienced or met this week, yesterday, today.

You can be grateful for learnings, family, lovers, friends.

Do this often as you can. Try to get into the habit of doing it everyday. It doesn't take long, and easily changes your mood and mindset regarding yourself and your life situation.

Another interesting take on gratitude is to apply it even to people you don't like or who you find difficult. After a short while, notice the changes that occur in that relationship. Simply by changing your attitude towards somebody else you can change the way they respond to you in the future, and you to them. Try it and see.

The idea of forgiveness – and being the bigger person

Jesus, in the New Testament, talked a lot about forgiveness and its tremendous power for transformation in relationships.

He talked about walking a mile with the person who is taking you to court, to resolve it before the issue gets to legalities. He talked about loving and forgiving your enemies, and praying for them too. He also talked about letting go of the negative power of holding grudges against others: 'As you judge others, so you too will be judged.'

I believe that these statements were originally intended and made for the good of all humankind, not just confined to people who practise this or that religious persuasion. Learning to forgive others shouldn't be a religious concept only, as gratitude has an amazing releasing power for all humanity.

Also just having the courage to apologise to somebody that you have fallen out with can release you both from its negative hold. Some people find this too hard to accept; however, you don't have to apologise for being wrong or that it was your fault, because it might not have been. The simple act of confronting it though, and simply saying: 'I'm sorry we have fallen out with one another over this issue, let's see if we can resolve it.' Regardless of whose fault it is, or who's to blame, this simple statement has transforming and generative significance. If after you have said this, however, the other person doesn't accept it, then that's okay too. This is because you have in effect forgiven them, and you have therefore released yourself from that person. If they still choose to carry a grudge, then that is their 'monkey' to bear on their back. It is no longer yours, and you can move on if you so wish. But don't be tempted to pick up the grudge again if they refuse your peace offer, because that just puts you back at square one.

The key to forgiveness is far from who's right or wrong, but instead is about allowing the issue to dissipate while maintaining regard for your relationship and being willing for it to be restored. I believe that even the most difficult situations that may have transferred across generations can be healed in this simple way.

Ideas of forgiveness really do loosen holds and break patterns of acquired conditioning that are unnecessary to bear. But many people choose otherwise. (Back to the example of Scrooge and *A Christmas Carol.*) To do this takes courage and at the same time opens your mind to being more open-hearted and open-minded. It takes courage and bravery to be the bigger person. The idea of forgiveness comes from the heart of the true authentic self. In this it is truly majestic.

Forgiveness and gratitude are two notions that truly make you feel good about yourself, and again this is evidence of your true authentic self shining through in difficult circumstances. The authentic self always leads to healing and feeling good about yourself, even in difficult circumstances.

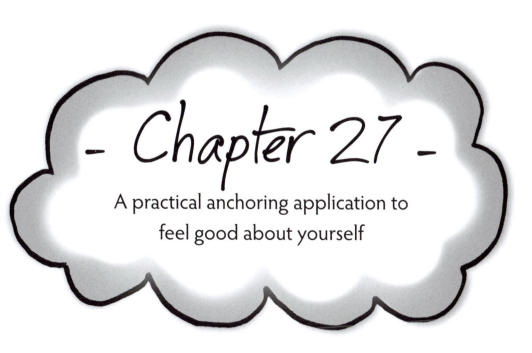

- Chapter 27 -

A practical anchoring application to feel good about yourself

Here's a small anchoring exercise to help you to recall at will a resourceful state.

Choose one or more of the options below, or find a time when you have experienced something similar and positive and powerful (these are all based on the resourceful changes you have read about in Part 4).

Remember back to…

A time when you felt proactive and achieved something significant because of it.

A time when you overcame something that seemed impossible, and achieved it.

A time when you learned to change your past that was limiting you in some way, and you were able to move forward and change your future.

A time when you had been graceful with another person.

A time when you had a great conversation with someone, which made you both feel really good about yourselves.

A time when you let go of controlling the outcome of something, and instead you just let it work itself out and unfold in front of you, and it sorted itself out really well.

A time when you held something loosely and it worked out, because you didn't control it.

The following instructions might feel illogical; however, this is the way your internal coding, used by your brain, translates all external experience into a mirrored internal representation version of that reality. It may feel unfamiliar simply because this technique uses the more story-based approach of your right brain by accessing the power of episodic and personal memory. If this is so for you, then it could be that you are more used to using the semantic impersonal factual-based memory constructs of your left brain. We discussed these types of memory in Part 2, and there I alluded to the transformational and generative power of using episodic memory to create change. Your right brain is a grand master at using these approaches to create change and return you to your authentic self.

Instructions to recall a state of mind...

Remember a time when... fill in with one of the statements above. (You can also use this approach to anchor something new you desire to become part of you.)

Spend a moment or two bringing a related memory back into your mind (or imagine it if it is something new for you).

Allow it to form fully in your mind. What you are doing with the following instructions is to access the way your mind–brain–body creates this experience via internal representations, which are the inner codings of all your experiences. The interesting thing is that through using episodic memory these representations start to rebuild the story behind the associated memory being recalled. You need to be in a relaxed and quiet state of mind to do this well.

In your mind's eye... what do you see as a visual representation? See it with as much full colour as you can, and as life size or larger if possible, right in front of you now. Imagine it as if you are seeing it again, re-experiencing it through your own eyes, as if you are there right now, and fully associate with it. If it's something new to you imagine how it might look to you. Imagine the scenario as a movie, or as a large photo picture. It may be that you can see this as a panoramic image, or framed, moving or still. It is fine however you visualise it. The way you represent your experiences will be entirely unique to you. (If you find that you only get very scant and opaque pictures in your head, or find this difficult don't fret over it, just move on to the next bit…)

Now, spend time becoming aware of any background sounds you hear and other voices that are relevant. Think about where these sounds come from and how loud or quiet they are. Are they nearby or far away? What can you distinguish?

With any voices you hear, what are the words being used and the tone and who's being addressed? Are they your words or someone else's? (Again don't fret if you get little or no auditory information, simply move on to the next bit…)

Next, turn your attention to the sensations in your body that this state of mind produces… your breathing, heart rate, what sensations can you feel in your torso, or head, arms or legs and your tummy? Become aware of your posture and how your spine and shoulders feel. What do you notice changing about your posture? What sensations are you aware of that are circulating inside you and how do they move around your body? Are you smiling, what about your face?

Once you have done all of these, break state for a moment and think about the following…

In the context of what you chose to re-experience, think about what it feels like to feel good about yourself.

What does it feel like to feel so good about yourself?

Now bring back that state again that you just spent time bringing back to life. You might notice that it comes back more quickly this time, with more detail or more information. This is because neurologically your mind produces millions and millions of all sorts of representations unconsciously. So your brain structure is designed to do this naturally. However, you may not be used to accessing your representational states like this as often. Indeed your brain is now learning to access this information and the more you do it the quicker it does this for you and places it into your consciousness. As I've already said, this is most likely a new experience, but it is entirely possible. So the more you recall it the more easily it will come back.

Instructions to anchor a positive state of mind…

To make it easy to come back at a moment's notice, follow these instructions in order to anchor it.

Bring back the internal representation again by turning your mind to imagining it. At the same time as you are imagining bringing back this feel-good state in your mind, use the index finger of one hand to press on the index knuckle of your other hand. As the state builds and intensifies in your mind, press harder with your finger onto your knuckle to match how your mind is intensifying the recall of the internal representation. This will take around three to five seconds or so.

This is called a kinaesthetic anchor.

When the image is stable in your mind, end the anchor by quickly pushing down hard on your knuckle with your finger and then let go.

You have now anchored an emotional mind–body state onto your knuckle.

Break the state by thinking of what you had for breakfast, say.

Now press your anchor again, that is, use your index finger to press back onto the knuckle of your other hand as described above, and be amazed at how your mind suddenly brings back the same emotional mind–body state as you anchored. The more you repeat this and press on your knuckle to bring back that anchored state the more readily accessible it will be for you. You can now practise this and keep firing this anchor whenever you wish or need to reach this emotional mind–body state quickly in the future. This is a great way to fast-track teaching your neurology to 'feeling good' about yourself.

- Part 5 -

Returning to the authentic self

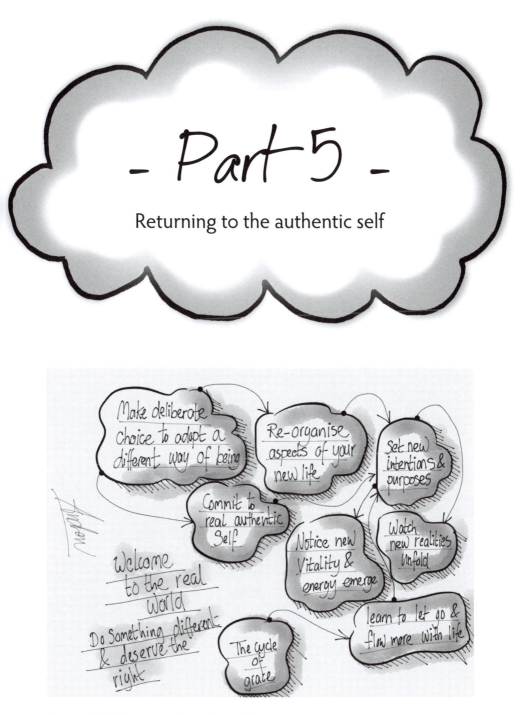

Figure 17: Welcome to the real world

- Chapter 28 -

Welcome to the real world of the authentic self

Baseline reality

Throughout this book I have referred to returning to your true authentic self. The reason for this is that the authentic self is your true baseline reality. It is your 'true north' compass point. It has always been a part of you, in your unconscious reality. The acquired self is an artificial layer of belief and conditioning that distorts your 'true north compass point' reality. The layers of acquired self are gradually superimposed layer by layer over your true baseline reality. These act like a heavy blanket that literally weighs down and stifles your true authentic self and restrains it. Its effect is that the authentic self becomes kidnapped and placed in keeping, hidden away from freedom.

Blinded from the truth

So, as you have seen in this book, you can become conditioned to the way you create your reality. You get accustomed to believing in the prevailing external reality that makes up your daily life, and can become addicted to it. This is far from the real truth. Your desires and dreams are the domain of your true authentic self; however, these end up being squashed by the conditioning of your acquired self. So you get conditioned to believe that what might be possible is nothing but pipe dreams. In this conditioned addiction you can be blinded and unaware of the vast possibilities available to you, simply by choice. You can become so habituated to believe in your limitations that you buy the idea that there is no choice at all. That you are governed by external circumstances that control and rule us all. You become persuaded that what happens to you in the external world cannot be changed. This is like a dream world that you end up believing in and sleepwalking through. Ludicrously, people will even end up fighting to protect this 'dream world'. This is because your acquired beliefs persuade you to believe that this is who you truly are. That this is your true identity, and nothing can change that. This is far from the real truth. This lie is as if wool has been pulled over your eyes and has blinded you to the real truth. The real truth is that when you wake up from sleepwalking through this acquired self 'dream world' in which you have been conditioned to living, you discover for yourself the real truth. As you will shortly see in these final chapters, when you wake up from this false reality, you discover that your true identity is much more than you dared to believe. To do this, you have to return back to your true authentic self.

In Part 1 I described some of the universal principles of the authentic self, and that rooted in the authentic self there are no boundaries to what might be possible. You will discover in this part that choice can lead you to different probabilities. It turns out that, with the authentic self, nothing is fixed. Whatever is rooted in the true nature of our authentic self can be made possible and can be made conscious. There are some sectors of reality that are destined to be experienced by your authentic self, others not. However, your acquired self will take you on a different and distorted route of fate. This is not the best of what is meant to be for you, but merely a compromise.

Becoming aware of the traits of the acquired self…

Part 4 was about learning strategies to break through the limiting effects of the acquired self. In Part 5 I turn your attention to learning how to return to your true authentic self and rediscover what true freedom means. Many people have memories from a happy and endless childhood; you may have too. Often this seemed to be a magical and uncomplicated time. A time where our imagination seemed to provide endless possibilities, and nothing seemed impossible. A time when we felt wide awake, and growing up was exciting and full of wonder. Yet those times, seen through adult eyes when we look back, now seem a faraway land, and bridges back to them have been forever burned. These were the times when your true authentic self ruled. The acquired self and its conditioning had not yet started to create its effect and addictive hold on you.

So to return to your authentic self, you have to 'wake up oh sleeper, awaken and rise from the dream world' of your conditioned self, and become aware of its effects and corresponding illusion. In Parts 3 and 4 you discovered how to break the hold of the acquired self, and as such you can now see more objectively, perhaps for the first time, the effects the acquired self can impose. Here are some examples to illustrate what the psychological traits of the acquired self include…

1. Inferiority and insecurity that is masked and hidden. A hidden world of mirrors that distract and distort.
2. Perfectionism and inadequacy produce a constant thirst and need for achievement.
3. Internal or external judgement is a constant tormentor. Others or one's self are never good enough; things could always be better. The thing being pursued and achieved provides the only mechanism for validation.
4. Obsession, habits, compulsions and high need for control are an ever-present indicator.
5. Over-responsibility or irresponsibility become cornerstones of our selves. Some vacillate between these two, creating uncertainty and misery.
6. Negative driver traits emerge and prevail, such as 'hurry up', 'try harder', 'people-pleaser', 'perfectionism', 'be strong'.
7. Overused, out of balance and unresourceful emotional states, such as unworthiness, powerlessness, depression, misery, anger, anxiety, worry and rage prevail and become default surface reactions that adversely affect our baseline homeostasis state.

Such are the consequences of the human condition.

Imagine a world where these psychological traits were no longer a part of you. This is the real world, it is the true reality created by the authentic self. We will explore these in detail in the subsequent chapters.

Welcome to the real world.

The return of your authentic self – a summary

Table 9 Contrasting the acquired and authentic selves – a summary

Acquired self	Authentic self
The conditioned self	The natural true self
The critical inner voice that constantly puts you and others down	The real you that the acquired self endlessly chatters to and berates
Uses control (learned strategies of protection, avoidance and accommodation)	The quiet and still voice deep within you, and is the 'human being itself', the real you
Learned from represented experience to be mistrusting, judgemental and critical	It embodies all inherent potential we were born with, including all capacities actualised and not yet actualised
Full of self-doubt, and defends itself rigorously by over-control	It embodies our innate ability to learn and to grow
Commanding, harsh and demanding	Gentle and graceful
It belittles and is like a parent or teacher that tells you and others off	It is the self that we enjoyed as children
It deludes you into thinking that you can't survive without its control	Best performance is when we get acquired self out of the way
Is always tense	Is relaxed, gentle and loving
Has very limited conscious resources	Accesses infinite unconscious resources
It is the monkey (not the organ-grinder)	It is the organ-grinder (not the monkey)
Affects everybody, and gets in your own way	Is always accepting, graceful, benevolent and helpful
Only operates on what is known and familiar, and then re-presents this as internal reality	Operates on what is new and emerging. Uses experience of the present moment
It's not okay not to be okay. Hates being vulnerable	It's okay with not being okay. It's fine with being vulnerable
Introduces distortion at every element of action, from perception, to how you react, to results you get and your self-image through feedback and distorted evidence	Learns by being proactive and adapting and being flexible to what is occurring in external reality
	Is able to learn from failure and mistakes and getting things wrong

Cause is greater than effect

In the context of this simple model, the conditioning of the acquired self is inclined to react to being an effect of a cause. When this happens it is because the reaction has not considered being a cause first. Whenever you react to your external circumstances and experiences you immediately find yourself an 'effect', of a cause.

So rather than being first at the 'cause' of an event, or circumstance, your acquired conditioning means you find you are usually in the grip of the inferior resources of 'effect'. So your reaction has defaulted to your selected 'effect' and is therefore narrowed to only that 'effect'. So you have limited your outcomes and your reality. 'Effect' in this way is a reactive consequence and you are already at the consequential end of that as your chosen reaction.

In contrast, by standing first in 'cause,' this greatly improves your choices of what subsequent 'effect' is best for you in that given circumstance. This is because 'cause' is always greater than 'effect'. In 'cause' you have greater resources and choices to better choose what 'effect' you wish to experience as a consequence. Being an 'effect' in this way, means you have chosen the 'effect' you prefer based on a variety of alternatives by having been first a 'cause'. This gives you greater options and possibilities.

So whenever you find yourself in reactive mode to any given circumstance, then choose not to accept this and purposefully choose to stand in 'cause' instead and then purposefully choose the 'effect' you want.

Now you have expanded your choices. Standing in 'cause' provides access to your authentic self and therefore you can make better choices. So by standing in 'cause' now, you have, in effect, allowed cause-and-effect to consciously alter your reality paradigm by interrupting the reactive cause-and-effect pathway you would have taken by default.

- Chapter 29 -

Okay not to be okay, and that's okay

What does it mean to have confidence?

I often get asked by people to help them to be more confident. So what is confidence? Confidence is often associated with the notion that it is only...

Okay to feel okay about yourself and your circumstances.

Only this paradigm is acceptable for being confident. If this is the prevailing belief, then it also follows that it is definitely...

Not okay, to feel not okay about yourself or your circumstances.

This paradigm is therefore considered or believed to be unacceptable. These two statements seem to set themselves up and work together as a cause-and-effect. In other words...

To be confident is to believe that it's only okay to feel okay.

But you may say: 'I don't feel okay about myself.' Therefore, it follows that it is...

Not okay to feel (or to be) not okay.

This means I'm not okay, because it's not okay that I feel not okay about myself.

So the more situations where I feel like this, then the more times I don't feel confident about myself.

And so this loop spirals downwards.

However, I propose that both of these statements lead one to 'presuppose', unresourceful assumptions and beliefs about yourself. They lead to creating internal representations that make you feel bad about yourself, and that in itself, as we have already learned, is not okay. They trigger associated dispositional negative forces of emotional body states, and that's not okay either, because again they make you feel bad about yourself.

Paul Jones, in his book *How to Live in the Here and Now*, came up with a much more resourceful and accurate way to perceive confidence. It is to presuppose or assume…

> It's okay not to be okay about myself… and that's okay.
>
> It's okay not to feel okay about my circumstances and my situation… and that's okay.
>
> It's okay that I feel rubbish today, because I made a mistake yesterday, but… that's okay, because I know I'm okay.
>
> I'm not feeling okay today, as I messed up and embarrassed myself in front of others, but even though I don't feel okay about this, I know I'm okay as a person.
>
> I feel very vulnerable because of x, y, or z, but that's okay, to feel not okay, and that's okay.
>
> It's okay not to feel okay about what has happened to me… but that's okay.

The above reframed presuppositions take a while to get your head around, but stick with them. In my experience, using these as 'presuppositions' in the present moment creates remarkable personal power.

The presupposition of 'it's okay to not be okay, and that's okay' generates an entirely different set of internal representations and emotional body states. This is because you are subtly recognising that you are not feeling okay, because of something that you have experienced. However, you are holding this in tension with being okay about this as a person. In other words you have not associated your situation with your personal identity, the you who you are.

This is a dissociated view. It is a clever indirect method of perceiving a difficult situation differently. That you, as a person, are separate from the experience that has made you feel bad. You are recalling that the event has simply made you feel bad, and you are recognising that's a natural feeling. But importantly you are not connecting the difficult situation to the 'real you'. It is merely something that has happened to you. This way of organising things that happen to you apart from your identity is important.

In other words it is similar to the presupposition we explored earlier in Part 4…

There is no failure, only learning and feedback.

This is an extremely powerful and important presupposition. It doesn't mean, by the way, that there is no such thing as failure. For example you can fail an exam.

However, what it actually means is that whatever goes wrong in your life, or whatever mistakes are made, it is nothing to do with your identity, the person you are. In other words, if you experience failure, or make a mistake or do something wrong, then it doesn't mean that you, as an individual, is a failure at all. You haven't failed, it is what you did that failed, not you as a person that is wrong or a mistake, or flawed, or broken or a bad person. You simply made a mistake, or did something wrong or failed at this or that.

Instead it means that when things go wrong or fail, or mistakes are made, then that experience is very useful to you. From this viewpoint you can learn from it. It teaches you something. It also doesn't mean that you can't feel upset by whatever occurred. That is fine too, it's okay to feel upset, as is that state of feeling and being vulnerable. However, it is important to recognise it as a strength, not a weakness.

It's okay not to be okay, and that's okay.

You see, it is all about how we perceive things. You can see anything proactively and positively, or negatively and reactively. This is the choice you make. So what I am saying is that neurologically speaking it is better to take the above perspective, as this allows us to access our true authentic self. 'It's only okay to be okay, and it's not okay not to be okay', merely create acquired dispositional limitations that end up ruling and conditioning you.

Being okay with vulnerability

By using this notion as a presuppositional statement about yourself, and about your difficult situations and experiences, you are learning to feel okay with yourself when you feel vulnerable. Vulnerability has power. It takes courage to be okay with yourself in difficult situations, and others will recognise this about you. It is okay not to be okay, and that is perfectly okay. It is okay to feel vulnerable about yourself.

However, the presupposition…

It's not okay not to be okay, and that's not okay.

… generates one set of neurological internal representations, while this presupposition…

It's okay not to be okay, and that's okay.

… generates a completely different set.

Practical application…

Starting with the first statement above, repeat it once in your head. Then remember a time when you might have felt something like this before, and feel the corresponding state that begins to generate from using this statement.

To help you to do this, coming up next is an abridged extract from the earlier script used at the end of Part 4 to recall a state of mind and its associated neurological emotional mind–brain–body elements. Remember this might feel illogical; however, this is how the internal coding, used by your brain, encodes all external experiences into a mirrored internal representation version of that reality.

Visualise how the statement re-presents itself in your mind. What do you see as a visual representation? Imagine the image as a movie, or as a large photo picture, or just as a metaphor of what it might look like. What colour do you represent it as? Is it large, small, near to you or far away in your mind's eye? It may be that you can see this as some sort of panoramic image, or framed image, moving or still. It is fine however you visualise it. The way you represent your experiences will be unique to you.

Now, spend time becoming aware of or imagine any associated background sounds you might be able to hear and any voices that are relevant. Think about where these sounds might come from and how loud or quiet they are. Are they nearby or far away? What can you distinguish? With any voices you hear, what are the words being used and the tone, and who's being addressed? Are they your words or someone else's?

Now, turn your attention to the sensations in your body that this state of mind produces inside you... your breathing, your heart rate. What sensations can you feel in your torso, or head, arms or legs and your tummy? Become aware of your posture and how your spine and shoulders feel. What do you notice changing about your posture? What sensations are you aware of that are circulating inside you and how do they move around your body?

This is the emotional mind–body state of 'It's not okay not to be okay, and that's not okay'.

Now repeat the above process and do the same for the statement 'It's okay not to be okay, and that's okay'.

Compare the two emotional mind–body states and what do you notice?

The latter one should feel much more positive and resourceful to you. Take note of how each feels so kinaesthetically different to you. This is therefore the way your neurology encodes and recreates these corresponding states inside you. It is amazing how easily we can consciously regenerate them. Remember, too, that your internal reality and external reality are connected and one co-creates the other.

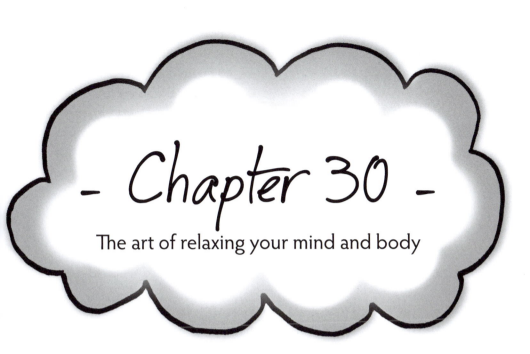

- Chapter 30 -

The art of relaxing your mind and body

Does meditation work?

Over the last few years there has been a concerted scientific interest in whether meditation techniques work. Can such simple and easy practices really help people to change the way they use their brains simply by changing their mindset and attitude?

Advancements in technology and instruments that can now accurately measure very subtle underlying neurological changes have made this research possible. Before this, the prevailing thought was that meditation was considered a 'bit out there and wacky' with no proof of its making a difference to people's lives. And so science, up until very recently, perceived such practice as irrelevant, simply because it couldn't be measured, validated or proved. As described in Part 2, Western psychological and neurological opinion overwhelmingly stated that, once our brain developed to its full maturity, its ways of working became a fixed construct.

Despite this, those who have consistently practised the art of meditation or used hypnosis as interventions for individual betterment and for personal change have insisted on their positive benefits: that there are no side effects to its use; that using meditation or self-hypnosis in a purposeful and positive way really does make a difference to changing the way people respond to their experience; and that it is possible to make a very real difference in positive ways to their lives. However, as said above, due to outdated scientific opinion, this has been driven out of mainstream thinking and sidelined as pop psychology and the weird Eastern art of the unknown. Today this viewpoint is at last changing.

Increasingly, neurological research is proving without question that the brain is 'plastic' and can learn 'new tricks' simply and easily by changing our mindset and attitude and then teaching our mind–brain–body. So this mind–brain–body connection to make permanent change at a personal level is very much possible and a reality after all. Many ancient philosophies and practices have quietly known empirically that this is so for thousands of years.

It is being proved from many neurological studies that ten minutes or so of meditation, or mindfulness as science often terms it, once or twice a day, or even just a few times a week, can make a huge difference to retraining our mindset to re-pattern neurological pathways, without the use of any medical or drug interventions. Meditation and mindfulness are the same thing. Sceptically I wonder if science has purposefully chosen to use the word 'mindfulness' so as to make a distinction between what it now believes as proven research, and 'meditation', which science in the past denied was of any benefit. Whatever the nuances here, it doesn't matter. Meditation works.

I have been regularly and successfully practising a combination of meditation and self-hypnosis for many years and have noticed the tremendous benefits it gives me. I am an advocate of this practice. I firmly believe that through purposeful and deliberate practice we can easily and simply begin to reconnect to our true authentic selves. Such practice is not onerous and only requires you to be sufficiently disciplined to make time for it.

Meditation and hypnosis are vastly fascinating subjects, and this book is not intended to be an exposition on them. Here I merely describe their benefits for a specific purpose. However, I will have more to say on these subjects in a future book perhaps.

The power of meditation and hypnosis, I believe, is their ability to connect you consciously to deeper parts of your mind and body. Your authentic self through meditation and hypnosis processes, connects and aligns with both your conscious and unconscious minds. Both brain hemispheres are accessed and rebalanced. To achieve this you have to be relaxed in both mind and body, as both are one system. By doing this you learn to suspend your inner critic and inner mind chatter. This takes a bit of practice, but over a short period of time you will be amazed at the results. I believe that the practice of meditation or self-hypnosis is a safe and easy intervention with no side effects, only benefits.

You can easily learn or be taught meditation techniques. There are lots of approaches. Whatever way you choose to learn the art of meditation, I encourage you to do so. The skills of meditation and self-hypnosis are easy to learn and have considerable benefits to you as a whole person. The more you practise them the more you will feel connected to who you are and your purposes and desires come more naturally to you.

Below is a guided approach that I have developed. I include it to allow you to understand an approach that combines meditation and hypnosis techniques. As I have said, though, there are many ways to do this. Below is one of a number of options and alternatives available to you.

A guided approach to meditation

Meditation and hypnosis used in the way I describe them here are gentle and powerful change agents and totally safe interventions. I recommend that you complement the change techniques described in this book with 30 or so minutes of a combined programme of guided self-hypnosis and meditation. And then you will be amazed at how quickly you can return to authentic ways of being.

Below is a process I have developed. If you choose to use it, then you need to commit to doing this three or more times a week, for a few weeks. After the guided programme of about four weeks or so, you then change the routine to meditate unguided, by yourself for about ten minutes twice a day, for the next four weeks.

Alternatively you could practise 20 minutes of meditation once a day for the same period. After that you should continue to meditate as a disciplined practice for around 20 to 30 minutes or more at least two to three times a week.

I find it best to meditate first thing in the morning, or early afternoon. However, you should establish a routine that suits you, as long as you make time for it. After only a few weeks of regular meditation, you will notice a significant difference in your overall being. It is amazing to think that the residual effects of years of conditioning can be significantly diluted in such short timescales. For example, a four to eight week period of sustained regular meditation will start to allow you to gain a return to feeling more like your true self. Only you will know what this means to you.

What will occur during meditation is that you learn to develop a relaxed and easy 'light trance-like state'. You are always awake and aware in this sort of relaxed light trance.

You will learn to quieten your inner mind chatter and internal thought streams and to stay awake. Don't fall asleep. Neurologically, your mind–brain–body is using this relaxed trance-like state for naturally rebalancing and realigning the unconscious and conscious parts of your overall consciousness. New pathways can be established easily and effortlessly using these techniques, and your mind–brain is able to start using different and more resourceful mechanisms within your brain.

I have observed that using and learning meditation and self-hypnosis techniques will enable you to shift the various limiting effects of your conditioning and previous mindset, sometimes quite dramatically. With sustained use, even over short periods of time, you will begin to notice that your constant background inner mind chatter will be much reduced, and its language changes too. This will be especially true if you followed the practical applications in Parts 3 and 4. The associated kinaesthetic effects created by your previous conditioned body states will begin to be replaced by feelings of calmness, positivity and often an underlying optimism in your thoughts, and general demeanour. Furthermore you will learn that it's okay to be not okay and that's okay too.

As I've said, meditation techniques are easy to learn and there are many books recommending several types of simple techniques to regularly practise. Mindfulness techniques seem to be the vogue of recommendation from the scientific community. However, I believe that you can choose what works for you, not just what is recommended by the scientists. There doesn't have to be one method that works better than others. You don't have to make a science out of it either. Meditation is simply a way of learning to flex and open your mind, so don't impose the limitations of one style against another. I don't believe it is the content that makes the difference; it is the act of spending time in a relaxed, trance-like or meditative state that opens the possibility for change to occur.

The practical application of meditation and hypnosis techniques...

I recommend and use a guided approach that combines meditation and self-hypnosis using a trance induction as the most effective way to learn and practically apply this skill. I have developed an approach that is specially scripted, and produced, using professional equipment, a pre-recorded (MP3 file) soundtrack of around 35 minutes or so duration.

I have developed standard guided scripts for general use by anyone at any time. I have also composed scripts that are adapted to specific circumstances or needs. Both are available for a small charge from my website (http://www.pdx-consulting.com/media.htm).

All my self-hypnosis guided scripts follow a specific strategy that I have developed empirically over many years of experience. The intentions of the pre-recorded scripts are to gently guide you through a particular set of mind–body self-relaxation directions. As we have all the necessary resources within us to achieve what we desire, the intention of my scripts is to induce mechanisms to re-establish such neurological mind–brain connections. Their purpose being to help people to easily and effortlessly return to their true authentic self.

The tone and language I use is purposefully hypnotically based. This optimises its effectiveness, and is a fundamental part of the meditation and trance induction. In addition, I have added a purposefully composed bespoke background trance soundtrack. This deepens the effect.

As you listen to my hypnotic voice together with the background trance-inducing sound track, their combined affect aids rapid relaxation.

Learning to relax your body is a key success criterion in meditation and hypnosis. As mind and body are one system, then a relaxed body implies a relaxed mind.

Learning to follow a guided approach to relaxing your body is also a fundamental part of eliminating conscious mind resistance from your inner critic (mind chatter). The two are symbiotically and inextricably linked.

For example, hyper-alert states, such as anxiety or control, have correspondingly hyper-tense body states, and are sometimes eventually accompanied by surface health issues such as skin and chest conditions. All such examples are a consequence of an over-reliance on conditioning of the acquired self. This is equally true for learning to breathe in a relaxed way. Having learned through the meditative script to relax your body and having established suitably good breathing patterns, your conscious mind calms down, as it learns to let go of its resistance. Your mind learns to do this remarkably quickly, especially if you allow your mindset to flow with the process and not put up resistance.

Neurologically, as already touched on above, through relaxation you are re-teaching the mind–brain–body connection to relearn to re-establish a calming of your entire neurological system. This helps to re-establish your balanced baseline homeostasis state. Furthermore, you are providing the opportunity to re-establish and realign brain hemispheres. As already covered, but worthy of note again, another essential effect of meditation is allowing your mind–brain to establish new neurological pathways, away from the downstairs trigger mechanisms and instead to build new circuits that rely more on the upstairs parts of your brain. These new pathways, once formed, have a calming effect on your neurology and mind–brain–body connection. So neurologically this leads to a return to the true authentic self.

Towards the end of the recorded script I introduce a variety of hypnotically based suggestions to help you to learn ways to change and to create new resourceful realities for yourself.

Listening to this three or more times a week for four weeks or so provides you with a pre-structured guided approach. This benefits you in learning how to relax, and use your mind in deliberate and purposeful ways. After this you will have developed the necessary skills to discipline your mind to be able to relax and to meditate effortlessly and rapidly on your own without the need for assistance.

The above is simply my approach; there are many other ways of learning meditation. For example some people may prefer to meditate for shorter periods instead, because that fits in with their lifestyle or busy life. Whatever approach you choose, meditation works and is a necessary vital part of reconnecting and returning to your authentic self.

Becoming aware of your body and your breathing

As you become more practised with these methods of relaxation, meditation and self-hypnotic trance states, you will discover that your whole body and mind begin to feel different. You notice you are able to feel good inside your skin more often. You can accelerate the process of your body and mind feeling good by consciously paying attention to your body and where you feel tension at various times during your day. The more you become aware of your physiology, and what is tense, the more choice you have to then consciously alter and improve your physiology in some way.

You'll be delighted with how quickly learning to relax any tension in your body contributes to you feeling good about yourself when your body is more easy and relaxed. Tension in the mind is always replicated by tension in the body. So reversing the process is essential to reinforce these messages. Eventually your conscious adaptations get picked up by your unconscious and it starts to break through the old tension habits and adapts your being to becoming more relaxed in both mind and body.

Noticing your body in everyday circumstances – practical application…

Become aware of any tension in your hands as you drive, or when sitting in a bus or a train, by noticing your hands on the steering wheel (or on your lap in the latter examples). Instruct your hands to then relax as you sit there, periodically making any corrections as and when you find your hands tense again.

As you drive or do other activities learn to become periodically aware of any tension in your facial features, particularly around your jaw, your eyes and your mouth. Learn to let go of tension in these areas too. It is amazing how much tension we hold in our facial muscles. Learning to hold these muscle groups loosely softens your facial features and corresponds to baseline homeostasis authentic self states. On long car, bus or train journeys, making these adjustments and changes are an ideal use of time, and your unconscious quickly learns with the constant corrections over a sustained period during a few journeys. The same applies to shoulders and neck and toes.

As above, the same goes for when you are about to go to sleep. Notice whether your hands are tense and consciously relax them and straighten them out. Instruct your unconscious mind to keep them relaxed as you sleep. Do an inventory of your entire body for any other tensions you have just before you go to sleep, and learn to soften these. This time at night is very effective for instructing your unconscious mind in these types of changes. The same applies when you first wake up. Notice any tensions and soften these too. If you clench your jaw while you sleep, then learn to simply relax your jaw at night. Give your unconscious mind permission to loosen your jawline and soften the muscles around this area.

Whenever you find yourself standing and are self-conscious about your arms and hands, then learn to relax your arms to your sides in a natural position, to avoid any nervous hand rubbing or fingers in the mouth or covering your mouth or face or hair etc.

Become aware of poor posture and take corrective action by straightening your back, shoulders and neck etc. This will create access to gently become more gracefully self-assured while being relaxed at the same time. This, again, is the nature of your authentic self.

Noticing your breathing

I wonder if you have ever watched a small baby in its cot breathing when it is asleep? As a father of three, I have had this pleasure.

It is a beautiful moment to witness. Babies use their tummies to breathe, they don't breathe from their chests. As a sleeping baby breathes in you see their tummy fill up and as they push the breath out their tummy relaxes. Breathing in and out in this way is exaggerated because of their small size. As they grow into young children and play outside on a hot day or on a beach you can notice the same thing. Their breathing in and out uses their stomach muscles. Their chest cavity and shoulders don't move.

This is how we are naturally supposed to breath. Our bodies are designed to breathe in and out by using our tummy muscles (actually our diaphragm) to do the work for us. My theory is that we were not intended to breathe from our upper torso, using our chest and shoulders. Instead, as we breathe (through our noses), the in breath expands our tummies, as we expand our diaphragm. Breathing out (via our mouths) then relaxes the diaphragm as we push the air out, moving our tummy muscles (diaphragm) inward.

I don't know if you have noticed the same thing that I have noticed about children's breathing, but I have observed that, for many children, their way of breathing seems to change when they go to school. I haven't researched this, it is merely empirically derived by watching my own children and their friends. I have, however, noticed in my extensive work with many people on a one-to-one basis and in groups that most adults breathe in and out by using their upper chest torso. At first glance this looks natural enough.

During my training to be a trainer and presenter we had an expert come and teach us about breathing properly again. Out of a group of around 30, all of us were breathing 'wrongly' from our chests. None of us was breathing naturally by using our diaphragm in the right way, which is situated under the ribcage cavity. The teacher's theory was that upper chest breathing is a physiological symptom of anxiety, stress, worry and over-control that prevails in our society and working cultures.

Just out of interest, notice how you are breathing right now. Do you use your tummy muscles (diaphragm) or your upper chest?

Our breathing expert gave us breathing exercises that showed us all how to do this and we practised this each day over the course of around three weeks. As I have already said, using the diaphragm to breathe means that our tummies expand during the in breath and contract inwards on the out breath to force the air outwards. Musicians such as trumpet players and singers know all about breathing correctly, and develop strong diaphragm muscles to aid them.

Our breathing expert reasoned that, in the West, we like to tuck our tummies in and puff out our chests, as this presents a nicer public profile. We don't like to push out our tummies; it somehow feels counter-cultural to us. Breathing the right way also physiologically teaches us to relax our mind and our bodies.

Neurologically, breathing in this way reconnects us to our natural authentic self baseline homeostasis state. This may be because your diaphragm area has many nerve endings that splay out to your midsection area. This area is often termed colloquially as the second brain, or intuitive brain, and is literally linked to your gut feel about things.

After my training, I dedicated around three to six months or so to retraining my breathing patterns, to use my diaphragm to breathe, rather than my upper chest, which I had become accustomed to. My intention was to feel optimally good about myself, by being more relaxed in my body and mind. I had noticed that underlying tension had crept into my body, and I wanted to change this. I knew that body tension was a result of tension in the mind, and I wished to discover ways of how I could access my own authentic self in different ways.

So, to do this practically, I consciously disciplined myself to alter my breathing during meditation sessions of around 30 minutes a day and also used to practise this whenever I was driving on long journeys. It took time to achieve this physiological alteration for me. That was around ten years ago now, and I am still breathing using my diaphragm as a result of this deliberate intention. However, this physiological change was certainly worth it, as I have continued to feel generally calmer and more relaxed in my overall demeanour since then.

Practical application...

If you feel underlying tension in your body then try practising this type of breathing during your meditation times. It is astonishing how relaxed it makes you feel. Breathing in this way is important, as it releases you from tension both in the body and in the mind.

For a short while during the first few minutes of your meditation time do the following exercise:

1. Take a deep breath in, slowly through your nose, and consciously concentrate on expanding your diaphragm and tummy.
2. As you reach the top of the breath hold the breath for a count of one, two, three or four.
3. Then start to slowly let the breath go, by consciously contracting your tummy muscles to push the air slowly out of your mouth to the count of five, four, three, two, one.

Do this five to six times and notice each time you do this how much more relaxed you feel.

Other people I have known have taken up singing lessons to help them to achieve this same purpose and of course it provides other benefits too.

As I have briefly mentioned already, I have a theory about why people develop unresourceful breathing patterns over time, and it is only that, a hypothesis. I have noticed that sustained anxiety, hyper-alert states and fear tend to adapt our physiology into more rigid postures. This is because tension builds up in the body as a consequence, especially around the shoulders, neck, upper chest and upper back. Over time this causes upper chest breathing patterns. This then becomes a habit.

Returning to my observation of schoolchildren, I wonder if it could be that being in a structured environment in a school setting perhaps triggers off this type of stress-related reaction (albeit at low subliminal but sustained level) in young children.

Anyway, the point I am making here is that your natural self uses your diaphragm to breathe.

Other unguided practical application meditation techniques

At this point you have learned the skill of meditating and from then on any other meditation technique that takes your fancy is useful. You should endeavour to organise your routine and discipline yourself to continue to meditate regularly. Preferably once a day, even if it is only for ten minutes or so.

I find that simply meditating on setting up my day with the right intentions and presuppositions highly beneficial. I often use a loose script based on the following words to guide me.

The power of the present moment...

...This is my time right now... and I desire and expect new and interesting successes to continue to surface before me.

New and exciting, inspiring opportunities and initiatives continue to emerge and come my way... today, this week and in the near future... that enhance, develop me, move me forward and contribute to my overall potential, and contribute to my family, and to my children's future.

I am intentionally setting up each day being emotionally excited and curious as to what will come my way this week. I am seeking and expecting joy and love each day and watch it come and meet me along my way in life.

That even better things are yet to come, and that life is kind always to me.

I am looking out for serendipitous events to continually and magically occur for me each day... and for my destiny to continue to unfold before me.

For each problem and challenge I remember to seek an answer that leads, grows and develops me to enable me to solve it. Problems are but one side of the coin. The answer lies hidden within each problem and is the other side of the coin.

Another beneficial meditation technique is to meditate around focusing your attention outside yourself. The idea of this one originates from mindfulness…

You start with focusing your attention on relaxing your body, and breathing as you learned by using my guided script.

Then you focus your attention on the sensations you can feel on the inside of your skin, and then begin to focus your entire attention onto the outside of your skin. What can you notice? Feel the sensations on parts of your skin, what you are sitting on and leaning your back on perhaps. Become aware of any temperature sensations you feel on your face. Even feel your hair on your arms and then on the top of your head.

Now become aware of the sounds and the 'feel' of the room around you.

Begin then to focus your attention on the whole house or building you are in.

What can you hear and feel and imagine in your mind's eye?

Now move your awareness and attention beyond these boundaries to the space around you, the gardens that might surround you, the roads and streets beyond that. Again become aware of what sounds you can hear outdoors.

Now continue expanding your awareness beyond this. See how far you can expand your consciousness.

This is a fantastically engaging meditation routine. It quickly teaches your neurology to take your attention away from you (Me! Me! Me!) and you learn to expand your consciousness to your external self and beyond your normal internal focus.

Setting your intentions…

Another meditation I have found useful is based on focusing your attention on a single aspect. Again this technique originated from mindfulness. However, instead of focusing your entire awareness and attention on a single object, I have adapted it to focus on a single idea, a concept, an intention, a goal or objective, or something you desire to achieve. Whatever is taking your interest at the time.

While you meditate, begin to focus your attention on this single idea. After a while open your mind, and begin to visualise and imagine how it would be as the idea takes hold in your mind. Focus on what it would look, sound and feel like if you achieved it.

Next, we look at setting intentions in more detail. My approach is to use a meditation or self-hypnosis routine to help to connect more to what it is that you desire, your purposes and to help you to manifest these into reality.

To me, the whole point of meditation is to open your mind and be flexible. Through these techniques you learn to focus your attention and awareness away from your old conditioned responses and move towards your true authentic self.

- Chapter 31 -

Techniques for setting intentions

Figure 18: Setting intentions directs external reality

Expanding your comfort zone

Expanding your comfort zone is a useful concept that helps you to clearly differentiate between acquired self conditioning and stretching towards the authentic self. To understand this more fully it is important to explore each of the notions of comfort, panic and stretch.

Comfort zone

Remaining in your comfort zone is the strategy of your acquired conditioning.

As we have already explored, the comfort of our conditioning means that many people become stuck at some point through life. It may be that certain patterns end up controlling your responses in unresourceful ways. Or that somehow you have begun to become aware that things have just become overfamiliar for you, and you are seeking something different. The strategies, patterns and principles adopted by the acquired self always end up being based on what is known and familiar. As we have seen, these end up becoming default responses. Neurologically, these lead to simply settling for the known patterns and ways of responding to experience.

If you find yourself:

Stuck in a rut or a groove or stagnating
In familiar circumstances all the time and nothing seems to change
Comfortably numb, lethargic, or in some sort of torpor
Where life seems somehow listless, has lost its sparkle or colour
Saying 'Is this all there is?'
Not taking risks, for fear of not being safe
Being bored, or feeling in some sort of dream world, or sleepwalk or stupor
Where growth and development has suspended
Content and satisfied (these are linked to authentic self as well and are discussed later)

Then in one way or another, you are in the comfort zone of your conditioning.

Neurologically this means that you have adopted a set pattern of internal representations that seem to set up default mind–brain–body states of thinking, feeling and being. I sometimes refer to this as 'the rust zone'. Spending too much time here in the longer term stunts your growth.

Many states that keep people in the comfort of their conditioning and therefore in their comfort zone are based on fear and avoidance. Fear and avoidance of the unknown, the unfamiliar, success, failure, making a mistake, being in the wrong, not being as good as others, being different, being unsafe or insecure, confrontation, change, putting oneself forward, making a fuss, or being noticed, or having to take or be in control, being controlling or judging yourself or others…

The reason perhaps that many people stay in the comfort of their conditioning, the comfort zone, is because they might very well suddenly find themselves in a panic.

Panic zone

If the acquired self is pushed too far out of its comfort zone, to the extreme, then you might find yourself flipping rapidly out of control, feeling overwhelmed and dropping into the panic zone. This is often because, for many people, their dispositional marked limiting beliefs have been triggered and consequently their mind–brain–body neurology becomes suddenly overwhelmed.

Panic states create huge imbalances in your overall neurology and are especially displayed in the emotional body.

Such states (as we have already described earlier in this book) are naturally triggered by flight, fight or freeze survival responses in reaction to immediate danger and threat, present in your external reality. These situations might typically last only a few milliseconds, and then they are soon over as the threat has passed. Our recovery to normality soon resolves itself, after the residue of the adrenaline dump has worn off.

If sustained, however, due to intense stress, anxiety and worry, or oversensitivity or hyper-reactions, for example, these instances are all triggered dispensational markers of acquired limiting belief systems. And our emotional body systems, let alone our mind–brain connection, are not designed to cope with our stress response mechanism being triggered indefinitely. In the longer term, if such artificially induced or acquired panic states persist they are inclined to lead to a degradation in physical and mental health.

Stretch zone

If you do the same things you will always get the same results. This is the strategy behind the acquired self and conditioning. You are not meant to lead your life in the above ways. Instead we are all designed and destined to continually experience new things, feel and learn, to grow and to develop as we mature. We are not meant to stay rooted and stuck to past and set ways of doing things and handling reality in the same way all the time using set preprogrammed ways. As we have learned, this has been acquired.

To get to your authentic self will require you to purposefully expand yourself by intentionally stretching towards new possibilities. To do this you have to plan ahead a little bit, move intentionally towards something that is worth achieving. In addition, you need to develop the awareness to divert your natural psychic energy to overcome the internal obstacles and interferences of your acquired self. After persisting for a while, however, the effort required to overcome your limiting conditioning, and to deserve the right to do so by stretching towards your intentions, begins to pay off. You end up having expanded your comfort zone. Neurologically it is known that once your mind–brain connection learns new patterns and strategies, that in turn expands your consciousness by altering and adjusting brain maps in new ways. In this way brain maps are constantly competing for brain 'real estate' and the brain dynamically reorders and changes its topology or neurological structure to encompass these new learnings. This is the miracle of neural plasticity at work and this competition and reassignment of brain 'real estate' is what takes mental effort and feels uncomfortable as we learn to expand our comfort zones.

So in contrast to acquired states, returning to your authentic self means that you have to unlearn and relearn something entirely different. That you have to change something. That means that you have to wake up from the stupor of your conditioned comfort, and stretch into something new. This willpower attracts your imagination that then provides the necessary psychic energy to then set the dynamics of neural plasticity into motion. To do this it is useful to set yourself some sort of goal, or objective or an outcome of one kind or another. This is so you give yourself some sort of purpose to move away from your acquired self and instead return to your authentic self. I prefer to use the expression 'setting intentions' to describe this new state of being, rather than goal setting.

The impetus to do this is best described by the notion of the stretch zone. Like the above notions of comfort and panic, it's a metaphor. All three zones, comfort, panic and stretch, are a different state of mind and body. The stretch zone provides you with the necessary psychic energy to overcome the lethargy and controlling influence of the conditioned states described in the comfort zone. It enables you to move towards your new intentions. This is because you intend it to be so.

For example, the ultimate intention of this entire book is to help you to develop strategies that motivate you to change what isn't working. So you can grow and develop and get the life that you desire and deserve. To do this, the techniques I have developed and outlined for you are intended to move you into your own 'stretch zone'. In this way you can overcome your acquired self, so you can expand into your true comfort zone – your authentic self. What I mean here is that by spending time in the stretch zone, growing and developing, then this will eventually expand into your new comfort zone.

In the stretch zone, you spend time evaluating and challenging your pre-programmed approaches to situations. If we don't do this, we risk getting ourselves stuck and not maturing and experiencing the whole of life.

In the stretch zone you find yourself:

Motivated
Stimulated
Ready for action
In a curious mix of excitement and risk
Challenged
Wanting to develop and grow

Curiously, once you have expanded your comfort zone, a mark of having returned to your authentic self is that you feel content and satisfied with yourself. You no longer have to strive and push or stretch. You can just let go, hold things loosely, accept yourself and what is happening to you in external physical reality, and simply relax into the new you.

So put another way, for a while you had to stretch to grow beyond the comfort zone of your conditioning. During that period of personal change and growth, what was once a stretch for you now becomes your new, larger and complete comfort zone, and you have the comforting satisfaction of having returned to your authentic self. Here, though, there will always be other fresh challenges to grow your authenticity further.

As we will see later in this final part of the book, returning to your true authentic self means that you have discovered ways of being that go beyond the mental constructs of your acquired conditioning and found new ways to expand and grow. For example, you learn to expand and grow by holding things loosely, letting go of control and learning to be accepting, and your intentions, once set, will come and find you along the way and unfold in front of you. Using these new paradigms opens up all sorts of new rabbit holes in which to explore how far they go.

Setting purposeful futures – practical application...

This next exercise is truly outstanding and I have used it with great success to help people to set up purposeful futures. It is based on setting intentions. I have adapted this from Paul McKenna's book, *The Hypnotic World of Paul McKenna*. Paul used this exercise in his hypnosis work to help people find what they want, and attributed this approach to Michael Breen. I have adapted it to be used as a conscious exercise.

Create a list of four goals or desires or qualities or experiences that you would like to have or achieve. Put each on a sticky note.

Pair them off in some sort of order logical to you. Place one pair of them at the top of a clear space, table or on a wall, and the other pair further down with plenty of space for a few more sticky notes in between.

Number each 1 and 2 for the top pair and 3 and 4 for the bottom pair.

Start with the top-paired sticky notes 1 and 2, and imagine in detail what it would be like to have already achieved these. Close your eyes and relax deeply if you want to.

Then ask yourself: 'Having achieved these two things, what does it do for me, get for me and give me?' You will find that the answers to these questions that emerge and come to mind now will be from a deeper part of you and be more profound than the first four sticky notes that recorded your goals. These statements now start to come from your authentic real self.

Write down these answers on another sticky note and place this under the first two paired goal notes 1 and 2.

Number this sticky note 5.

Do the same for the bottom pair of sticky notes 3 and 4 and number this sticky note 6. Place number 6 just above sticky notes 3 and 4.

Now take the two statements for sticky notes 5 and 6 and look at them as a pair, and again repeat the same process as you did for the above pairs.

Ask yourself: 'Having achieved the things written on the two sticky notes 5 & 6… what does it do for me, get for me, or give me?'

The answers here will be deeper still; now you will be accessing the things that really matter to you, that you care about and that come more from the heart and your dreams and desires. These will represent your deepest intentions. Spend time allowing the answers to flow and trust that they will come. Be true to yourself and the answers will emerge.

Write down these statements on a final sticky note and place this in the centre of sticky notes 5 and 6. Label it 7.

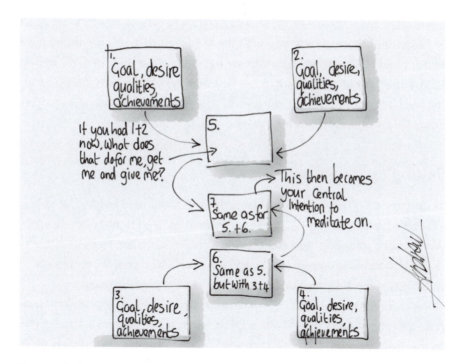

Figure 19: Setting goals and intentions exercise

The key statement(s) in sticky note 7 is what you need to put into place, believe in and continue to act as if you have right now. The power of the present moment is used to set your future intention. Intentions work because you behave as if it is yours now. As you regularly do this you create the internal representations required to set your feelings and emotions to feel good about yourself, and secure that your intention is being fulfilled. Every fibre of your body is involved in the intention: it is a mind–brain–body thing. As you continue to intend this, watch as your intention sets its sails and starts to bear a course that unfolds little by little and moves towards you step by step from now on. Eventually, your intention will steer you to the right sector in reality where external reality manifests accordingly. This is a conscious, unconscious and cognitive harmonious process. Below we take this further still. We will explore how to use the power of meditation to access other more powerful parts of your mind–brain–body, to set your intentions and watch them work themselves out in your reality.

Also remember that this practical exercise first started from the outside and worked inwards. However, what I want you to notice now is that it actually works the other way round, from the inside out. When you look at the content on sticky notes 1–4, you might begin to see these now as more goals or milestones that provide you with the evidence that you are in the right sector of reality because your intention has manifested itself. In so doing you have ended up also achieving what you desired on the outside. By focusing your attention from the inside-out, you also get what you first desired. Bonus! Focusing on the intrinsic sill also give you the extrinsic.

Setting up intentions

In Chapter 3 in Part 1, 'Universal principles', I introduced you to the notion of reality being created through your intentions. An intention focuses and directs your attention into the future, with the purpose to get what you desire. By thinking about your intentions regularly, your awareness then watches out for the intention to unfold in external physical reality.

A dictionary definition of an intention describes it as a plan, aim, purpose, objective, goal, target. While this is correct, an intention in the context of this book is a lot broader, and goes much further, than this definition. Although setting an intention has similarities and parallels to goal, objective or outcome setting, for me these familiar terms just seem a bit too mechanical, too structured and contrived. They rely too much on cognition.

Goals seem to work on conscious mind principles only, based on you imposing them on yourself. They are often based on what you materially want or based on logic and objectivity and predominantly as left-brain tendencies. Intentions are far more subtle. Goals are always worked out by what is known and familiar to you and possible for you. With goals you are always in control of them, and they require you to achieve them; the power of intentions work on what is *not* known, and what is unfamiliar. They chart new water and sail in new seas of other possibilities. They can be outrageous, providing they acknowledge your dreams and desires and are somehow linked to who you truly are and your authentic self. With intentions you *never* control the outcome, you let it shape up before you, in the way it is meant to work out. You are *not* in control of how it works out at all. With intentions, you set them, let them go, hold them loosely and patiently wait for reality to correspondingly manifest itself into being. This will work out in a way that is unique to you and right for your authentic self. All you need to do is to trust and believe in them and they will come to you. What you build in your mind, and trust in with all your soul, will come to you every time.

In my opinion, goals don't allow for the even greater power, resources, possibilities or options of using the 'infinite' abilities of your unconscious mind. Setting an intention requires the use of balancing and aligning both conscious and unconscious minds. My working hypothesis is that as the starting point is often unfamiliar and new, the intention starts with perhaps more right-brain inclinations and as it unfolds gradually the conscious mind gets involved, too, to look out and watch for evidence on the horizon of external reality. In this way both brain hemispheres collaborate in the purpose of intention. I find setting intentions far more satisfying, as they seem to have a kind of 'magic' quality about them. I find that they align better to your neurological constructs than goals or outcomes do.

Setting intentions is a process that only the authentic self can do, and it does it very well indeed. And to do this it needs a cooperative balance between both your minds. So intentions are the domain of your authentic self. Because of this, whenever you set an intention, they have an elegant gracefulness about them. Setting intentions and watching them manifest and unfold into your life is a truly beautiful art. You have to be wide awake, generate positive resourceful emotional body states and trust implicitly in its manifestation.

Be careful though that your conscious mind, doesn't dismiss it and throw its hands in the air and walk away angrily saying: 'This stuff doesn't work, it's not real, it's too fuzzy and unrealistic.' If this happens then your mindset collapses back to doubt and frustration and you quickly get what you have just emotionally created. And so the winds of that possibility change direction, the mist of confusion sets in and the energy of the imagination is popped and bursts, so what was behind the intention is no more and it is quickly taken away. And your boat steers back to the familiar waters of the comfort of your conditioning and you go back to your slumber.

Practical application...

Whenever you set intentions, if you follow the principles below, I believe that they will work well for you. In your own way you uniquely manifest the authentic reality you truly desire.

What is it that you desire?

When setting an intention, the first step is to allow it to form from within you, to manifest and come to you from within yourself. In the previous practical application I gave you a cognitive approach or method using sticky notes as a prop to consciously start the process of forming your intentions. So in the following paragraphs, I now teach you how to apply intentions to yourself, using relaxation techniques. We discussed these in detail in Chapter 30 on meditation and self-hypnosis.

Choose a time when you can be in a relaxed state of mind, and when you are at your very best and at peace with yourself. You will need to set some time aside for this and take your time. Pick an environment in which it is conducive for you to think.

Setting up intentions requires balance and cooperation of both your conscious and unconscious minds. Therefore I recommend meditation or a light self-hypnotic trance as an ideal mechanism to quietly spend quality time allowing your intentions to come to you. We discussed this in a preceding chapter.

Remember, do not fall asleep; this is about sharpening the keenness of your mind. Keep practising your ability to hold an idea loosely in your mind, while you relax in a trance-like state.

Use the output of the previous practical application as a starting point to set up your meditation. Alternatively, use the meditation process to discover what it is you wish to intend. Let your ideas of what it is that you truly desire to shape in your future to form naturally, so they can come to you. To do this, purposefully invoke your imagination. Consciously give your imagination permission to wonder purposefully about your desires and intentions.

Imagine these emerging from your unconscious mind and flowing easily into your consciousness so they come from within you without you imposing them on yourself. This is important.

If necessary spend several meditation sessions practising this approach. Deliberately doing this will strengthen and considerably develop your meditation skills as well. Remember, meditation and self-hypnosis are methods to engage your authentic self; they have access to your unconscious mind, and this might be at first unfamiliar to you. Remember unfamiliarity is the domain of your unconscious and it thrives in new unknown situations. If you find yourself a bit twitchy or panicky about this, then this, too, is a useful learning for you. It is teaching you to let go of the 'sticky' nature of your conscious mind that feels out of control when it is in unfamiliar waters and doesn't know what to do. In this case, give yourself permission to learn from the unconscious part of you to relax and go with the flow.

If you are more of a logical person, and find it hard to use ideas and imagination, then be patient and kind to yourself. Keep practising – the more you meditate the better you become at it. The purpose of using meditation in this way is to use the power of your authentic self and to trust the power of that present moment to do the work for you. You must suspend any self-critical and sceptical inner mind chatter. Eventually you will find that you won't ever lose your logical abilities but simply be able to augment them with further inner resources. Remember that wisdom comes from multiple perspectives.

Be bold; use your imagination to go beyond limiting constraints. Allow your whole self to engage in the process. Don't over-think, but allow your thoughts, feelings and emotions to emerge and come to you. The more you do this the easier it becomes for you.

Now, connect the intention to who you are, who you are meant to be and your purpose. It might be that you are not aware of this just yet, so in that case, you could set an intention to discover this and use the purpose of the intention to connect to this for yourself.

Always avoid material things and money; these are simply the means or evidence that let you know that your intentions have manifested themselves into your reality. Instead, focus on what they do for you.

When you set an intention, you look at it with 'soft eyes'. It is not some dragon you have to slay, or something to yank and wrench into existence. As you desire it, it will find you and correspond with your longing for it. It will do this in a way totally unique to you and no one else. To do this you have to trust in yourself. That is why intentions work best when you are connected to your authentic and true self.

Shaping your intention

When you have decided on what it is that you want to intend then you need to shape it. To do this follow the principles below:

Your intentions you set for yourself need to be positive, present and personal. I find it best to write down intentions. (You can use your self-inventory journal for this.) The act of writing them is an exercise that helps you to engage and involve the whole you in the process.

However you write it, make it easy to say to yourself, so it seems to uniquely satisfy you and sit well with you, as if you are pleased with it when you read it.

Even though the intentions are based on manifesting a future desire, set them as if they are present today. So imagine you are at the point now where your intention has manifested and you have what you want. From this point start your intention with these words:

I am…
Or
I have…
Or
I am and I have…

By doing this you are beginning with the end in mind. You are pretending that you are already experiencing its manifestation in external and internal reality. This is important, because you are using your internal language in a connective way.

Neurologically, your brain uses the same representational map-making abilities it uses to store a memory of something experienced as it does to generate a completely new idea.

Remember from earlier in the chapter about expanding your comfort zone; intentions are intended to stretch you, but they do this gently, gracefully and naturally. You are not yanking, forcing, wrenching or manipulating reality to do as you command. It's useful to keep reminding yourself that the discipline is in letting go of control, holding things loosely and letting things flow in the moment and watching what happens, not trying to herd reality down your predefined pathway, but to let the intention unfold itself into reality as you watch. By all means expect things to happen, but allow it to surprise you as they do.

Intend your intention

Now that you have shaped your intention, the key is to use the power of your imagination to intend the intention. The best way of doing this is to spend time everyday specifically focusing on your intention. As mentioned already, meditation or a light self-hypnotic trance is the ideal way to do this.

So the whole idea with an intention, once determined and set, is to imagine it as if you have already got it and you are pleased and excited about it. Being emotionally connected to and motivated by the thought of it working its way out in reality is important. In this way you are also influencing your mind–brain–body connection to really associate with it. You may begin to connect it to other things too, in your life and the reality that you desire to lead. That's fine, go with the flow, learn what you learn, notice what you notice along the way.

While you meditate, begin to focus your attention on this single intentional idea. For a while repeat the words you have set up previously in your head and then let them go into your mind. Give your unconscious mind the instruction to work on this intention for the next 10 or 20 minutes or so. You don't need to know what it is thinking, just give it permission and trust that it is working on your behalf in the background.

As you open your mind, begin to visualise and imagine how it would be as the idea takes hold. Let it germinate and grow like a seed in your mind. Let go of forcing it in any way. Instead, let the power of your unconscious and conscious minds work on it together for you. Spend a little time focusing on what having this as part of your life might look, sound and feel like.

Once you have spent all the time you need setting your intention, instruct your mind that it holds it loosely; your conscious mind lets go of controlling the outcome; it hands it over completely to your unconscious mind; and it trusts the power of your unconscious resources to work it out into reality. You have done the 'what's' and that's all that's needed. Let the 'how's' sort themselves out. Finally direct your conscious mind to expect the interplay between the internal intention and external reality to gradually reveal and manifest the intention into external reality. Simply ask your consciousness to look out for it unfolding before you.

As for your ongoing meditations, I have found that it is useful to continue to repeat this intention setting process regularly for a while. This reinforces the intention into your neurology and continues the discipline, as well as reminding you to expect it to manifest somehow into your reality.

So, in the ways described above, regularly set aside time each day to purposefully imagine, desire and anticipate your intention becoming part of your reality. What we desire and imagine consciously creates consistent thought patterns that have sufficient energy and purpose to attract and generate the corresponding physical materialisation of it into our reality. What we attract we get.

Alternate between this and meditating on just expecting the outcome to begin to work out before you. You won't know your 'how' and that is fine, just expect things to happen, and be happy and surprised as they do begin to unfold before you. As you walk towards them, they also come towards you. This is not a passive process, but requires you to act, but act gently and gracefully and intentionally and with purpose.

Consciously, it is important to keep your attention on expecting it to turn up in various forms in your external experience. You have to look out for and recognise subtle changes in things that serendipitously occur, and most importantly seize those 'by chance' moments as the intentions manifest and emerge into your awareness. As things happen, follow them up, see where they lead. You will need to respond, act and do things along the way, and whatever those actions are, only you will know as reality shifts towards your intention becoming part of your desired reality.

Remember you only set the intention. Trust that all the rest is worked out for you. It is as if you are journeying toward the intention you have set and, at the same time, you are expecting the outcome of what you want and desire to come and meet you halfway.

How do intentions work?

Once you have handed over your intention to your unconscious mind, the intention is taken up as an instruction by your unconscious mind. Consciousness is incredibly complex and highly versatile and, to all intents and purposes, is infinite in its capacities. So via the constructs of your unconscious mind–brain connection it acts as a vehicle that connects consciousness to the infinite, endless and universal nature of All That Is. This little-understood interconnection naturally attracts and directs external physical reality to match the implicit intentional instructions.

My working hypothesis is that the universal principles of All That Is somehow appear to be highly attracted and tuned to correspond to the wavelength of your intentional thought-forms, which we as human beings can direct. These interconnections then enable the necessary energy for your intentions to be manifested into your external physical reality. This in itself is apparently effortless and certainly a graceful process that is continuously operating, everywhere, all the time, without fail. It is a profound mystery. All I know from my own observations is that we co-create our reality.

However, because these kinds of processes are unfamiliar and are so abstract and obscure, with such an esoteric nature, they are therefore not widely accepted and therefore seen as 'pie in the sky', not proven science. And yet, over recent decades, these sorts of notions are being better under-stood and accepted as research in neuroscience and quantum physics moves into the mainstream.

As we have already covered, what seems to be true is that while you are responsible for setting the intention of intending what you desire, you are not responsible for how your intentions are worked out. This is not your domain. The hows are somehow mysteriously worked out somewhere in the attraction process between your unconscious and its relationship with All That Is. So once you have set your intention and then let it go, your respon-sibility is simply to expect it to unfold into reality in some way.

Vadim Zeland, in his series *Reality Transurfing*, eloquently describes the processes of attracting different realities to ourselves. Throughout this book I have purposefully used nautical analogies to describe the journey of return-ing to your authentic self and this seemingly mysterious process of shaping our own reality and setting intentions and patiently expecting the outcomes to manifest. Your desired intention is the sail. According to Zeland, your sails then get filled with the winds of intentionality that bear your ship on a heading towards the sea of infinite potential and across oceans of possibility, where your corresponding reality will be discovered and manifested. As you are sailing on uncharted waters it takes time for you to get there and to feel your way by new winds, and unfamiliar seas. Along the way, while waiting for your intentions expectantly, be patient and don't doubt. Doubt simply turns your ship right around and quickly takes you back to familiar waters once again. Don't expect a smooth passage and calm seas. There may be storms ahead.

As we are in a physical reality, there is often a delay in our mental intentions to their corresponding manifestation into reality. This is due to many things, including sometimes a natural time lag, or that we have so many competing and confounding thoughts that come and go that are too vague or woolly to create the required energy to materialise the intention. The clearer and more disciplined and sustained attention the intention is given, the more energy it has available to correspondingly manifest itself into reality at some point. It may be, too, that you reshape your intention to match what is consequently occurring, or not occurring, in your external experience. In other words, you might modify your intention according to what you learn from the process and the way in which reality correspondingly emerges and unfolds.

Beginner's luck, synchronicity and intending answers to questions, or next steps

Having talked about possible time lags above, it is also important to recognise the power of beginner's luck. Beginner's luck is often part of the initial process of your intention beginning to unfold quickly into reality. I have found that people who have used this process I am outlining to you frequently report that things seem to just happen and align, or line up and unfold quickly. That a series of linked events just seem to somehow work and sort themselves out, as if by magic.

When this happens, you need to capitalise on these winds of fortune and go with them, exploiting the energy and flow of this jet stream of good luck. Not only is this the principle of beginner's luck operating, it is also the power of serendipity that is playing its hand. In Chapter 8 I described the universal principle of the natural state of joy. When we are experiencing the state of natural joy, then the power of serendipity is always present. Serendipity creates happy chances, pleasant surprises, flukes, fortunate mistakes and, of course, luck. The same principles are in play for the opposite emotional forces too, but the outcomes in those cases are always negative.

As an example, before travelling anywhere by train or plane, I often set up an intention to wonder about who I might meet that is interesting or will provide me with something. I then expect this to work out as I am travelling and so look for interesting people amongst those I happen to bump into. This is also true whenever I am at a place where I happen to be with a lot of other people that I have never met before (like a conference or when I am presenting to others). And so very often this accords with my experience. I get what I ask for. So often I have engaged with interesting people in this way that have influenced me, or I them. I have also often meditated around intentions simply to meet someone who will provide me with an answer to something important I need, or am seeking: a next step, or a solution to a problem. This is synchronicity in action. I often wonder and marvel at the graceful beauty of the way this principle so effectively and effortlessly operates. I have many real life examples of this principle happening to me and to people I have taught to set intentions for themselves.

Intending destiny versus being controlled by fate

I believe it is necessary to clearly differentiate fate and destiny. They are often considered to be the same thing. However, I feel that they shouldn't be confused with one another. While similar, they are intentionally different and initiate different results.

Fate is popularly defined as being predestinated, or predetermined. However, in the context of this book, it is more about believing that circumstances and events seem to develop in your life that appear outside of your control. My thinking about fate is that it is what happens to you, if you do not follow your purpose.

If you don't set intentions for yourself then you are effectively allowing yourself to be led by fate. Fate will therefore direct you and is therefore in the driving seat of your life. If you are not in control of your life, you are in effect allowing the situations you face to have control over you.

Fate is a characteristic of an over-conditioning of the acquired self, when we end up buying the idea that we have no choice in the reality we experience. Instead it seems easier to simply give up fighting our conditioning and follow its direction. So fate is what sets up corresponding headings in life. As such we set no bearings for ourselves. We end up experiencing being tossed around on the waves of fate, going nowhere in particular. The inner compass of our authentic self is ignored. Life might feel a bit like a soap opera.

Destiny, on the other hand, is something subtly different. When you set intentions for yourself you are defining inner purpose. As you have already learned in this chapter, setting intentions in the ways previously outlined means you are purposefully connected to your true authentic self.

Your authentic self, via your consciousness (and the vast resources of your unconscious mind), knows it is universally connected to All That Is. This is the infinite and universal source of life force that is some sort of unknown form of collective consciousness, far bigger than you as an individual. This remains a mystery as yet. Through this connection, however, your deeper dreams, desires and purposes are somehow implicitly understood by your authentic self. This is destiny. The authentic self knows this as your authentic inner compass is always pointing to your true direction. It wholeheartedly knows what it is you are meant to be in this life. So, if you spend time listening to its quiet whispering you can understand it consciously too. Through regular meditation you will develop a sense of its calling in your life.

Through the practical applications in this chapter, you have learned the graceful art of setting intentions. As you set your intentions, be aware that you are connecting to your authentic self and at the same time your greater destiny is unfolding as it meets you along your way as you head towards it.

See also the final chapter of this book, about vision boards (Chapter 33). Using a vision board as a tool will help you to connect with your intentions each and every day that you look at it.

Chapter 32 -

Generating authentic purpose

Raising the bar of your thinking – a practical application

Robert Dilts, one of Richard Bandler and John Grinder's earliest NLP students, designed a simple model for thinking about personal change and learning. It provides a framework in which we organise, plan ahead and develop ourselves. There may be parts of our lives that we want to change. But how do we go about it? This model can help you to identify where and what development will be most helpful for you.

For example, exploring how holding a particular mindset, belief or attitude affects the way you think about yourself, and where that thinking might get stuck, and what level of your thinking might need enriching in some way. You may want to learn from an interaction with someone else that affected you in some adverse way, and want to understand where your thinking might be improved for the future. Perhaps you might desire to change yourself in some way, and you want to ensure that the change is integrally aligned from different perspectives of thinking about yourself.

I have found this tool effectively illustrates how the thinking patterns of the authentic self operate. By doing this, you can learn to raise the level of your own thinking to higher levels.

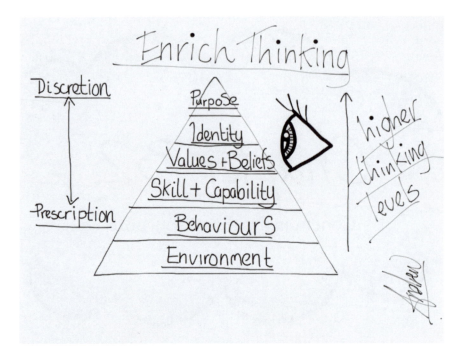

Figure 20: Enriching your thinking levels (Influenced from Robert Dilts)

The tool is best used by checking out your own thinking about a particular context: any personal issue, situation or experience. By practically applying the following process, you are guided to sequentially vary your thinking perspectives as you go. The perspectives at the higher levels tend to align more to your authentic self. Once you have aligned your thinking to your authentic self, it has a knack of ensuring that your various other levels and perspectives of thinking about your life and your experiences also perfectly realign. Any disconnects between different thinking levels or perspectives means that some aspect of your acquired conditioning needs to be adjusted in some way.

Each of the six levels of thinking patterns sequentially builds one on the other from the bottom upwards. The higher levels in the hierarchy tend to have more influence and impact on those below it. By applying the next practical exercise to yourself you learn how thinking differently produces different results. The higher your thinking, the greater the impact you have on your reality.

Practical application…

Choose a personal issue, or something you want to do better, or a situation that you would like to further explore, or take stock of.

With this context in mind, start at the bottom of the table below, at Environment, and work upwards to Purpose. Once you are at the top, then work downwards, from Purpose to Environment, by going the other way this time. You may wish to write your answers down in your self-inventory journal.

Notice what changes or is different when you go down, compared to when you went up as you do this. Which level has the most effect or impact on you? At which level is there a disconnect?

Table 10 Enriching your thinking exercise

Purpose/vision/connection – What else? Who else?   What is my purpose? Close your eyes and imagine connecting with the best and highest thing about you, which is beyond anything you have been exploring (faith, spirituality, higher self, your connection with others). How does this all connect with the big picture of your life?
Identity – Who am I in this area of my life? Who am I when I do the things I do – at my best/worst?   What is my mission?
Values and beliefs – Why?   What motivates me in this area? What do I believe about myself/others (values, meanings, rules I/others operate by)? What's true, or not true to me? What's important about me to tell other people who know me well, so they understand me and what I stand for?
Skill and capability – how?   What capabilities, skills, expert knowledge, strategies and resources can I draw upon and have available (maps and plans)? What is missing or needs bettering?
Behaviours – What?   What specific behaviours do I do when I engage in this area of my life? What supports me, or gets in my way? What behaviours do not support me (actions and reactions)?
Environment – Where am I when I think about this area of my life? What do my senses tell me? What do I see, hear and feel? What happens to me here? Where and what are my external constraints, concerns, boundaries of influence and opportunities?   What would others see me do?

Source: Influenced by Roger Terry.

The top three thinking approaches, Purpose, Identity and Values and Beliefs connect more to who you really are, so they tend to be more aligned to your true authentic self. They are less prescriptive or rule bound and are more about discretion, and use more of your inner resources, than the bottom three, Environment, Behaviours, and Skill and Capability. These are more adapted to imposed rules, control and more rudimentary ways of thinking.

Often people's thinking can focus on the bottom three ways of thinking only, and stop at Skill and Capability as being considered the pinnacle of experience. Too much reliance on capability thinking can lead to becoming trapped in the cycle of grief we explored in Part 3. However, there is far more thinking scope available to you, by developing higher capacities of thinking for yourself. So this often creates a void or a separation between Skill and Capability and the levels below it, and Values and Beliefs and the levels above that.

To move beyond your choices and possibilities it is important to expand and enrich your thinking to beyond Skill and Capability, to bridge this gap and extend and expand your thinking towards Values and Beliefs, Identity, and Purpose.

In this way you engage the additional resources of your authentic self. These have always been available to you, but it does require you to learn how to access them. This tool helps you to develop the language to engage with the thinking patterns of your authentic self.

Your thinking at these higher levels does, however, require you to be more engaged with who you are, your desires, dreams and higher purposes. The more you stretch your thinking to these levels, the easier it becomes.

That doesn't mean that capabilities and behaviours aren't important, because they are. However, the more you focus on the higher levels of thinking, the more impact they have on the context of the lower levels of thinking. These then tend to align and be influenced more by your authentic self and its thinking patterns. This does not happen with so much effect going up through the levels from the lower primary or elementary levels. In other words, this model of thinking about your thinking works best and has significantly more impact when you open your mind to raising your thinking, using top-down strategies, rather than from the bottom up.

Aligning to what you want and desire – practical application...

This exercise is adapted from a book called *Brand New You* by Simon Middleton. This is an exercise that enriches your thinking by you focusing on what is important for you in your life. It helps you step by step to connect more deeply to what is behind your plans and your overall purposes and direction in your life from different perspectives.

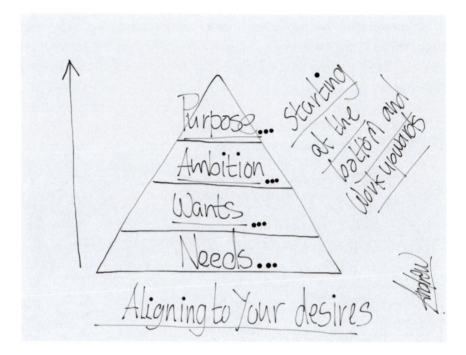

Figure 21: Aligning to what you desire (Source: Simon Middleton)

Using your self-inventory journal follow these simple instructions to plan ahead for your life. It starts with more materially based aspects that build to support aspects of your authentic self. If you find it hard to connect to your overall purposes, as many people do, then this exercise is really useful, as it helps you to build up to this more abstract concept from a practical starting point:

Needs are basically what it is that you practically require as a base to build from. For example, money, work, savings, lifestyle stuff and things you need to support your wants.

Wants in this context are materially based desires to possess, or do something; job certainty or role, cars, houses and earnings would be examples, as would potential pay rises, promotions, etc. These are more specific than your basic needs.

Ambitions are more emotionally based than wants. They are linked to your motivations, enthusiasms, eagerness and drives. These now start to support your authentic self in your hopes, dreams and desires. What you want to become, where you live, what you earn, when and where you retire, what you do, be, have, etc.

Purpose. What are you doing it all for, what's behind your life, what legacy do you leave? Altruism and goodwill to others, what is greater than you, etc. These all help to consolidate your connection to return to your authentic self.

The cycle of grace

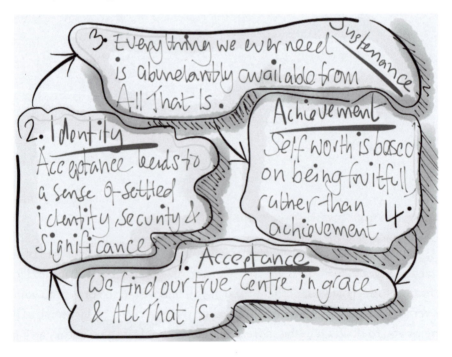

Figure 22: The cycle of grace (Source: James Lawrence)

As we learned earlier in this chapter, to access authentic self resources your thinking needs to be different. Your thinking strategies and principles need to include perceptions about your beliefs and values, your identity, and understanding your sense of purpose and connection. Importantly, using these levels of thinking, you will become aware of experiencing external reality from these higher principle contexts.

This next model, by James Lawrence in his book *Growing Leaders*, builds on the cycle of grief we explored in Part 3, Chapter 20. The cycle of grace model is the antidote to the cycle of grief. It is a useful guide to help you to approach your life with authenticity, and is graceful and effective.

It practically embodies these higher level thinking principles, so you start to personally experience them in action as you apply them to yourself. In this way you go beyond thinking, and start to live your life by authentic self principles.

In the cycle of grief model, we discovered that the cycle was highly addictive and was acquired through the limiting effects of conditioning. This in turn evolved into a cycle based on achievement through capability, which led to never-ending grief. The antidote, or alternative, in the cycle of grace model reverses that cycle and returns you to the way you are meant and intended to be. This relies on your identity being at the core, rather than your achievements. To do this means you have to rely on the presence and resources of your authentic self. It is pictured on page 306 and is called the cycle of grace.

The cycle of grace starts in the context of having applied the learning of Part 5. As you start letting go of control, holding things loosely and trusting more in things greater than you, you will notice changes in how you are being. This is because you are unconsciously allowing room for the cycle of grace to naturally form within you.

Believing that things will work out if you let them take shape will gently centre you into a feeling of acceptance and grace about yourself. That you are okay, even if you don't feel okay about what is happening to you. These are the principles of acceptance we described earlier in Part 5. They shape your identity and your belief in who you are, give you a clearer understanding of who you are meant to be, and give you purpose and connection to others.

This kind of acceptance about yourself leads to a greater sense of satisfaction, of a sustained and lasting sense of settled and stable identity, which is rooted in your true authentic self. You become comfortable in your own skin and who you are. This now becomes your inner compass of enduring security and significance – your belief that the world abundantly takes care of you, helps sustain you and that you no longer have to strive to achieve.

Instead you now strive towards a different, higher purpose.

The way you perceive your achievements changes. Self-worth is no longer solely based on your capabilities as the prize, and on what you have done, but rather believing you are fruitful because of who you are, and that this is more than enough to achieve your intentions. By taking the cycle of grace to heart and consciously and deliberately intending it to be your way of being, you will then indeed experience being this way and your internal and external reality will, without question, naturally and easily correspond to it. I have this model on my vision board (see Chapter 33).

Creating a present point of power – a centred state of now

When accessing your authentic self, it is important that you feel good about yourself more of the time. We have discussed this many times so I hope you are getting this now? To do this you have to create habits that generate resourceful representations that create good 'pictures' in your head and corresponding emotional states in your body. When you feel good about yourself more of the time you are able to gain access to your *present point of power in the moment* more often. When you do this it therefore means you build up your ability to rapidly connect and use the resources of your authentic self.

Being centred means being in a state of 'here and now', where our attention is totally absorbed on simply being, being in the here and now. It is a time when we can be aware of our uniqueness in the present moment.

When you are totally centred, you access the state of your true authentic self. Way back in Chapter 12 we described this as being your homeostasis, your baseline balanced state. In this state you find yourself simply being. Being in a state of the 'here and now', where you have emptied yourself of yourself, and your attention is totally focused on the world around you. Your internal dialogue and inner chatter is quiet, and your intuition is quickened and able to operate without any distractions.

To get to this state you have to relax your mind, and then let your centred state of being find you. See Chapter 30 for more details on meditation and self-hypnosis. Spend time being open to tuning onto the wavelength that your authentic self operates within. Remember, you don't have to yank it or wrench it into being, instead all you need to do is get out of its way and let it return into you.

Now to help you to access this state more easily…

Remember a time when you were last aware of being highly present… when you were in a state of being totally focused on what was going on around you.

> This state is counter to those where you are 'in your own head', and accessing painful stories (unresourceful beliefs) about yourself or others, worrying about the past or being anxious about the future.

As you access this resourceful state of being highly present, become aware of it with soft eyes; this is no dragon you have to slay.

Bring back that memory of being fully present and fully associate with it.

Bring back any visual pictures, auditory information and kinaesthetic sensations that are associated with your emotional body state.

What else do you notice about the way you feel now?

Use the simple anchoring technique you learned earlier in Chapter 27 to anchor this state.

Alternatively, use this process as an intention during meditations that you have learned in Chapter 30.

As I continue to reinforce… It is really important that you spend time planning ahead to feel good about yourself, as this accesses the resources of your authentic self.

Lessons from the warrior's way

Warriors are experts at accessing a state of deliberate purpose and centredness. You can learn a lot from modelling their way of being to access your true authentic self.

They have understood that to become a true warrior you have to be in a relaxed state of mind. This sounds counter-intuitive; however, any martial arts teacher will tell you that this is true. To fight well, you have to empty yourself first of your fears and to use fear as a driving force, not an inhibitor. This is impossible if your body is not relaxed. So these go hand in hand.

While the art of relaxing in this way under threat may take years of practice, the important thing is the warrior mindset. Through the ability to centre themselves, warriors understand all about the challenges of accessing true authenticity. Over time adept warriors understand themselves from the

higher ways of being that we discussed earlier in this chapter. Their identity and values and beliefs are clear, as is their sense of purpose. Purpose
is based on defending a higher principle than themselves, for example the
protection of others or a way of life that is greater than the warrior. The
warrior implicitly understands this. Their mindset is based on the following
understandings.

That risk is something that they accept and no longer question. Life and
death are all part of experience and so they have learned that risk is part of
life. The unknown is faced every day. Every day is a new day with new possibilities and options and choices. They discipline themselves to face their
fears. The thing that a warrior fears the most might be fear itself and things
being overfamiliar.

Part of the test of their skill is not only to regularly practise their method
of fighting and their skilled use of weaponry, but also to test out their state
of mind in extreme and everyday situations. This could result in living or
dying. However, this is part of the experience. As is being able to calculate
the risks, and test out their chosen responses as situations unfold.

Ultimately, warriors become able to acknowledge that all of life and
death is simply play and sport – a game to be lost or won. Living is a privilege
as is being prepared to die for a purpose that is beyond themselves, and
for the greater good. This is something that earns respect. Perhaps acting in
these ways in any situation, not just in battle, develops courage and bravery
to face life and what it throws at you. By disciplining your mind to adopt
these same attitudes, you may discover that you are more than you think and
that you are able to overcome your fears. Like the warrior, you too can face
and overcome your own enemies within and win the battles in life.

In this way warriors avoid the trappings of the acquired self, which would
condition them in less resourceful ways. A true warrior is connected to their
authentic self. By using the warrior's way as a model you too can connect to
life in similar ways. We can all learn a lot about the warrior's way. You too can
choose to live your life in similar ways: even though you may not have to ever
literally face a battle situation, you can still adopt the same principles, and
face situations and reality in ways akin to the warrior's brave and courageous
spirit. It is the warrior spirit that is useful to model.

Like the cycle of grace, the warrior's way mantra also features on my vision
board. It reminds me that life is just a test of skill; that I have to take risks from
time to time to feel alive; and that my work needs to be fun and playful too.

You can deliberately intend such ways to become part of you. As we learned earlier, you simply adopt the idea and intend it consciously to be. Purposefully adapt your language and use meditation as the vehicle to presuppose it into being. Over a short while your neurology swiftly adapts.

You see, when you reconnect to the real you, you are more than you think.

Figure 23: The warrior's way

- Chapter 33 -

The new reconnected you

So here we are at the final pages of this book. My hope is that you have enjoyed reading it and going on a personal journey of discovery for yourself. I hope, too, that you have found it useful to make changes for yourself and to help you to return to your true authentic self.

I hope that you have discovered more about who you really are, and that you are more than you think.

By this point I hope, too, that the changes you made for yourself during your journey of reading and participating in the practical applications within this book will be leaving you feeling very different about yourself.

By now you understand the universal principles that open your mind to experiencing a reality that you desire and deserve.

That you now understand who you are neurologically as well. That neurologically you can practically apply yourself to change whatever it is that isn't working for you and do something different until you have what you want for yourself. You can change whatever you want about yourself through your mind–brain–body connection. Your mind–brain connection is powerful, adaptive, dynamic and plastic. All change is possible.

You understand that the difference that makes all the difference to the reality you co-create is the resourceful pictures you generate in your head and the emotional states in your body. It is not the content of your thoughts that makes this happen, but the states of mind and body that your thoughts and feelings generate.

By now you understand, too, all about the way you acquired limiting beliefs, and how you conditioned yourself into limited realities. That these are all the actions of what we described as the acquired self. You now have had many opportunities to loosen and break the hold of these patterns for yourself using the many techniques in this book. These are the same techniques that I use with the people I have the privilege of working with to create personal change for themselves.

I hope that your attention is now more tuned to your authentic self and its return and that you can feel good about yourself and can feel whole again.

So by now I hope that you truly are a new you, that you have rediscovered yourself and have a sense of who you really are and that you:

1. Are now proactive about co-creating your reality in a positive way.
2. Have opened your mind as to how powerful you are and how the choices you make co-create the reality that you desire.
3. Are practising meditation, and as such you feel relaxed about yourself and your external reality is corresponding to this.
4. Are aware that the use of your language and what you presuppose about yourself has shifted your internal and external reality.
5. Are okay about not being okay, and that that is okay.
6. Are deliberately shaping reality through the power of intentions to shape the reality you seek.
7. Are purposefully generating authentic purpose and using your 'brain for a change'.
8. Have found your true authentic self and that as you shape reality it easily and effortlessly finds you along the way.

So you truly are more than you think, are you not?

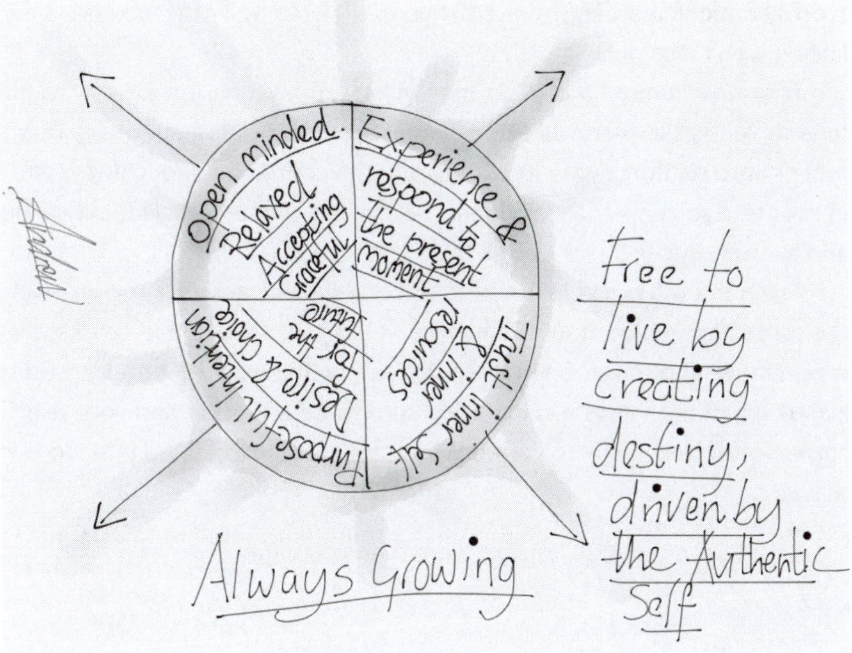

The diagram shows a circle divided into sections with handwritten text reading: "Open minded.", "Experience & respond to the present moment", "Relaxed", "Accepting", "Grateful", "Trust the future", "Desire & Choice", "Purposeful Intention", "Trust inner self", "Precious inner resources". Arrows point outward from the circle. Surrounding text reads: "Free to live by creating destiny, driven by the Authentic Self" and "Always Growing".

Figure 24: Free to live by creating destiny driven by the authentic self

Final practical application – vision boards

I hope that you will find that this last practical application is an ideal end to this book.

I want you to create a vision board for yourself. This is a simple white, cork or metal board that you can buy cheaply from any stationery store or office store. Hang it up, or fix it on a blank wall somewhere, anywhere convenient for you, such as in your office, or in a private space, or the kitchen, or bedroom or wherever.

Then think about what it is that you dream for, desire or want and find pictures of it in magazines and on the internet or from your photos that represent it. Whatever you put on your vision board, make it inspiring to you. Use images, quotes, inspiring messages, hopes and dreams; these all go on this board as a collage. Draw, sketch, write, doodle and so on. This is your story about you and what you want now, in the short term and longer term, in your future. Use magnets or sticky tack or pins to put these on your board. Remember, if it feels unfamiliar to you, then it is because it is the right-brain modality that you are using and that your left brain will catch up and join in later. It won't miss out.

Take your time. Once you have filled up your vision board, spend time looking at it every day and purposefully and deliberately use it as a reminder to reinforce your intentions. It is never finished and is always work in progress, so keep adapting it and be flexible with it; it is always dynamic and ever-changing.

Again this is a powerful process and one to be enjoyed. Keep changing the content as you go along. Remember it is a fluid and flexible process that is generative and transformative. As you review this, you will be surprised at how many of the things you intended start to be achieved, and your reality corresponds beautifully to your dreams, desires, purposes and intentions in this way.

You are more than you think.

About the author

Andrew Jenkins is a very dynamic and skilled facilitator, coach, mentor, presenter and teacher of new thinking. He is the MD of PDx Consulting Ltd, a consultancy dedicated to developing leaders, managers and executives to perform at their very best in many well known organisations across the world.

Andrew also presents for one of the world's leading coaching training organisations. He is a fully qualified psychotherapist, hypnotist, coach and internationally accredited trainer.

Andrew qualified as a Chartered Engineer, and was employed as an engineer for a number of years, before changing and broadening his career to work and consult with many leading global organisations. With operational change expertise he developed a knack of helping businesses transform at a time of unprecedented shifts in globalisation, competition from new emerging economies and increasingly rapid advances in new technology, all against a backdrop of ever-diminishing resources. He now also speaks and writes about new ways of thinking, leading and being, in order to encourage people and companies to grow and change.

It is Andrew's belief that macro economics will continue to radically change employment, demographics, wealth distribution, job security. 'Old world jobs' are being swept away and new opportunities are arising and emerging to build the 'new world economies.'

Through his commercial experience and acumen, Andrew's consulting practice is dedicated to engaging with organisations to lead and act in new ways. To do this requires influencing new and different thinking at strategic levels in order to support ongoing future growth. This is important, as changes of this kind cannot simply come from efficiencies in new systems and processes alone. This is now old news. Alert to the radically different context in which businesses are now forced to function, Andrew has become an active advocate of economic prosperity being revolutionised through investing in human capital in unique ways. It is his strongly-held belief that, in the new emerging global economy, executives will need to be significantly more supported and encouraged so that they can reach their full potential, and use their talents and creative abilities whilst doing the 'stuff of work.' New organisational strategies need to be adopted to engage and influence senior people at all levels to connect much more emotionally to facilitate these sorts of necessary transformations, so organisations can meet the challenges and seize the opportunities that lie ahead. This is the purpose and philosophy behind Andrew's company PDx Consulting Ltd.

In Andrew's view, such new thinking will require the knowhow of specialised and skilled individuals to encourage and coach in this sort of new investment within our organisations. He passionately believes that it is vital for us all that we each find our purpose, and make our life and work count to make tangible differences. To do this, leaders will need to support their people so that they can each find their unique edge alongside doing their work, playing to their own unique strengths, and not wasting time, energy and investment on covering up and coping with weaknesses. In the new global economy, people will be regularly changing careers and continually learning and honing new skills, and entrepreneurial mindset, so we will all need to learn to adapt quickly to change, bring our very best selves to work, and be at the 'top of our game' during our varied and multi-faceted careers. Andrew has become one of these leading change experts and is committed to enabling business leaders, teams and individuals to engender this type of altruistic spirit, in order to help people overcome the obstacles that are holding them back, so that everyone can become the person they are meant to be and make a living from what they enjoy doing best. That way, says Andrew, all of us can find a sense of purpose and be fulfilled, so that we come to work whistling in the morning and go back home again singing once work is done.

www.pdx-consulting.com
www.youaremorethanyouthink.co.uk

Further information

Further reading

Andreas, Steve (2012) *Transforming Negative Inner Self Talk: Practical Effective Exercises.* W. W. Norton & Company

Begley, Sharon and Davidson, Richard J. (2012) T*he Emotional Life of your Brain.* Hodder

Checkland, Peter (1990) *Soft Systems Methodology.* John Wesley & Sons

Cope, Mick (2004) *The Seven Cs of Coaching.* Pearson Prentice Hall

Damasio, Antonio (2008) *Descartes' Error.* Vintage Digital

Dilts, Robert (1990) *Changing Belief Systems with NLP.* Meta Publications

Doidge, Norman (2008) *The Brain Changes Itself.* Penguin

Eide, Brock and Eide, Fernette (2011) *The Dyslexic Advantage.* Hay House

Gallwey, Timothy W. (2000) *The Inner Game of Work.* Orion Business

Goleman, Daniel (1996) *Emotional Intelligence.* Bloomsbury

Goleman, Daniel, Boyatzis, Richard and Mckee, Annie (2003) *New Leaders.* Sphere

Helmstetter, Shad (2011) *What to Say When You Talk to Yourself.* Park Avenue Press

Horsely, Jake (2003) *Matrix Warrior. Being the One.* Orion Publishing Group

James, Bev (2011) *Do It Or Ditch It.* Virgin Books

Jones, Paul (2009) *How to Live in the Here and Now.* O Books

Lawrence, James (2004) *Growing Leaders.* BRF

Levine, Peter A. (2012) *In an Unspoken Voice: How the body releases trauma and restores goodness.* North Atlantic Books

McGilchrist, Iain (2010) *The Master and His Emissary.* Yale University Press

McKenna, Paul (1993) *The Hypnotic World of Paul McKenna.* Faber & Faber

Middleton, Simon (2012) *Brand New You: Reinventing work, life and self through the power of personal branding*. Hay House

Moss, Richard (2007) *The Mandala of Being*. New World Library

Robbins, Anthony (2001) *Awaken the Giant Within*. Pocket Books

Robbins, Anthony (2003) *Unlimited Power*. Free Press.

Roberts, Jane (c. 1997–2011) *The Seth Books* series. Amber Allen Publishing

Rosen, Sidney and Erickson, Milton H. (1991) *My Voice Will Go with You: The teaching tales of Milton H Erickson*. W. W. Norton & Company

Zeland, Vadim (2008–2012) *Reality Transurfing*. Books 1 to 5. O Books

Films

The Matrix. Warner Home Video 1999

Happy. Passion River Film 2012

The Secret. Prime Time Productions 2006

What the Bleep. Revolver Entertainment 2004

Adjustment Bureaux. Universal Pictures 2010

NLP resources

Use of various NLP practical resources from certificated International NLP Trainers Association (INLPTA) Practitioner, Master Practitioner and Train the Trainer qualifications.

Particular thanks to Roger Terry of Evolution Training for his kind permission for the use of his NLP belief material in Tables 1-5, 8 and 10. Original source of Table 1 adapted by Roger Terry from original source: Anthony Robbins, *Awaken The Giant Within*, Pocket Books, 2001. Table 4 and 5 idea taken and further adapted by Roger Terry from: Anthony Robbins, *Unlimited Power*, Free Press, 2003.

NLP resources are widely distributed for general use; however, I acknowledge the influence and the great work done by Richard Bandler, John Grinder, Robert Dilts, Joseph O'Conner, Michael Hall, Wyatt Woodsmall and Steve Andreas in their outstanding contribution to the creation of NLP for the good of the world. My thanks also to Bev James, MD of The Coaching Academy for her inspiration and for giving me so many opportunities to present on the topic of limiting beliefs and Pam Lidford, an exceptional trainer whose own work in the field is outstanding.